We Know Pies!

and now you can too...

The complete guide to perfect
filling, meringues and crusts!

Written by:
Marlene Wyatt and Mona Elliott

Illustrated by:
Ashley Jo Baker

Wood Family Enterprises

P.O. Box 299

Pyatt, AR 72672

1-800-456-0851

First Edition

Third Printing

ISBN: 0-9649375-1-4

Printed in the USA by
Enterprise Printing Company, Inc.
P.O. Box 258 • Bull Shoals, AR 72619
www.EnterprisePrintingWeb.com

About the Authors . . .

The roots grow deep in the Ozark Mountains for Marlene Wyatt and Mona Elliott. Marlene is number eight in a family of twelve. Mona is Marlene's oldest niece with only a ten year age difference between them.

They feel their relationship is more like being best friends or sisters rather than aunt and niece. Even Marlene's daughter Rebecca thought they were sisters and called Mona aunt for years.

They have played together, cried on each others shoulders, were pregnant together. . . even visited their doctor together, and have worked together (having been in business together for the past fifteen years). They started in the day care business but now have Wood Family Enterprise where they develop and manufacture baking products.

Marlene can't remember actually teaching Mona how to bake, but does remember how Mona would always observe as she prepared a delicious pie to eat!

Both Mona and Marlene's kitchen drawers were stuffed full of recipes, so the only natural thing for them to do was create this book to share with everyone. Both can remember how intimidating baking could be when they first started out, so they have prepared easy to follow, step-by-step directions with illustrations for anyone to follow. Their recipes and instructions are so easy, you will feel like they are in the kitchen with you as you create your own work of art.

Enjoy the recipes and have fun. Create some wonderful memories for your family too!

Table of Contents

Step-by-Step Perfect Pie Crust

Step 1:

Try to make sure <u>all</u> your ingredients are chilled before you begin. Combine all your dry ingredients together first... flour, salt, sugar, spices, etc.

Use a pastry blender or two knives to cut the butter, margarine or shortening into dry ingredients. Press down quickly, using as few strokes as possible. The mixture should resemble coarse cornmeal. It is ok if you have a few "pea-sized" pieces.

Step 2:

Always use a fork to stir in liquids. Add liquids slowly, one or two tablespoons at a time, just until dough comes together and leaves sides of bowl. (Remember too little water will make your dough dry and brittle and hard to roll out. Too much water will make it sticky.) Just have a little patience and with a little practice, before long you will know exactly how much water to add.

Important Note: <u>Do Not Over mix or Over handle</u> - The less you handle the dough the better. A light hand really does make a light flaky crust.

1

Tips for Baking Double Crust Pies

Follow one of the methods in Step 4 to transfer the bottom crust to the pie plate. Remember to leave at least a 1-inch overhang. Fill with filling as per individual recipe.

Roll out top crust. If you wish to cut out decorative cutouts in the top crust now is the time to do so. Brush edge of bottom crust with water. Place the top crust over filling.

If there is more than a 1-inch overhang of dough left around pie plate, trim to 1-inch. Tuck top crust under bottom crust and crimp to seal edges together. Flute (See Fluting Techniques).

If there are no cutouts in top crust, make three or four 1-inch slits to help steam escape during baking and to prevent spill overs. Slits can be as plain or as fancy as you want.

For pretty crust, brush with egg, egg whites, water or milk and sprinkle with sugar. For brown crust brush with milk; for golden crust brush with a mixture of milk and egg yolk; for shiny crust brush with egg white. Sugar adds sparkle!

Decorative Top Crusts:

Roll out crust. Cut out decorative shapes. Place overlapping, all over top of filling. For a festive Christmas pie, cut out several different sizes of holly leaves and place over a cranberry or cherry pie. Roll pea size balls of dough for berries and place between leaves. Star and heart shape cutters also make pretty top crust.

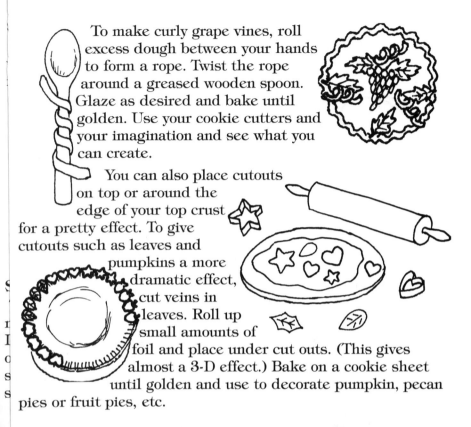

To make curly grape vines, roll excess dough between your hands to form a rope. Twist the rope around a greased wooden spoon. Glaze as desired and bake until golden. Use your cookie cutters and your imagination and see what you can create.

You can also place cutouts on top or around the edge of your top crust for a pretty effect. To give cutouts such as leaves and pumpkins a more dramatic effect, cut veins in leaves. Roll up small amounts of foil and place under cut outs. (This gives almost a 3-D effect.) Bake on a cookie sheet until golden and use to decorate pumpkin, pecan pies or fruit pies, etc.

To prevent your crust from becoming too brown around the edges, cover the outer edges with foil or a pie crust shield.

Freezing Pastry:

Preparing pie crust ahead and then freezing can save a lot of time. Unbaked crust can be frozen for up to two months. Baked crusts can be kept frozen for up to four to six months.

Tips for Rolled Pie Crust Success

Even though the basic techniques for creating the perfect piecrust are fairly simple, (with a little practice) I hope the following tips and hints will help you to understand the techniques and make you a Master Pie Baker!

• The best pie pans are those made from dull-finished aluminum or glass. (My favorite is glass.) Shiny pans can result in a soggy pie bottom.

• All your ingredients including your mixing bowl should be as cold as possible . . especially the water. The water should be added gradually. Too much water will make your pastry tough, too little will cause it to crumble and be difficult to roll out. Even your hands should be kept as cool as possible.

• Roll your dough out on a lightly floured surface. The less flour used while rolling out the flakier your pastry will be. Always take care not to over handle or overwork your dough. . . . there is an old saying, "Light hands make light dough!" If your dough becomes hard to roll out, allow to rest for awhile. Dough tends to toughen when humidity is high, so chill during rolling if necessary.

• Glazes give pies a wonderful finish and also help to keep them fresh. For a brown crust, brush with milk, for golden crust brush with milk and egg yolk mixed together. For shiny crust, brush with egg white. To add sparkle, sprinkle with sugar.

• Flavorings make a great addition to crust. They can be added to the pastry after the fat has been cut into the flour. Add ground nuts, grated lemon or orange zest, sesame seeds, wheat germ, etc. or even a little brandy or rum for sweet pies. For savory pies, try adding chopped fresh herbs, dry mustard or grated cheese.

Tips continued

- Unbaked pie shells can be frozen for up to two months. Baked shells will keep frozen for four to six months.

- When a recipe calls for shortening, solid vegetable shortening is best. Too much shortening makes pastry greasy, too little will make your pastry tough. Also when a recipe calls for shortening, don't substitute oil or butter, these could cause undesired results.

- Always sift your flour before measuring. Unless a recipe calls for a different type flour, always use a good all-purpose flour for your pie crust. And remember, too much flour makes pastry tough. While too little flour can leave your pastry sticky.

- To keep the bottom crust of juicy berry pies from becoming soggy, sprinkle the crust lightly with equal amounts of a sugar and flour mixture.

- To cut in butter, use a pastry blender, fork or two knives in a scissors motion.

- To prevent meringue from weeping, spread meringue on hot or warm filling and make sure you spread all the way to edge of pie crust to seal well. All ovens are different so when browning your meringue, make sure you watch it closely to prevent over browning or burning.

Classic Pie Crust

8, 9 OR 10-INCH SINGLE CRUST

1-1/3 cups flour   1/2 cup shortening
1/2 teaspoon salt   3-4 tablespoons cold water

FOR SINGLE CRUST, form dough into disc shape.. Roll dough into circle. See pie instructions.

FOR BAKED SINGLE CRUST - prick bottom and sides thoroughly with fork to prevent shrinkage. You can line the inside of crust with foil and fill with pie weights. If you don't have weights, dried beans work great. Bake at 425 degrees for 10 to 15 minutes or until golden brown.

8 OR 9-INCH DOUBLE CRUST

2 cups flour   3/4 cup shortening
1 teaspoon salt   5-6 tablespoons cold water

10-INCH DOUBLE CRUST

2-2/3 cups flour   1 cup shortening
1-1/4 teaspoons salt   7-9 tablespoons cold water

FOR DOUBLE CRUST PIES - Divide dough in half, roll each half separately. Place bottom crust into pie plate; add desired filling. Moisten crust edge with water. Top with top crust. Trim 1/2 inch beyond edge of pie plate. Fold top edge under bottom crust. Seal; flute edges. Cut slits in top crust to allow steam to escape. Bake according to specific recipe directions.

When making pie crust always combine flour and salt in medium bowl. Cut in shortening. Blend until mixture is cornmeal texture. Sprinkle with water, 1 tablespoon at a time. toss lightly with fork until dough forms a ball then follow directions for either a single or double crust.

Easy Rich Butter Crust
Makes 10-inch single crust

1-1/2 cups flour

1 cup softened butter or margarine

1/2 cup powdered sugar

Beat all ingredients with mixer on low speed for 1 minute. Beat on medium speed for 2 more minutes or until creamy. Spread onto bottom and up sides of 9-inch pie pan or in bottom of a 10-inch springform pan. Bake at 400 degrees for 12 to 15 minutes or until golden.

Cream Cheese Pastry
Makes 9-inch single crust

1/4 cup butter, cut in small cubes

4-ounces cream cheese, cut in small cubes

1 cup flour

1/4 teaspoon salt (omit if using salted butter)

Combine all ingredients with pastry blender. With hands, knead and shape into disc shape. Roll out. Bake at 375 degrees for 10-12 minutes or until golden. This is a very dry dough and is a little more difficult to roll out, but if you like cream cheese it's worth the extra work!

Buttery Sweet Pastry
Makes 9-inch single crust

1-1/2 cups flour

3 tablespoons sugar

1/2 cup cold butter

1 egg slightly beaten

1-2 tablespoons cold water

Stir together flour and sugar. Cut in butter to pea-sized pieces. Mix egg and water together. Using a fork, stir liquid in flour mixture until all dough is moistened. Form a ball. Roll out on floured surface. For baked shell, bake at 375 degrees 12 to 15 minutes or until golden.

15

Puff Pastry

3/4 cup plus 2 tablespoons
and 2 teaspoons flour

1/3 cup cake flour

Pinch of salt

1/4 cup plus 2 teaspoons ice
water

1/2 cup (1 stick) plus 5-1/2

tablespoons unsalted butter,
at room temperature

2 teaspoons freshly squeezed
lemon juice

In a medium mixing bowl, stir together flours and salt. Remove 3 tablespoons and set aside.

In an electric mixer bowl, using paddle attachment on low speed, mix 4 tablespoons butter with the remaining flour. Combine just until the mixture has the texture of coarse meal.

Combine the water and lemon juice and add to the flour and butter mixture. Mix until the dough comes together and is slightly sticky.

With your hands, shape the dough into a 4-inch thick square. Wrap the dough in plastic wrap and refrigerate for 45 minutes.

In the bowl of an electric mixer, using the paddle attachment on medium-low speed, beat the remaining butter until soft and smooth. Add the reserved 3 tablespoons flour and beat until incorporated. Wrap the butter in plastic wrap. With your hands, shape the butter into a 6-inch square. Refrigerate 45 minutes, or until cold but still pliable.

Remove the square of dough from the refrigerator. Unwrap and place it on a lightly floured board and roll it into a 13-inch square. Unwrap and put the 6-inch square of butter in the middle of the dough. Turn the edges of the dough over the butter, completely covering the butter block. Roll the dough into a 19-by 6-1/2-inch rectangle. Fold the dough toward the center in thirds as you would a business letter. Turn the dough so that the seam is on the left and the open end is on the right. Roll and fold the dough once more in the same manner. The dough has now been given two turns. Wrap in plastic wrap and refrigerate the dough for one hour.

(Continued on next page)

(Puff Pastry continued...)

Remove the dough from the refrigerator. Roll and fold the dough twice as before. Wrap and refrigerate the dough for 1 hour.

Once again, remove the dough from the refrigerator. Roll and fold the dough twice more. Wrap and refrigerate the dough 1 hour.

The puff pastry is now ready to be rolled as required for recipes.

Note: Puff pastry can be made several days in advance, and can be frozen for several weeks. Store well wrapped in plastic wrap. Defrost overnight in the refrigerator before rolling. If possible, roll out the pastry on a lightly floured work surface in desired shape before freezing. In this instance, place the pastry pieces in the oven directly from the freezer. Puff pastry should be eaten the same day it is baked.

No-Fail Pie Crust
Makes three single crusts

3 cups flour	*1 egg*
3/4 teaspoons salt	*1 teaspoon white vinegar*
1 cup shortening	*7 to 10 tablespoons cold water*

Mix flour and salt, cut in shortening until texture of cornmeal. In separate bowl, mix egg, vinegar and water. Add liquid to flour mixture. Toss gently with fork.

Divide dough into thirds. Form in balls and roll out on lightly floured surface. Bake according to recipe. For single baked crust, bake 12 to 15 minutes at 400 degrees.

If not using all crust at once, wrap dough in plastic wrap and store in refrigerator for up to a week. Let dough reach room temperature before rolling out.

*This is my favorite rolled pie crust recipe.

Sesame Seed Crust
Makes 9-inch single crust

2 tablespoons sesame seeds
1 cup flour
1/2 teaspoon salt

1/3 cup shortening
3 to 4 tablespoons cold water

Preheat oven to 450 degrees. Toast sesame seeds until golden brown. Remove and cool. Combine flour and salt, add seeds. Cut in shortening to form coarse crumbs. Gradually add water and mix lightly until dough forms. Form dough into ball. Roll out on floured surface. For baked shell, bake 10-12 minutes at 450 degrees until golden brown. Or bake according to recipe.

Chocolate Pie Shell
Makes 9-inch single crust

1 cup all-purpose flour
1/4 teaspoon salt
1/3 cup shortening

1/2 square semi-sweet chocolate, grated
2 tablespoons water

Combine flour and salt; cut in shortening. Stir in grated chocolate. Sprinkle water over and mix gently until dough holds together. Form into ball and roll out. For baked shell, bake at 385-400 degrees for 12-15 minutes or bake according to recipe.

Chocolate Pat-in-Pan Crust
Makes 9 or 10-inch single crust

3/4 cup plus 2 tablespoons flour
1/2 cup softened butter or margarine

1/4 cup powdered sugar
2 tablespoons baking cocoa
1/4 cup finely chopped pecans or walnuts

Mix together all ingredients until a soft dough forms. Press onto bottom and sides of an ungreased pie plate. Bake 12 to 15 minutes at 400 degrees or until light brown.

Variations: For plain crust, omit baking cocoa.

Chocolate-Vanilla Wafer Pastry Shell

Makes 9-inch single crust

1-1/3 cups vanilla wafer crumbs

4 ounces sweet baking chocolate chopped or grated

1/4 cup packed brown sugar

1/3 cup melted butter or margarine

Combine crumbs, chocolate and sugar. Add butter or margarine. Press onto bottom and up sides of pie plate. Bake 10 minutes at 350 degrees. Crust can also be chilled for 3 hours instead of baking.

Sweet Cream Graham Crust

Makes 9-inch single crust

1 cup graham cracker crumbs

1/2 cup melted butter

1/4 cup powdered sugar

1 tablespoon light cream

Combine crumbs and sugar, mix in butter and cream. Press over bottom and up sides of pie plate. Bake 10 minutes at 325 degrees.

Peanut Butter Pastry

Makes 9-inch single crust

1 1/4 cups flour

1/3 cup crunchy or creamy peanut butter, chilled

1/2 teaspoon salt

6 tablespoons cold water

Combine flour and salt. Cut in peanut butter; add water.

Roll out dough. Bake at 375 degrees 12-15 minutes until golden. This is not a real flaky pie crust, but delicious!

Macadamia Nut Crust
Makes two 9-inch pie crusts

2 1/2 cups flour
3/4 cup cold butter or
margarine, cut up

6-8 tablespoons water
1 1/2 cups macadamia nuts,
finely chopped

Cut butter into flour until crumbly. Add water; form into a ball.
Turn out onto floured surface and knead in nuts. Roll out on
floured surface. Bake at 375 degrees for 15-20 minutes or until
golden.
Variations:
Makes wonderful tart shells. For tarts, divide into 12 equal
portions. Press each portion into a 3 to 4-inch tart pan. Prick
bottoms and side with fork.

Sweet Pistachio Crust
Makes 9-inch single crust

1/2 cup softened butter or
margarine
1/3 cup sugar
1 cup flour

1 teaspoon vanilla
2/3 cup chopped pistachios

Cream butter and sugar together. Gradually add flour until well
blended. Stir in vanilla and pistachios. Press into bottom and
up sides of a 9-inch pie plate or springform pan. Bake at 350
degrees for 12 to 15 minutes or until golden.

Cookie Nut Crust

1/2 cup softened butter or
margarine
1/3 cup brown sugar, packed
1 1/4 cups flour

1/2 cup chopped nuts (your
choice)
1/2 teaspoon vanilla

Mix butter and sugar; stir in remaining ingredients until
crumbly. Press mixture in bottom and 1/2 inch up sides of 9-
inch pie plate. Bake at 350 degrees for 10-12 minutes or until
golden.

Almond Chocolate Wafer Crust
Makes 9 or 10-inch single crust

1 cup sliced almonds
25 chocolate wafers

1/4 cup butter or margarine, melted

Grind almonds in food processor, place in bowl. Pulse wafers in processor or crush with rolling pin. Add to almonds with melted butter. Press mixture on bottom and up sides of pie plate. Bake at 350 degrees for 10 minutes. (This makes enough mixture to fit into a 10-1/2-inch tart or springform pan.)

Butter Almond Pie Crust
Makes two 9-inch single crusts

2 cups flour
1/4 cup finely chopped almonds
1/4 teaspoon salt

2/3 cup cold butter (no substitutes)
5 to 8 tablespoons cold water

Combine flour, almonds and salt. With pastry blender, cut in butter until mixture resembles coarse crumbs. With fork, add water one tablespoon at a time, just until flour is moistened. Divide dough in half. Shape each into a ball. Wrap and chill. Roll out each half on a lightly floured surface into 12-inch circle. Place in pie plate. Bake at 375 degrees for 15 to 20 minutes for single baked pie crust, or follow individual recipe instructions.

Pressed Nut Crust

1 cup flour
1/2 cup softened butter or margarine

1/4 cup finely chopped nuts (your choice)

Mix all ingredients until soft dough forms. Press in bottom and up sides of 9-inch pie plate. Bake at 400 degrees for 12 to 15 minutes until golden.

No-Weep Meringue

1 tablespoon cornstarch	3 egg whites
1/2 tablespoon cold water	6 tablespoons sugar
1/2 cup boiling water	1 teaspoon vanilla

Mix cornstarch with cold water in small saucepan. Add boiling water; cook until thick. Set aside to cool.

Beat egg whites to soft peaks. Add cooled cornstarch mixture; continue beating until stiff. Add sugar 1 tablespoon at a time; beat until well mixed. Add vanilla; spread on pie.

Bake at 350 degrees for 15 minutes or until brown; turn off heat. Let cool in oven with the door open.

Meringue for 9-inch Pie

3 egg whites
1/4 teaspoon cream of tartar
6 tablespoons sugar

Beat egg whites and cream of tartar until foamy; add sugar two tablespoons at a time. Beat until stiff. cover cooled pie filling, sealing edges. Bake in hot oven at 425 degrees for 5 minutes.

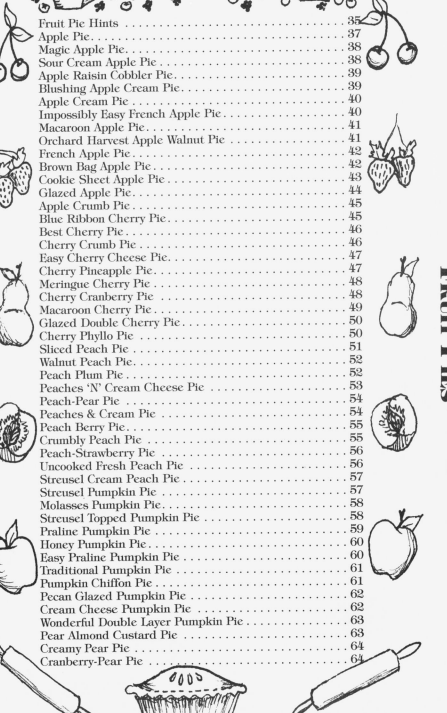

FRUIT PIES

FRUIT PIES

Fruit Pie Hints

FLAKY CRUST

• To keep the bottom crust from becoming soggy when making juicy berry pies, sprinkle the bottom of crust with equal mixture of sugar and flour.

APPLES

• To make peeling apples easier, halve and core apples then place them in double boiler steamer for 4 to 5 minutes. When they soften the peel can easily be pulled off.

• To core apples easily, use the small end of a melon baller to neatly scoop out the core from halved apples.

• To freeze apples properly, peel and slice then drop into Fruit Fresh to keep from discoloring. Place the slices in boiling water for 2 minutes then cool in cold water 2 minutes. Drain. Place slices into plastic freezer bags. Seal, label and freeze. For diced or chopped apples, cut the slices after they are defrosted.

• Look for firm flavorful varieties of baking apples such as Golden Delicious, Granny Smith, Rome and Northern Spy. Combine several types for interesting flavor. Avoid soft-eating apples such as McIntosh, they will fall apart during baking and lose their flavor.

APRICOTS

• Fresh or dried apricots can be substituted for fresh or dried peaches.

BLUEBERRIES

• Frozen blueberries can be substituted for fresh berries but be sure to reduce the liquid and increase the thickener in the recipe. **Do not thaw before baking.**

• If you are lucky enough to find them, wild blueberries can be used . . . they have a more intense flavor.

• Fresh blueberries are usually available from May through October.

Fruit Pie Hints

CHERRIES

- Tart cherries make the best pies. Did you know February is National Cherry Month?

- If cherries are in season, two cups of pitted fresh cherries can be substituted for one can canned cherries. If liquid is needed substitute cranberry juice for equal amount of cherry juice.

CRANBERRIES

- If using frozen cranberries, do not thaw before using in pie recipes.

PEACHES

- Peak season for fresh peaches is June through September. Fresh peaches aren't always in season, so you can use frozen or canned peaches for substitute. Thaw and drain frozen peaches and well-drain canned peaches. One pound of frozen or canned peaches equal three medium fresh peaches. (Save the syrup from canned peaches to pour over pancakes, waffles, ice cream, angel food cakes etc.)

PINEAPPLE

- Pineapple is low in calories, has no fat, a good source of fiber and rich in vitamin C.

PUMPKIN

- Fresh pumpkin can be substituted for canned. Wash, peel and remove seeds. Cut into chunks and steam until soft. Puree using a blender or food processor. Cool and pack into freezer bags or containers. Use exact amount for canned pumpkin.

RHUBARB

- Rhubarb is at its peak April through June.

STRAWBERRIES

- Before storing strawberries, remove any damaged ones. You can cut off the bad spots and use these berries in sauces or recipes where appearance doesn't matter. Store berries in the refrigerator with the hulls intact, unwashed and lightly covered.

Apple Pie

Pastry for double crust pie
3/4 cup flour
1/2 teaspoon each ground nutmeg and cinnamon
1/4 teaspoon salt

6 cups thinly sliced and peeled tart apples
3/4 cup sugar
2 tablespoons butter or margarine

Mix sugar, flour, spices and salt. Stir in apples.

Turn into pastry-lined pie plate. Dot with butter. Cover with top crust, seal and flute. Bake at 425 degrees for 40 to 50 minutes or until pie is brown and juice begins to bubble thru slits.

Variations:

Dutch Apple Pie:
Make extra large slits in top crust; 5 minutes before end of baking, pour 1/2 cup whipping cream thru slits in top crust. Best served warm.

French Apple Pie:
Omit margarine, do not top with top crust, instead use **Crumb Top:** Mix 1 cup flour, 1/2 cup cold butter or margarine and 1/2 cup packed brown sugar. Cover top with aluminum foil the last 10 minutes of baking.

Easy Apple Pie:
Substitute 2 cans (20-ounces each) sliced apples, drained for the 6 cups fresh apples.

Tip: Jonathan, Granny Smith and Golden Delicious apples are the best baking apples.

Magic Apple Pie

1 egg
3/4 cup sugar
1/2 cup flour
1 teaspoon baking powder
Pinch of salt

1 medium tart apple, peeled
1/2 cup raisins
Whipped cream or ice cream, optional

In a mixing bowl, beat egg. Add sugar, flour, baking powder and salt. Stir in apple and raisins. Spread into a greased 9-inch pie plate.

Bake at 350 degrees for 25-30 minutes or until golden brown and a toothpick inserted near center comes out clean. Serve with whipped cream or ice cream if desired. This pie will form its own crust.

Sour Cream Apple Pie

9-inch unbaked pastry shell
2 eggs
1 cup sour cream
1 cup sugar
6 tablespoons flour, divided
1 teaspoon vanilla
1/4 teaspoon salt

3 cups peeled, chopped tart apples
3 tablespoons butter or margarine
1/4 cup packed brown sugar

In large bowl, beat eggs; add sour cream. Stir in sugar, two tablespoons flour, vanilla and salt; mix well. Stir in apples.

Pour into pie shell. Bake at 375 degrees for 15 minutes.

Combine butter, brown sugar and remaining flour. Sprinkle over top of pie. Return to oven for 20-25 minutes or until set. Cool completely.

Apple Raisin Cobbler Pie

1 shortbread pie crust
2 cans (20-ounce each) apple pie filling
1 cup raisins
1/4 teaspoon ground ginger

1/3 cup flour
1/4 cup packed brown sugar
3 tablespoons melted butter or margarine
3/4 cup chopped walnuts

Preheat oven to 375 degrees. Combine apple filling, raisins and ginger. Spoon into crust. Combine flour and sugar; cut in butter until crumbly. Stir in walnuts; sprinkle over filling.

Bake 35 to 45 minutes or until topping is golden.

Blushing Apple Cream Pie

Pastry for double crust pie
3/4 cup whipping cream
2 tablespoons red cinnamon candies
1/2 teaspoon ground cinnamon

1 cup sugar
1/4 cup flour
2 tablespoons vinegar
4-1/2 cups thinly sliced peeled tart apples

In a mixing bowl, combine whipping cream, cinnamon candies, cinnamon, sugar, flour and vinegar. Mix well. Add apples and stir gently to mix. Pour into pastry lined pie plate.

Roll out remaining pastry to fit top of pie. Cut slits in top crust; place over apples. Seal and flute edges. Bake at 400 degrees for 50 minutes or until pastry is golden and apples are tender.

Apple Cream Pie

9-inch baked pastry shell
4 cups thinly sliced peeled tart apples
2 tablespoons sugar
2 tablespoons lemon juice
1/4 cup butter or margarine
8-ounces cream cheese, softened

1-1/2 cups cold milk, divided
1 package (3.4-ounces) instant vanilla pudding mix
1 teaspoon grated lemon peel
1/4 cup apricot preserves or strawberry jelly, melted

In a large skillet, sauté apples, sugar and lemon juice in butter until apples are tender. Cool.

In a large mixing bowl, beat cream cheese until smooth. Gradually beat in 1 cup milk, dry pudding mix and lemon peel. Add remaining milk; beat until thickened. Spread into pastry shell. Arrange apples over filling. Brush with preserves. Refrigerate for 1 hour before serving. Brush with additional preserves if desired.

Impossibly Easy French Apple Pie

1 cup original Bisquick, divided
1/4 cup chopped nuts
1/4 cup packed brown sugar
3 tablespoons butter or margarine, divided
3 cups sliced peeled apples

1 teaspoon ground cinnamon
1/4 teaspoon ground nutmeg
1/2 cup sugar
1/2 cup milk
2 eggs

In a bowl, combine 1/2 cup Bisquick, nuts and brown sugar. Cut in 2 tablespoons butter until mixture resembles coarse crumbs; set aside.

In a bowl, combine apples, cinnamon and nutmeg; spread into a greased 9-inch pie plate. In another bowl, combine sugar, milk, eggs and remaining butter and Bisquick; stir until smooth. Pour over apples. Sprinkle with crumb mixture. Bake at 325 degrees for 40-45 minutes or until knife inserted in center comes out clean. Cool 5 minutes.

Macaroon Apple Pie

9-inch unbaked pastry shell

Filling:

4 cups sliced peeled tart apples

1/2 cup sugar

1/4 teaspoon ground cinnamon

Topping:

1/2 cup flour

1/2 cup sugar

1/2 teaspoon baking powder

1/4 teaspoon salt

1 egg

2 tablespoons butter or margarine, melted

1/2 teaspoon vanilla extract

1/4 cup flaked coconut

Toss apples with sugar and cinnamon; pour into crust. Bake at 375 degrees for 20 minutes. Meanwhile, combine the first four topping ingredients in a bowl. Stir in egg, butter and vanilla until smooth. Add coconut. Spoon over hot apples, carefully spreading to cover. Bake 30 minutes longer or until apples are tender.

Orchard Harvest Apple Walnut Pie

1 shortbread pie crust

2 cans (20-ounces each) apple pie filling

1/4 teaspoon ground nutmeg

6-ounce bag sweetened dried cranberries

Topping

1/3 cup flour

1/4 cup packed brown sugar

3 tablespoons melted butter or margarine

3/4 cup chopped walnuts

Heat oven to 375 degrees. Combine apple pie filling, 1 cup sweetened dried cranberries and nutmeg. Spoon into crust.

Topping: Combine flour and sugar; cut in butter until crumbly. Stir in walnuts; sprinkle over filling.

Bake 35 to 45 minutes or until topping is golden.

French Apple Pie

9-inch unbaked pastry shell
Filling:
1/2 cup firmly packed brown sugar
1/4 cup flour
1/4 cup golden raisins
1/4 cup chopped walnuts
2 teaspoons finely chopped fresh ginger root

5 medium (5 cups) Granny Smith apples, cored and thinly sliced
Topping:
3/4 cup flour
1/2 cup firmly packed brown sugar
1/2 cup cold butter
1/4 cup walnuts

Preheat oven to 375 degrees. In large bowl, combine first five filling ingredients. Add apple slices; toss gently to mix. Spoon into pie shell.

In small bowl, combine 3/4 cup flour and 1/2 cup brown sugar; cut in 1/2 cup butter until crumbly. Stir in 1/4 cup walnuts. Press evenly over apple mixture.

Bake **55** to 60 minutes or until apples are fork tender. If crust is browning too quickly, cover with pie shield. Serve warm or cool.

Brown Bag Apple Pie

9-inch unbaked pastry shell
4 large tart apples
1 cup sugar
1/2 cup butter

1 teaspoon cinnamon
3/4 cup flour
1 large brown paper bag

Peel and core apples. Arrange in bottom of pie shell. Mix cinnamon and 1/2 cup sugar together; sprinkle over apples.

In a separate bowl, sift remaining sugar with flour. Cut in butter until crumbly. Sprinkle over apples.Place pie into brown paper bag and bake 50-60 minutes in a 375 degree oven.

Cookie Sheet Apple Pie

3-3/4 cups flour
1-1/2 teaspoons salt
3/4 cup shortening
3 eggs, lightly beaten
1/3 cup milk
1-1/2 cups sugar

8 cups sliced peeled tart apples
1 teaspoon ground cinnamon
1/2 teaspoon ground nutmeg
1 cup crushed cornflakes
1 egg white, beaten

In a bowl, combine flour and salt. Cut in shortening until mixture resembles coarse crumbs. Add eggs and milk. Mix to form dough. Chill for 20 minutes.

Divide dough in half; roll one half to fit the bottom and sides of a greased 15x10x1-inch baking pan. Arrange apples over crust.

Combine sugar, cinnamon, nutmeg and cornflakes. Sprinkle over apples. Roll out remaining dough to fit top of pan. Seal edges; cut slits in top. Brush with egg white.

Bake at 400 degrees for 15 minutes; reduce heat to 350 degrees and bake 25-30 minutes or until golden brown.

*This recipe is great for a large crowd!

Glazed Apple Pie

Crust:
5 cups flour
4 teaspoons sugar
1/2 teaspoon salt
1/2 teaspoon baking powder
1-1/2 cups shortening
2 egg yolks
2/3 cup ice water

Filling:
4 cups thinly sliced peeled tart apples
4 teaspoons lemon juice
1 teaspoon vanilla extract
3/4 cup sugar
3/4 cup packed brown sugar
2 teaspoons ground cinnamon
1/4 teaspoon salt
3 tablespoons butter or margarine
2 tablespoons milk

Glaze:
1/2 cup confectioners' sugar
1 tablespoon water
1/8 teaspoon vanilla extract

In a bowl, combine flour, sugar, salt and baking powder. Cut in shortening until crumbly. Beat egg yolks and water; add to flour mixture, tossing with a fork until dough forms a ball. Divide dough in half. Roll out one half to fit the bottom and up the sides of an ungreased 15x10x1-inch baking pan.

Toss apples with lemon juice and vanilla; set aside. Combine sugars, cinnamon and salt. Place half of the apples over crust and sprinkle with half of the sugar mixture. Repeat; dot with butter.

Roll out remaining pastry to fit top of pie; place over filling. Seal and flute edges. Brush with milk. Bake for 50-55 minutes or until golden brown in a 350-375 degree oven. Cool for 10 minutes. Combine glaze ingredients and drizzle over pie.

Apple Crumb Pie

9-inch unbaked pastry shell
6 cups peeled, chopped, tart apples (approximately 6)
2 tablespoons butter or margarine, melted
2 tablespoons sour cream
4 teaspoons lemon juice
1/2 cup sugar

1 tablespoon flour
1/2 teaspoon ground cinnamon
1/2 teaspoon ground nutmeg
Topping:
1/2 cup flour
1/2 cup sugar
1/4 cup cold butter or margarine

In a bowl, combine the apples, butter, sour cream, lemon juice, sugar, flour, cinnamon and nutmeg. Spoon into pastry shell.

Topping: Combine flour and sugar in a bowl. Cut in butter until mixture resembles coarse crumbs. Sprinkle over filling.

Bake at 375 degrees for 45-50 minutes or until the apples are tender. Cool on wire rack.

Blue Ribbon Cherry Pie

Pastry for double crust 10" pie
2 (16-ounce each) cans tart cherries
7 tablespoons flour

1-1/2 cups sugar
1 teaspoon cinnamon
2 tablespoons berry wine
1/2 teaspoon red food coloring

Preheat oven to 400 degrees. Drain cherries, reserving 1 cup juice. Mix flour, sugar and cinnamon in saucepan. Add reserved cherry juice, wine and food coloring; mix well. Cook over low heat until thickened, stirring constantly. Pour over cherries in bowl; mix gently.

Pour filling into lined pie plate. Top with top crust. Seal and flute; cut vents. Bake for 40 to 45 minutes or until golden brown. May bake in 2 small pie plates if preferred.

Best Cherry Pie

Pastry for double crust pie

1 cup sugar

2 tablespoons plus 1-1/2 teaspoons cornstarch

1/8 teaspoon cinnamon

1/8 teaspoon salt

1/2 cup peach nectar

1/3 cup Chambord liqueur (optional)

2 tablespoons butter or margarine

3-1/2 cups thawed frozen dry pack pitted red tart cherries, well drained

Combine sugar, cornstarch, cinnamon and salt in medium saucepan. Stir in nectar and Chambord, if desired. Cook and stir over medium heat until thickened and clear. Add butter; stir until melted. Cool. Add cherries; stir until well blended.

Pour into unbaked pie crust. Cover pie with top crust or woven lattice top, if desired. Flute edge high then shield edge to prevent over browning.

Bake at 425 degrees for 30 minutes. Remove shield. Bake for 10 minutes. Do not over bake. Cool until barely warm or to room temperature before serving.

Cherry Crumb Pie

9-inch graham cracker crust

1 tablespoon cornstarch

1 tablespoon cold water

1 can (21-ounces) cherry pie filling

Topping:

1/3 cup flour

1/3 cup quick cooking oats

2 tablespoons sugar

2 tablespoons brown sugar

3 tablespoons cold butter or margarine

In a bowl, combine cornstarch and water until smooth. Stir in pie filling. Pour into crust.

Topping: Combine flour, oats and sugars in a small bowl. Cut in the butter until crumbly. Sprinkle over filling. Bake at 375 degrees for 35-40 minutes or until crust is golden brown and filling is bubbly. Cool on a wire rack then refrigerate until chilled.

Easy Cherry Cheese Pie

3/4 cup flour
3 tablespoons sugar
1/4 teaspoon salt
1/4 cup butter or margarine, softened
21-ounce can cherry pie filling

8-ounces cream cheese, softened
1/3 cup sugar
1 egg
1 teaspoon vanilla extract

In a bowl, combine flour, sugar and salt. Add butter; stir until combined. Press onto the bottom and up the sides of a 9-inch pie plate. Bake at 350 degrees for 10-12 minutes or until lightly browned. Pour cherry pie filling into crust.

In a mixing bowl, beat cream cheese, sugar, egg and vanilla until smooth. Carefully spread around outside edges of pie, leaving a 3-inch circle of cherries exposed in the center. Bake for 30-35 minutes or until edges begin to brown. Cool on a wire rack. Refrigerate for several hours before serving.

Cherry Pineapple Pie
If you like cherry pie, you will love this pie!

Pastry for double crust 9-inch pie
1 cup sugar
1/3 cup all-purpose flour
1/8 teaspoon salt
2 (16-ounce) cans pitted tart red cherries, well drained

2 (8-ounce) cans crushed pineapple, well drained
2 tablespoons butter or margarine
1 tablespoon milk
Additional sugar

Combine sugar, flour and salt. Stir in cherries and pineapple. Pour mixture into pastry lined pie plate. Dot with butter. Top with top crust. Brush with milk and sprinkle with sugar. (This pie looks great with a lattice topping.) Bake at 375 degrees for 50-60 minutes or until bubbly and golden brown.

Meringue Cherry Pie

9-inch unbaked pastry shell
Filling:
2 cups boiling water
1 cup dried cherries
3 egg yolks (save whites for meringue
2 cups sour cream (regular, light or non-fat)

1 cup firmly packed brown sugar
2 tablespoons flour
1 teaspoon almond extract
Recipe for meringue (See crust section)

Preheat oven to 425 degrees. Pour boiling water over cherries; let soak for 5 minutes then drain.

In a large mixing bowl, beat egg yolks until thick and lemon-colored . . 3 to 4 minutes. Stir in sour cream, brown sugar, flour and extract. Beat at medium speed, scraping bowl often, until well mixed . . . 1 to 2 minutes. By hand, stir in cherries.

Pour filling into pie shell. Bake for 20 minutes then reduce oven to 350 degrees. Bake for 20 minutes more.

Prepare meringue; spread over filling. Bake for 12-15 minutes or until lightly browned.

Cool at room temperature for 2 hours. Refrigerate at least 1 hour before serving.

Cherry Cranberry Pie

Pastry for 9-inch double crust
3/4 cup sugar
2 tablespoons cornstarch

1 can (21-ounces) cherry pie filling
2 cups cranberries
Milk and additional sugar

Combine sugar and cornstarch in a bowl. Stir in pie filling and cranberries.

(Continued on next page)

Line a 9-inch pie plate with bottom pastry. Pour filling into crust. Roll out remaining crust to fit top of pie. Cut slits in top or cut out stars with star-shaped cookie cutter.

Place pastry over filling; trim, seal and flute edges. Arrange star cutouts on pastry. Brush with milk and sprinkle with sugar. Cover edges with pie shield and bake at 375 for 55-60 minutes or until crust is golden brown and filling is bubbly. Cool on a wire rack.

Macaroon Cherry Pie

9-inch unbaked pastry shell

3 cans (14-1/2-ounces each) pitted tart cherries

1 cup sugar

1/3 cup cornstarch

1/2 teaspoon ground cinnamon

1/4 teaspoon red food coloring, optional

Topping:

1 egg, lightly beaten

2 tablespoons milk

1 tablespoon butter or margarine, melted

1/4 teaspoon almond extract

1/4 cup sugar

1/8 teaspoon salt

1 cup flaked coconut

1/2 cup sliced almonds

Line a 9-inch deep dish pie plate with pastry. Flute edges. Bake crust for 6 minutes in a 400 degree oven. Set aside.

Drain cherries, reserving 1 cup juice. Set aside.

In a saucepan, combine sugar and cornstarch. Gradually stir in cherry juice until blended. Bring to a boil over medium heat; cook and stir for 2 minutes or until thickened. Remove from heat; stir in cinnamon and food coloring if desired.

Gently fold in cherries. Pour into crust. Cover edges with pie shield. Bake at 400 degrees for 20 minutes.

Meanwhile, in a bowl, combine the first six topping ingredients. Stir in coconut and almonds. Remove pie shield from pie; spoon topping over pie. Bake at 350 degrees for 20 minutes or until topping is lightly browned. Cool on wire rack for 1 hour. Chill for 4 hours before cutting.

Glazed Double Cherry Pie

Pastry for double crust pie

1/2 cup sugar

3 tablespoon cornstarch

16-ounce package frozen unsweetened pitted dark sweet cherries

1/2 teaspoon vanilla

3/4 cup sliced almonds, toasted

21-ounce can cherry pie filling

1/4 cup sifted powdered sugar

1 to 1-1/2 teaspoons milk

In a bowl, stir sugar and cornstarch together. Add frozen cherries and vanilla. Toss. Let stand at room temperature for 1 hour or until a syrup forms. Stir occasionally.

Preheat oven to 375 degrees. Place 1/2 cup almonds in bottom of pastry-lined pie plate. Stir sweet cherry mixture and spoon on top of almonds. Spoon cherry pie filling over sweet cherry mixture; spread evenly.

Place top pastry over filling; trim and flute edges. Cover edge to prevent over browning. Bake 50 minutes. Remove cover and bake about 30 minutes more or until top is golden brown and filling is bubbly. Remove from oven; cool on wire rack for 1 to 1-1/2 hours. Stir powdered sugar and enough milk to make a drizzling consistency. Drizzle over pie. Sprinkle remaining almonds on top of pie. Cool completely before serving.

Cherry Phyllo Pie

10 frozen phyllo leaves, thawed

1/2 cup margarine or butter melted

3 tablespoons cornstarch

1 teaspoon lemon juice

1 cup sugar

3 drops red food coloring, if desired

2 cans (16-ounces each) pitted red tart cherries, drained

Heat oven to 350 degrees. Cut stack of phyllo leaves into 12-inch squares; discard remaining strips. Cover squares with damp towel to prevent them from drying out. Carefully separate

(Continued on next page)

(Cherry Phyllo Pie - *continued*)

1 square; brush with margarine. Place in ungreased 9-inch pie plate, allowing corner of phyllo to hang over edge of pie plate. Repeat with 4 squares.

Mix sugar and cornstarch. Stir in lemon juice, food coloring and cherries. Spread in phyllo-lined pie plate. Fold overhanging corners phyllo over filling. Spread each remaining phyllo square with margarine. Arrange on filling to make top crust allowing corners to hangover edge of plate. Fold overhanging corners of phyllo under, between bottom layers and rim of plate. Cut through top layers of phyllo with scissors to make 8 sections.

Bake until crust is golden brown and juice begins to bubble through cuts in phyllo . . about 45 to 50 minutes.

Sliced Peach Pie

9-inch baked pastry shell
15-ounce can sliced peaches
2 tablespoons brown sugar
1/4 teaspoon ground ginger
1 cinnamon stick (3-inches)
1 (3-ounce) package peach gelatin

4 ounces cream cheese, softened
2 tablespoons butter or margarine, softened
1/8 teaspoon ground nutmeg
8-ounces frozen whipped topping, thawed
Fresh mint, optional

Drain syrup from peaches into a 2-cup measuring cup. Add enough water to measure 1-1/3 cups. Chop peaches and set aside.

In a saucepan, combine the syrup, brown sugar, ginger and cinnamon stick. Bring to a boil. Reduce heat; cook and stir for 5 minutes. Remove from heat. Discard cinnamon stick. Stir gelatin into syrup mixture until it is dissolved. Add peaches. Refrigerate until partially set . . about 40 minutes.

In a mixing bowl, beat cream cheese, butter and nutmeg until smooth. Spread over the bottom and up the sides of the crust. Pour gelatin mixture over cream cheese layer. Chill until serving. Spread with whipped topping. Garnish with mint if desired.

Walnut Peach Pie

1 shortbread pie crust

10 tablespoons butter or margarine, softened

2/3 cup sugar

1 egg

1 teaspoon vanilla

1 cup finely ground walnuts

1/3 cup raisins

2 cups fresh, canned or frozen and thawed peach slices

1/3 cup peach preserves

In a mixing bowl, beat butter and sugar until light and fluffy; beat in egg and vanilla. Stir in raisins and walnuts. Spoon filling into piecrust.

Drain peach slices between layers of paper towel. Arrange on top of pie, slightly overlapping the edges. Bake at 350 degrees for 55 minutes or until pie is browned and set in center. Cool on wire rack.

In a small saucepan, heat preserves to boiling; boil until slightly thickened. . . about 1-1/2 minutes. Strain; brush preserves over pie.

Peach Plum Pie

Pastry for double crust pie

2 cups peeled fresh peaches or frozen peaches, thawed and drained

2 cups sliced peeled purple plums

1 tablespoon lemon juice

1 1/2 cups sugar

1/4 cup quick-cooking tapioca

1/4 teaspoon salt

2 tablespoons butter or margarine

In a large bowl, combine peaches, plums and lemon juice. In smaller bowl, combine sugar, tapioca and salt. Add to fruit mixture. Stir gently and let stand for 15 minutes.

Pour into pastry lined pie pan. Dot with butter. Cover with top crust, flute and seal. Slit top. Bake at 450 degrees for 10 minutes. Reduce heat to 350 degrees and bake for 35 minutes longer or until crust is golden and filling is bubbly.

Peaches 'N' Cream Cheese Pie

10-inch unbaked pastry shell

1/2 cup butter or margarine, softened

2/3 cup sugar

2 eggs

1 cup flour

1 teaspoon baking powder

1 teaspoon vanilla

8-ounces cream cheese, softened

1 tablespoon peach juice

1/3 cup sugar

1/4 cup sour cream

1 egg

1/4 teaspoon salt

Sliced fresh peaches

1 cup sour cream

2 tablespoons brown sugar

Preheat oven to 325 degrees. Cream butter with 2/3 cup sugar in large mixing bowl until fluffy. Beat in 2 eggs. Add mixture of flour and baking powder; mix well. Stir in vanilla and peach juice. Spread over pie shell.

Blend cream cheese and 1/3 cup sugar in medium mixing bowl until light. Beat in 1/4 cup sour cream, 1 egg and salt. Spread over cream cheese mixture. Arrange peach slices over top.

Bake for 30 to 35 minutes. Blend 1 cup sour cream and brown sugar in small bowl. Spoon over pie. Bake for 5 minutes longer. Chill until serving time.

Peach-Pear Pie

1 unbaked 9-inch pastry shell
1/3 cup packed brown sugar
1/4 cup sugar
3 tablespoons cornstarch
1/2 teaspoon ground cinnamon
1/4 teaspoon ground allspice
1-1/2 cups sliced peeled fresh peaches
2-1/2 cups sliced peeled fresh pears
1 tablespoon lemon juice

<u>**Walnut Streusel:**</u>
1/2 cup flour
1/4 cup sugar
3 tablespoons brown sugar
1/4 teaspoon each ground cinnamon and nutmeg
1/4 cup cold butter or margarine
1/3 cup chopped walnuts

Combine sugars, cornstarch, cinnamon and allspice in bowl. Set aside. Sprinkle peaches and pears with lemon juice. Add to dry ingredients. Toss to coat. Pour into pastry shell.

For streusel, combine dry ingredients; cut in butter until mixture resembles coarse crumbs. Stir in nuts. Sprinkle over filling. Cover edges with pie shield. Bake at 375 degrees for 1 hour or until bubbly. Remove shield.

Peaches & Cream Pie

9-inch unbaked pastry shell
3/4 cup sugar
1/4 cup flour
1/4 teaspoon salt
1/4 teaspoon nutmeg
1/4 teaspoon cinnamon
3 cups peeled, sliced peaches (about 5 medium)
1 cup whipping cream
Whipped cream garnish

Preheat oven to 350 degrees. Prick pastry shell with fork. Bake 10 minutes. Set aside to cool. Increase oven temperature to 400 degrees.

Combine sugar, flour, salt, nutmeg and cinnamon in large bowl. Add peaches, toss gently. Spoon mixture into pie shell. Pour whipping cream over top. Bake until set, about 40 to 45 minutes. Let cool to room temperature. Serve with whipped cream.

Peach Berry Pie

Pastry for double crust pie
1 1/2 cup sugar
1/4 cup all-purpose flour
2 tablespoons cornstarch
1/2 teaspoon salt
1/2 teaspoon nutmeg
1 3/4 cups sliced, peeled fresh or frozen peaches (drained)

3/4 cup fresh or frozen blueberries
3/4 cup fresh or frozen cranberries or raspberries
1 teaspoon vanilla
1 tablespoon butter or margarine

Combine sugar, flour, cornstarch, salt and nutmeg together in a large bowl. Add fruit and vanilla. Mix well. Let set for 15 minutes; stir.

Pour into pastry lined pie pan. Dot with butter. Cover with top crust or lattice top. Bake at 375 degrees for 50-55 minutes or until golden brown and bubbly.

Crumbly Peach Pie

9-inch unbaked pastry shell
1 cup sugar
2 tablespoons flour
1/8 teaspoon nutmeg

1/2 cup butter
6 or 8 large ripe peach halves
4 tablespoons water

Blend sugar, flour, nutmeg and butter until crumbly. Put half of the crumbly mixture in the pastry shell. Arrange peach halves on top with the cut side down. Cover with remaining crumbly mixture. Add water.

Bake at 450 degrees for 10 minutes then reduce heat to 350 degrees and bake until peaches are tender. Be sure to use only soft, ripe peaches. . . otherwise the crust will burn before peaches are cooked.

Peach-Strawberry Pie

Pastry for double crust pie

4 cups sliced, peeled fresh peaches or 4 cups frozen unsweetened peach slices

1 cup sugar

3 tablespoons flour

2 tablespoons quick-cooking tapioca

2 cups coarsely chopped fresh strawberries

4 teaspoons butter

1 tablespoon sugar

Thaw peaches if frozen; drain and set aside. Preheat oven to 400 degrees. In a large bowl, combine 1 cup sugar, flour and tapioca. Add peaches and strawberries. Toss gently to combine; spoon into pastry-lined pie plate. Dot with butter.

Top with top crust, slit and flute edges as desired. Sprinkle with 1 tablespoon sugar. Bake for 45-50 minutes or until filling is bubbly in center. To prevent over browning, cover edge of pie while baking. Cool completely on a wire rack before serving.

Uncooked Fresh Peach Pie

9-inch baked pastry shell

3 cup fresh sliced peaches

3/4 cup sugar

1 tablespoon lemon juice

3 tablespoons cornstarch

1/4 teaspoon salt

2 teaspoon butter or margarine

1/4 teaspoon vanilla or almond flavoring

Combine peaches, sugar and lemon juice. Let stand one hour. Drain; measure 1 cup syrup. Add cornstarch to syrup. Cook over low heat until thick. Add salt, butter and flavoring. Cool.

Place sliced peaches in pastry shell. Pour syrup over peaches. Serve with whipped cream or ice cream if desired.

Hint: To save time, combine peaches, sugar and lemon juice and let stand while you are preparing your pie crust

Streusel Cream Peach Pie

9-inch unbaked pastry shell
4 cups sliced peaches
3/4 cup sugar
1/2 teaspoon nutmeg, optional

1 egg
2 tablespoons cream or milk
1/2 cup flour
1/4 cup butter

Preheat oven to 375 degrees. Arrange peach slices in crust. Combine 1/2 cup sugar and nutmeg. Sprinkle over peaches. Beat egg and cream together. Pour over peaches. Mix flour, remaining sugar and butter until crumbly. Sprinkle over peaches.

Bake 35-45 minutes or until brown. Serve warm. Pie may be served topped with ice cream or whipped cream, if desired.

Streusel Pumpkin Pie

Filling:

1 (30-ounces) can pumpkin pie mix

1 (14-ounces) can sweetened condensed milk

1 egg, lightly beaten

Topping:

1/2 cup packed brown sugar

1/4 cup all-purpose flour

1/4 cup chopped pecans

1/2 teaspoon ground cinnamon

3 tablespoons cold butter or margarine

This recipe makes two 9-inch pies. You will need two unbaked pie shells. I suggest the Crunchy Pecan Crust. (See crust section)

Combine pumpkin pie mix, condensed milk and egg. Pour into pastry shells.

For topping, combine sugar, flour, pecans and cinnamon in small bowl. Cut butter in until crumbly. Sprinkle over filling. Bake at 375 degrees for 40-45 minutes or until knife inserted in center comes out clean.

Molasses Pumpkin Pie

9-inch unbaked pastry shell
2 eggs
1/2 cup sugar
1 teaspoon ground cinnamon
1/2 teaspoon salt
1/2 teaspoon ground ginger

1/2 teaspoon ground nutmeg
1-3/4 cups canned or cooked pumpkin
3 tablespoons molasses
3/4 cup evaporated milk
Whipped topping

In a mixing bowl, beat eggs, sugar, cinnamon, salt, ginger and nutmeg. Beat in pumpkin and molasses; gradually add milk. Pour into crust. Cover edges with pie shield.

Bake in a 425 degree oven for 10 minutes. Remove pie shield and reduce heat to 350 degrees. Bake an additional 28-32 minutes or until a knife inserted near the center of the pie comes out clean. Cool on a wire rack for 2 hours then chill until ready to serve. Serve with whipped topping. Refrigerate leftovers.

Streusel Topped Pumpkin Pie

1 graham cracker crust
15-ounce can pumpkin
14-ounce can sweetened condensed milk
1 egg
1-1/4 teaspoons ground cinnamon

1/2 teaspoon each ground ginger, nutmeg and salt
1/4 cup firmly packed brown sugar
2 tablespoons flour
2 tablespoons cold butter or margarine
3/4 cup chopped walnuts

With mixer or wire whisk, beat pumpkin, sweetened condensed milk, egg, 3/4 teaspoon cinnamon, ginger, nutmeg and salt. Pour into crust. Bake 15 minutes.

Meanwhile, combine sugar, flour and remaining 1/2 teaspoon cinnamon; cut in butter until crumbly. Stir in walnuts. Remove pie from oven; reduce oven to 350 degrees. Sprinkle streusel mixture over pie. Bake 40 minutes or until set. Cool. Serve warm or at room temperature. Refrigerate leftovers. Top with whipped cream if desired.

Praline Pumpkin Pie

9-inch unbaked pastry shell
Praline Layer:
3 tablespoons butter or margarine
1/3 cup firmly packed brown sugar
1/3 cup chopped pecans
Custard Layer:
1 cup evaporated milk
1/2 cup water

3 eggs
1-1/2 cups pumpkin (from a 1-pound can)
1/2 cup granulated sugar
1/2 cup firmly packed brown sugar
1-1/2 teaspoon pumpkin-pie spice
1 teaspoon salt
1/2 cup heavy cream, whipped

Cream butter or margarine with the 1/3 cup brown sugar in small bowl; stir in pecans. Press over bottom of prepared shell evenly.

Bake in 450 degree oven for 10 minutes; remove and cool on wire rack 10 minutes. Reduce heat to 350 degrees.

Custard Layer: Scald evaporated milk with water in small saucepan. Beat eggs slightly in large bowl; stir in pumpkin, granulated sugar, brown sugar, pumpkin-pie spice and salt. Beat in scalded milk mixture. Pour into cooled pastry shell.

Bake in 350 degree oven 50 minutes or until center is set but still soft. Do no over bake. Custard will set as it cools. Cool pie completely on wire rack. Top with whipped cream,

Honey Pumpkin Pie

9-inch unbaked pastry shell
1 can (16-ounces) solid pack pumpkin
1 cup evaporated low-fat milk
3/4 cup honey

3 eggs, lightly beaten
2 tablespoons flour
1 teaspoon ground cinnamon
1/2 teaspoon ground ginger
1/2 teaspoon rum extract

In a large bowl, combine first eight ingredients; beat until blended. Pour into pie shell. Bake at 400 degrees for 45 minutes or until knife inserted near center comes out clean. Cool on wire rack.

Easy Praline Pumpkin Pie

1 graham cracker crust
4 tablespoons butter or margarine
1/2 cup chopped pecans
1/3 cup packed brown sugar
1 package (3 ounces) cook and serve custard mix
1/3 cup sugar
1 teaspoon ground cinnamon

1/4 teaspoon ground cloves
1/4 teaspoon ground allspice
2/3 cup evaporated milk
2/3 cup milk
1 can (16-ounces) solid pack pumpkin
Whipped topping
Additional chopped pecans

In a medium saucepan, melt butter; stir in pecans and brown sugar. Cook and stir over low heat until bubbly. Spoon into pie crust.

In a medium saucepan, combine custard mix, sugar and spices. Stir in milks and pumpkin. Cook and stir over medium heat until bubbly. Cover and cool for 20 minutes. Pour filling over pecan mixture. Refrigerate 3 hours or until set. Garnish with whipped topping and chopped pecans.

Traditional Pumpkin Pie (makes two pies)

Two (9-inch) unbaked pastry shells

6 eggs

1 can (29-ounces) solid-pack pumpkin

2 cups packed brown sugar

2 teaspoons ground cinnamon

1 teaspoon salt

1/2 teaspoon each ground cloves, nutmeg and ginger

2 cups evaporated milk

Beat eggs in a mixing bowl. Add pumpkin, sugar, salt and spices. Beat just until smooth. Gradually add milk. Pour into pastry shells. Bake at 450 degrees for 10 minutes. Reduce heat to 350 degrees and bake an additional 40-45 minutes longer or until knife inserted near the center comes out clean. Cool on wire racks. (For one pie just use half of the above ingredients.)

*What moistens the lips,
what brightens the eye,
What calls back the past
like rich pumpkin pie?*

Pumpkin Chiffon Pie

9-inch baked pastry shell

3 eggs, separated

1 cup sugar

1-1/4 cups cooked or canned pumpkin

1/2 cup milk

1/2 teaspoon salt

1/2 teaspoon ginger

1/2 teaspoon cinnamon

1/2 teaspoon nutmeg

1 tablespoon unflavored gelatin

1/4 cup cold water

Beat egg yolks and 1/2 cup sugar until thick. Add pumpkin, milk, salt and spices. Cook in double boiler until thick. Remove from heat. Soften gelatin in cold water; stir into hot mixture. Beat egg whites and remaining sugar; add to pumpkin mixture.

Pour into cooled baked shell; chill. If desired, spread sweetened whipped cream over top of pie.

61

Pecan Glazed Pumpkin Pie (makes 2 pies)

Two (9-inch) unbaked pastry shells

2 eggs

16-ounce can pumpkin

12-ounce can evaporated milk

1 cup brown sugar, divided

2 teaspoons pumpkin pie spice

2 tablespoons butter, melted

1 cup pecan pieces

Beat eggs, pumpkin, evaporated milk, 3/4 cup sugar and pumpkin pie spice. Pour filling into crusts. Bake 20 minutes in a 375 degree oven.

Combine 1/4 cup sugar, pecans and melted butter together. Crumble over top of partially baked pies. Bake 20 to 30 minutes more or until knife inserted in center comes out clean.

Cream Cheese Pumpkin Pie

9-inch unbaked pastry shell

8-ounce package cream cheese, softened

1 egg yolk, slightly beaten

2 tablespoons honey

1/2 teaspoon vanilla

1 cup canned pumpkin

5-ounce can evaporated milk (2/3 cup)

2 slightly beaten eggs

1/3 cup packed brown sugar

1 teaspoon ground cinnamon

1/4 teaspoon ground nutmeg

Preheat oven to 375 degrees. In a bowl beat cream cheese, egg yolk, honey and vanilla with an electric mixer on low to medium speed until smooth. Set aside.

In another bowl, stir together pumpkin, evaporated milk, the remaining 2 eggs, brown sugar, cinnamon and nutmeg. Pour pumpkin mixture into pastry-lined pie plate. Dollop the cream cheese mixture over pumpkin mixture. Pull a thin metal spatula or knife gently through dollops to swirl fillings.

Bake for 50 minutes or until top is puffed and a knife inserted near the center comes out clean. Cool 1 hour on a wire rack. Cover and chill at least 2 hours before serving.

Wonderful Double Layer Pumpkin Pie

1 graham cracker crust
4-ounces softened cream cheese
1 tablespoon sugar
1 tablespoon half & half or milk
1-1/2 cups frozen whipped topping, thawed
1 cup cold milk or half & half

2 packages (4-ounces each) vanilla instant pudding and pie filling
16-ounce can pumpkin
1/2 teaspoon ginger
1 teaspoon cinnamon
1/4 teaspoon cloves

Combine cream cheese, 1 tablespoon half & half and sugar in large bowl. Beat with whisk until smooth. Carefully add whipped topping. Spread on bottom of crust.

Pour 1 cup half & half into bowl. Add pudding mixes and beat 1 to 2 minutes with whisk. Stir in pumpkin and spices. Mix well. Spread over cream cheese layer.

Refrigerate 4 hours or until set.

Pear Almond Custard Pie

1 graham cracker crust
1/2 cup unsalted butter, softened
1/2 cup sugar
1 egg
1 cup ground almonds

1 teaspoon almond extract
1 tablespoon flour
1 can (29-ounces) pear halves, drained and patted dry with paper towel

In a mixing bowl at medium speed, cream butter and sugar until light and fluffy, scraping bowl frequently. Add egg, almonds, almond extract and flour. Mix until combined.

Slice 4 pear halves about 1/2 inch thick and place in the bottom of the pie crust. Arrange remaining pears in the pie crust. Spoon almond mixture evenly over the pears.

Bake at 350 degrees for 35 minutes or until almond mixture is golden brown. Cool on wire rack.

Creamy Pear Pie

9-inch unbaked pastry shell
4 cups sliced peeled pears
1/3 cup sugar
2 tablespoons flour
8-ounces sour cream
1/2 teaspoon vanilla extract
1/2 teaspoon lemon extract

1/2 teaspoon almond extract
Topping:
1/4 cup flour
2 tablespoons butter or
margarine, melted
2 tablespoons brown sugar

In a large bowl, toss pears with sugar and flour. Combine sour cream and extracts; add to pear mixture and mix well. Pour into pie shell. In a small bowl, mix topping ingredients until crumbly. Sprinkle over pears. Bake at 400 degrees for 10 minutes. Reduce heat to 350 degrees and bake 45 minutes longer or until pears are tender.

Cranberry-Pear Pie

Pastry for double crust pie
1 cup sugar
1/4 cup water
4 cups thinly sliced, peeled
and cored pears

2 cups cranberries
3 tablespoons cornstarch
1/4 cup cold water
1/2 teaspoon aniseed,
crushed, optional

In a large saucepan combine sugar and the first 1/4 cup water. Bring to boil; stir to dissolve sugar; reduce heat. Simmer, uncovered for 5 minutes. Add pears and cranberries. Return to boiling; reduce heat. Simmer fruit mixture, uncovered, over medium-high heat for 3 to 4 minutes or until cranberries pop, stirring occasionally.

In a small bowl combine cornstarch and 1/4 cup cold water. Stir cornstarch mixture into the cranberry mixture. Bring to boiling; reduce heat. Simmer for 2 minutes, stirring occasionally. remove from heat and stir in aniseed, if desired.

Transfer cranberry mixture to the pastry-lined pie plate. Cover with top crust. Bake in a 375 degree oven for 55 to 60 minutes or until the top is golden. Cool on a wire rack. Serve warm or at room temperature.

Pear Streusel Pie

9-inch unbaked pastry shell
__Filling:__
4 cups peeled and sliced pears
1/4 cup butter or margarine
3 tablespoons light corn syrup
1 tablespoon lemon juice
1/4 cup all-purpose flour
1/4 cup sugar
2 tablespoons cornstarch

1/2 teaspoon each ground cinnamon and allspice
1/8 teaspoon salt
__Topping:__
1/2 cup all-purpose flour
1/2 cup sugar
1/4 cup butter
1/2 cup chopped pecans

Combine pears, butter, corn syrup and lemon juice. Toss gently.

Combine flour, sugar cornstarch, spices and salt. Add to pear mixture. Pour mixture into unbaked pie shell.

To make topping, combine flour and sugar. Cut in butter; add pecans. Sprinkle over pie. Bake at 450 degrees for 10 minutes then reduce heat to 350 degrees and bake for 45 more minutes or until golden.

Fresh Pear Crumb Pie

10-inch unbaked pastry shell
6 cups thinly sliced firm pears
3 tablespoons lemon juice
1/2 cup sugar
2 tablespoons all-purpose flour

__Topping:__
1/2 cup all-purpose flour
1/2 cup sugar
1/2 teaspoon ginger
1 teaspoon cinnamon
1/4 cup butter or margarine

Drizzle pears with lemon juice. Toss with mixture of 1/2 cup sugar and 2 tablespoons flour in bowl. Spread into pie shell.

For topping, combine 1/2 cup flour, 1/2 cup sugar, ginger and cinnamon in medium bowl. Cut in butter until crumbly. Sprinkle over pears. Bake in a 375 degree oven for 50-55 minutes or until pears are tender and top is brown.

Pear Crumb Pie

9-inch unbaked pastry shell
Filling:
1/2 cup packed brown sugar
2 tablespoons cornstarch
1/2 teaspoon ground cinnamon
1/4 teaspoon ground ginger
1/8 teaspoon salt

Dash ground nutmeg
6 cups thinly sliced peeled pears
1 tablespoon lemon juice
Topping:
2/3 cup flour
1/3 cup packed brown sugar
1/3 cup cold butter or margarine

Combine filling ingredients; spoon into crust. Bake at 400 degrees for 25 minutes.

For topping, combine flour and brown sugar; cut in butter until crumbly. Sprinkle over filling. Bake 40 minutes longer.

Triple Fruit Pie-1

Pastry for double crust pie
1 cup dried apricots, quartered
3/4 cup dried cherries
1 cup water or orange juice
4 cups peeled & sliced pears
1/2 teaspoon ground ginger

1 tablespoon finely shredded lemon peel
1 cup sugar
2 tablespoons instant tapioca
2 tablespoon flour

In a small saucepan, combine apricots, cherries and water or orange juice. (Use orange juice if you want a tarter pie.) Bring to boil, reduce heat. Simmer uncovered until most of liquid is reduced and fruit is moist.

Peel, core and slice pears into 1/4-inch slices. In a large bowl, combine pears, apricot mixture, ginger, lemon peel, sugar, tapioca and flour.

Transfer mixture to a 9-inch pie plate lined with your favorite pastry. (I suggest wheat germ pastry for this pie.) Adjust top crust over filling. Seal and flute. Bake at 350 degrees for 75 minutes or until pastry is golden and fruit is tender.

Mincemeat-Pear Pie

Pastry for 9-inch double crust pie

3 cups thinly sliced, peeled and cored pears (3 medium)

27-ounce jar mincemeat (2-2/3 cups)

1 tablespoon lemon juice

Milk, optional

Coarse sugar, optional

Hard Sauce:

3/4 cup butter

1-1/4 cups sifted powdered sugar

3 tablespoons brandy, rum or orange juice

1/2 teaspoon vanilla

Filling: In a medium mixing bowl stir pears, mincemeat and lemon juice together. Transfer filling to pastry-lined pie plate.; flute edge. Cover edge of pie with pie shield and bake in a 375 degree oven for 25 minutes. Remove cover and continue baking for 20-25 minutes or until pastry is golden brown. Cool on a wire rack.

Meanwhile, on a lightly floured surface, with a knife or cookie cutter cut remaining piecrust into stars or other decorative shapes. Place pastry cutouts on an ungreased cookie sheet. If desired, brush cutouts with milk and sprinkle lightly with coarse sugar. Bake cutout alongside the pie about 10 minutes or until golden brown. Transfer cutouts to a wire rack to cool. To serve arrange baked cutouts atop pie. Serve slices of pie with Hard Sauce if desired.

Hard Sauce: In a medium mixing bowl, beat butter and sifted powdered sugar until fluffy. Beat in brandy, rum or orange juice and vanilla. Store, covered in refrigerator for up to 2 weeks. Let stand at room temperature for 30 minutes before serving.

Baked Pineapple Pie

10-inch unbaked pastry shell
4 eggs
16-ounce can crushed
pineapple
1-3/4 cups sugar
3 tablespoons all-purpose flour

Salt to taste
3 tablespoons melted
margarine
3 tablespoons lemon juice
1/2 teaspoon vanilla

Preheat oven to 375 degrees. Beat eggs slightly in medium bowl with fork. Add pineapple, sugar, flour, margarine, lemon juice, vanilla and salt. Mix gently. Spoon into pie shell and bake for 60 minutes.

Pineapple Pie

9-inch baked pastry shell
1 small can crushed pineapple
3/4 cup sugar
1 small box lemon or lime
flavored gelatin

1 (12-ounce) can evaporated
milk, chilled
2 tablespoons lemon juice
Green food coloring, optional

Combine crushed pineapple, sugar and gelatin in the top of a double boiler. Heat slowly until gelatin dissolves. Stir well and cool, but do not allow it to gel. Whip milk with lemon juice. Combine the two mixtures. Add a few drops of green food coloring, if desired.

Pour mixture into shell. Chill until set . . .about 2 hours.

Pineapple Meringue Cream Pie

9-inch baked pastry shell
1 package pineapple cream pie filling
1-3/4 cup milk
1/4 cup pineapple juice
2 egg yolks
1/2 cup drained crushed pineapple

1/4 cup chopped maraschino cherries
Meringue:
2 egg whites
1/4 teaspoon salt
1/4 teaspoon cream of tartar
4 tablespoons sugar

Cook pie filling, milk, pineapple juice and egg yolks over medium heat; stir constantly until mixture boils and is thick and smooth. Remove from heat and fold in pineapple and cherries. Pour into pie shell.

Meringue: Beat egg whites with salt and cream of tartar until soft peaks form; gradually beat in sugar until stiff peaks form. Pile on pie and bake at 375 degrees for 8 to 10 minutes.

Coconut Pineapple Pie

9-inch unbaked pastry shell
1 cup sugar
3 tablespoons flour
1 cup light corn syrup
1 cup flaked coconut

8-ounce can crushed pineapple, drained
3 eggs, beaten
1 teaspoon vanilla extract
1/4 cup butter or margarine, melted

In a bowl, combine sugar and flour. Add corn syrup, coconut, pineapple, eggs and vanilla. Mix well. Pour into pie shell and drizzle with butter.

Place pie shield over edges to prevent over browning. Bake at 350 degrees for 50-55 minutes or until a knife inserted near the center comes out clean.Cool on wire rack and chill before serving.

Glazed Pineapple Pie

Pastry for double crust pie
1 can (20-ounces) crushed pineapple
1 cup sugar
1/4 cup flour
1 tablespoon lemon juice

1 tablespoon butter or margarine, melted
1/4 teaspoon salt
3/4 cup flaked coconut
1/2 cup confectioners' sugar
1/4 teaspoon vanilla extract

Drain pineapple, reserving 1 tablespoon juice for glaze. In medium bowl, combine pineapple, sugar, flour, lemon juice, butter and salt; mix well then set aside.

Line a 9-inch pie pan with the bottom pastry. Sprinkle with coconut. Spread pineapple mixture over coconut. Top with remaining pastry; flute edges and cut slits in top.

Bake at 400 degrees for 35-40 minutes or until golden brown. Cool 20 minutes on wire rack.

Glaze: Combine confectioners' sugar, vanilla and reserved pineapple juice until smooth. Spread over the top of warm pie. Serve warm or at room temperature.

To decorate top of pie, use a small pineapple-shaped cookie cutter to cut shapes from top pastry before placing pastry over filling. Place dough shapes on an ungreased baking sheet and bake at 350 degrees for 8-10 minutes or until golden. Cool slightly; arrange on top of baked pie after glazing.

Perfect Rhubarb Pie

Pastry for 9-inch double crust pie

4 cups sliced fresh or frozen rhubarb

4 cups boiling water

1-1/2 cups sugar

3 tablespoons flour

1 teaspoon quick cooking tapioca

1 egg

2 teaspoons cold water

1 tablespoon butter or margarine

Place rhubarb in a colander and pour boiling water over it. Set aside. In a bowl, combine sugar, flour and tapioca. Mix well. Add rhubarb; toss to coat. Let stand for 15 minutes. Beat egg and 2 teaspoons cold water; add to rhubarb mixture and mix well.

Line a 9-inch pie plate with bottom pastry. Add filling. Dot with butter. Cover with remaining pastry; flute edges, cut slits in top crust. Bake at 400 degrees for 15 minutes. Reduce heat to 350 degrees. Bake 40-50 minutes longer or until crust is golden brown and filling is bubbly.

Oat-Topped Rhubarb Pie

9-inch unbaked pastry shell

1-1/2 cups packed brown sugar

1/3 cup water

4 tablespoons plus 1-1/2 teaspoons quick cooking tapioca

4-1/2 cups fresh or frozen chopped rhubarb, thawed

Topping:

1 cup old-fashioned oats

1/2 cup packed brown sugar

1/4 cup cold butter or margarine

Toss brown sugar, water, tapioca and rhubarb together in bowl. Let stand for 15 minutes. Pour into crust.

Topping: Combine oats and brown sugar in a bowl. Cut in butter until crumbly. Sprinkle over filling.

Cover edges with pie shield and bake at 375 degrees for 45 minutes. Remove shield and bake 10-15 minutes longer or until browned and bubbly. Cool 3 hours before cutting.

71

Rhubarb Crunch Pie

9-inch unbaked pastry shell
2 cups chopped rhubarb
1 egg, slightly beaten
2 tablespoons all-purpose flour
1 cup sugar

1 teaspoon vanilla extract
1/2 cup packed light brown sugar
1/3 cup butter or margarine
3/4 cup all purpose flour

Combine rhubarb, egg, 2 tablespoons flour, sugar and vanilla in bowl; mix well. Spoon into pie shell. Mix brown sugar, butter and 3/4 cup flour until crumbly. Sprinkle over pie.

Bake for 15 minutes in a 425 degree oven. Reduce oven temperature to 350 degrees. Bake for 30 minutes longer. May replace flour with blended oats or add a few cornflakes.

Strawberry-Rhubarb Crumb Pie

9-inch unbaked pastry shell
Filling:
1 egg
1 cup sugar
2 tablespoons all-purpose flour
1 teaspoon vanilla
3 cups rhubarb, cut into 1/2-inch pieces

1 pint strawberries, halved
Topping:
3/4 cup all-purpose flour
1/2 cup brown sugar, packed
1/2 cup rolled oats
1/2 cup cold butter or margarine

Beat egg in mixing bowl; beat in sugar, flour and vanilla. Gently fold in rhubarb and strawberries. Pour into pie shell.

For topping, combine flour, sugar and oats in small bowl. Cut in butter until crumbly. Sprinkle over fruit.

Bake at 400 degrees for 10 minutes. Reduce heat to 350 degrees, bake for 35 more minutes or until golden and bubbly.

Raisin Meringue Pie

9-inch baked pastry shell
1 cup packed brown sugar
2 tablespoons flour
8-ounces sour cream
3 eggs, separated
1/2 teaspoon each ground
nutmeg, cinnamon and
allspice

1/4 teaspoon salt
1 cup chopped raisins
1/4 teaspoon cream of tartar
6 tablespoons sugar

In heavy saucepan, combine brown sugar and flour. Stir in sour cream, egg yolks, spices and salt until smooth. Cook and stir over medium heat until mixture comes to a boil. Remove from the heat. Stir in raisins; cover and set aside.

In a mixing bowl, beat egg whites and cream of tartar on medium speed until foamy, about 1 minute. Gradually beat in sugar, 1 tablespoon at a time, on high until stiff glassy peaks form and sugar is dissolved, about 3 minutes. Pour hot raisin filling into pastry shell. Spread meringue evenly over filling; seal edges to crust.

Bake at 350 degrees for 15 minutes or until golden brown.

Raisin Pie

9-inch unbaked pastry shell
3 eggs, separated
3 tablespoons butter
1-1/2 cups sugar
1 tablespoon vinegar or lemon
juice

2 cups raisins, plumped (soak
in hot water for a few
minutes)
1 teaspoon vanilla

Cream butter and sugar, then add beaten egg yolks, vinegar or lemon juice, raisins and vanilla. Fold in beaten egg whites. Pour into pastry shell. Bake at 325 degrees about 45 minutes until a knife inserted in pie comes out clean.

73

Raisin-Apple Cider Pie

9-inch unbaked pastry shell
6 cups apple slices
1 cup apple cider
3/4 cup sugar
1/4 teaspoon salt
2 tablespoons cornstarch

2 tablespoons lemon juice
1/4 teaspoon nutmeg
1/4 teaspoon cinnamon
2 tablespoons butter or margarine
1 cup seedless raisins

Heat apples, cider, sugar and salt to boiling. Cover; simmer until apples are barely tender. Drain, measuring liquid. If less than 1-1/2 cups liquid, add cider to make required measure. Blend liquid, cornstarch, lemon juice, spices and butter; simmer until thickened. Add apples and raisins; pour into pastry shell. Bake in 425-degree oven 20 to 25 minutes. (Decorate with leftover pastry cut in petal shapes and baked separately on cookie sheet if desired.) Serve warm or cold.

Southern Dixie Pie

9-inch unbaked pastry shell
3/4 cup raisins
Water
1/2 cup butter or margarine, softened
1/2 cup sugar
1/2 cup packed brown sugar
3 eggs

1 teaspoon vanilla
1 to 2 teaspoons ground cinnamon
1/2 cup chopped nuts
1/2 cup flaked coconut
Whipped topping
Additional chopped nuts for garnish, optional

Bake pastry shell at 450 degrees for 8-10 minutes only.

Place raisins in saucepan and cover with water. Bring to boil. Remove from heat.

Cream butter and sugars together; beat in eggs, vanilla and cinnamon until smooth.

Drain raisins. Add raisins, nuts and coconut to creamed mixture. (Mixture will appear curdled.) Pour into pastry shell.

Bake at 350 degrees for 30 to 35 minutes or until set. Cool. Garnish with whipped topping and nuts if desired.

Sour Cream Raisin Pie

9-inch unbaked pastry shell
1 cup sour cream
1 cup light brown sugar, packed
1 teaspoon allspice

2 tablespoons flour
3 egg yolks
3 tablespoons buttermilk
1 teaspoon vanilla
1 cup chopped raisins

Combine sugar, spice and flour. Mix well. Add beaten egg yolks, sour cream, buttermilk, vanilla and raisins. Pour into unbaked pastry shell.

Bake 40-50 minutes in a 350 degree oven.

Grandma's Sour Cream Raisin Pie

9-inch baked pastry shell
1-1/2 cups dark raisins
3/4 cup sugar
1/4 cup cornstarch
1/2 teaspoon cinnamon
1/4 teaspoon nutmeg
1/4 teaspoon salt

2 cups milk
3 egg yolks. beaten
1 cup sour cream
1 tablespoon lemon juice
1 cup whipping cream, whipped (optional)

Combine first six ingredients in 2-quart saucepan. Stir in milk. Bring to a boil over medium heat, stirring constantly. Boil for 1 minute; remove from heat. Stir a small amount of hot mixture into egg yolks; stir egg yolks into hot mixture. Stir in sour cream. Cook just until mixture begins to bubble; remove from heat. Add lemon juice. Cool for 10 minutes. Spoon into pie shell. Chill for 2 hours or until set. Top with whipped cream.

Ruby Grape Pie

Pastry for 9-inch double crust

4 cups halved seedless red grapes (about 2 pounds)

2/3 cup sugar

1/2 teaspoon ground cinnamon

3 tablespoons cornstarch

2 tablespoons lemon juice

1 tablespoon grated lemon peel

2 tablespoons butter or margarine

In a bowl, combine grapes, sugar and cinnamon; toss to coat. Let stand for 15 minutes. Combine cornstarch, lemon juice and peel; stir into grapes.

Line a 9-inch pie plate with bottom crust. Pour grape mixture into crust. Dot with butter. Roll out remaining pastry to fit top of pie; place over filling.

Trim, seal and flute edges; cut slits in top. Cover edges with pie shield. Bake at 375 degrees for 30-40 minutes or until golden brown.

Easy Berry Pie

Pastry for 9-inch double crust

5 cups blackberries, blueberries or raspberries

3/4 to 1 cup sugar (for blueberry use 3/4 cup sugar)

1/2 cup all-purpose flour (for blueberry use 3 tablespoons)

2 tablespoons lemon peel or 1/2 teaspoon cinnamon

Mix the sugar and flour together in a large mixing bowl. Stir in berries and lemon peel or cinnamon. Gently toss until berries are coated.

Pour mixture into pastry lined pie pan. Top with top crust or lattice top. Bake at 375 degrees for 40-50 minutes or until golden.

<u>Variation:</u> Mixed Berry Substitute for the 5 cups of berries:

2 cups strawberries

2 cups blueberries

1 cup blackberries or raspberries

Granny Ruby's Raisin Pie

Pastry for double crust pie
2 cups water
2 cups raisins
1 teaspoon cinnamon
1 teaspoon pumpkin pie spice

1 teaspoon vanilla
1 cup sugar
5 teaspoons flour
1/2 cup water

Mix water and raisins together and cook over low heat until tender. Add spices, vanilla and sugar. Bring to a boil. Stir flour and water together. Add to hot mixture. Stir until thickened. Pour into pastry-lined pan. Adjust top curst. Flute edges. Bake at 400 degrees for about 40 minutes.

When I smell the wonderful aroma of cinnamon, nutmeg and allspice, it still brings back one of the sweetest memories of my childhood. I can remember coming home from school and smelling my mom's raisin pies as soon as I opened the door.

I come from a large family (twelve children) so when my mom made pies, she always had to bake several. She would bake two or three and then stack them together and then bake two to three more.

I can still remember how amazed I was to see how perfectly she stacked those pies. And to this day, when I smell sweet spices or bake my mom's raisin pie, it takes me back to those sweet days of my childhood. But I still have not figured out how to stack pies!!

Ozark Mountain Berry Pie

Pastry for 9-inch double crust
1-1/2 cups sugar
4 tablespoons plus 1-1/2 teaspoons cornstarch
3/4 cup cold water

3 tablespoons lemon juice
3 cups fresh blueberries
1 cup fresh raspberries
1 cup fresh blackberries

In a saucepan, combine sugar and cornstarch. Stir in water and lemon juice until smooth. Add berries; stir gently. Bring to a boil over medium heat; cook and stir for 2 minutes or until thickened and bubbly. Remove from heat; cool.

Line a 9-inch pie plate with bottom crust. Add filling. Roll out remaining pastry; make a lattice crust. Seal and flute edges. Cover edges with pie shield. Bake at 400 degrees for 10 minutes. Reduce heat to 350 degrees and remove pie shield. Bake 40-50 minutes longer or until crust is golden brown and filling is bubbly. Cool completely before serving.

Blueberry Pie

Pastry for 9-inch double crust
4 cups fresh or frozen blueberries
1 tablespoon lemon juice
1-1/4 to 1-1/2 cups sugar
1/4 cup quick cooking tapioca

1 tablespoon cornstarch
1/2 teaspoon grated lemon peel
1 tablespoon butter or margarine

In a bowl, combine berries and lemon juice. Add sugar, tapioca, cornstarch, and lemon peel; toss gently. Let stand 15 minutes.

Line a 9-inch pie plate with bottom crust. Add filling; dot with butter.

Place remaining pastry over filling. Cut slits in top. Trim, seal and flute edges. Cover edges with pie shield and bake at 350 degrees for 30 minutes. Remove pie shield and bake 20-30 minutes longer or until crust is golden brown. Cool on wire rack.

Triple Berry Pie

Pastry for double crust 9-inch pie (I suggest crunchy pastry - see crust section)

1-1/4 cups each fresh blueberries, raspberries and chopped rhubarb*

1/2 teaspoon almond extract

1-1/4 cups sugar

1/4 cup quick cooking tapioca

1/4 teaspoon ground nutmeg

1/4 teaspoon salt

1 tablespoon lemon juice

In large bowl, combine fruits and extract; toss to coat. In another bowl, combine sugar, tapioca, nutmeg and salt. Add to fruit; stir gently. Let stand for 15 minutes. Add lemon juice. Pour into pastry lined pie plate. Cover with top crust. Seal and flute edges. Bake at 400 degrees for 20 minutes. Reduce heat to 350 degrees and bake 30 minutes longer or until the crust is golden brown and filling is bubbly.

*Frozen berries and rhubarb may be substituted for fresh; thaw and drain before using.

Blackberry-Sour Cream Pie

9-inch unbaked pastry shell

4 cups fresh blackberries

1 cup sugar

1 cup sour cream

6 tablespoons flour

1/4 teaspoon salt

1 cup fine dry bread crumbs

2 tablespoons sugar

1 tablespoon melted butter or margarine

Preheat oven to 375 degrees. Place blackberries in pie shell. Combine 1 cup sugar, sour cream, flour and salt in bowl; mix well. Spread over blackberries.

Combine bread crumbs, 2 tablespoons sugar and butter in bowl; mix well. Sprinkle over pie.

Bake 40-45 minutes or until golden brown. May substitute 2 cans blackberries for fresh blackberries.

Raspberry Glaze Pie

9-inch baked pastry shell

5 cups fresh raspberries, divided

1 cup water, divided

1 cup sugar

3 tablespoon cornstarch

2 tablespoons lemon juice

3 ounces cream cheese, softened

1 tablespoon butter or margarine, softened

1 tablespoon milk

Combine 2/3 cup berries and 2/3 cup water in saucepan. Simmer for 3 minutes. Strain berries; reserving liquid, and discard seeds.

In another saucepan, combine sugar, cornstarch and remaining water until smooth. Add raspberry juice. Bring to a boil over medium heat; cook and stir for 2 minutes or until thickened. Remove from heat and stir in lemon juice. Cool.

Beat cream cheese, butter and milk in small mixing bowl until smooth. Spread in the bottom and up the sides of baked pastry shell. Top with remaining berries. Slowly pour glaze over berries. Refrigerate until serving.

Fresh Raspberry Pie

1-1/4 cups flour

3 tablespoons confectioners' sugar

1/2 cup cold butter or margarine

Filling:

1 cup sugar

1-1/2 cups cold water

3 tablespoons plus 2 teaspoons cornstarch

3 tablespoons corn syrup

1/4 cup strawberry gelatin powder

1/2 teaspoon vanilla

1 quart fresh raspberries

(Continued on next page)

Combine flour and confectioners' sugar; cut in butter until crumbly. Press onto bottom and up the sides of an ungreased 9-inch pie plate. Bake at 350 degrees for 18-22 minutes or until edges are golden brown. Cool on a wire rack.

In a saucepan, combine sugar and cornstarch. Stir in water until smooth; stir in corn syrup. Bring to a boil; cook and stir for 2 minutes or until thickened. Remove from the heat; stir in gelatin and vanilla until gelatin is dissolved. Cool to room temperature, about 30 minutes. Add raspberries; gently stir to coat. Spoon into crust. Refrigerate until set about 3 hours.

Raspberry Topped Lemon Pie

9-inch graham cracker crust

3 egg yolks

14-ounces sweetened condensed milk

1/2 cup lemon juice from concentrate

10-ounces frozen red raspberries in syrup, thawed

1 tablespoon cornstarch

Whipped topping

Preheat oven to 325 degrees. With mixer, beat egg yolks and sweetened condensed milk until well blended. Stir in lemon juice. Pour into crust.

Bake 30 minutes.

Meanwhile, combine raspberries and cornstarch in saucepan. Cook and stir until mixture thickens and is clear. Spoon on top of pie.

Chill at least 4 hours. Top with whipped topping. Garnish as desired and refrigerate leftovers.

White Chocolate Strawberry Pie

9-inch baked pastry shell

4 (1-ounce) squares white baking chocolate

2 tablespoons milk

3-ounces cream cheese, softened

1 teaspoon grated orange peel, optional

1/3 cup confectioners sugar

1 cup whipping cream, whipped

2 cups fresh sliced strawberries

Whipped cream or one square melted chocolate for garnish, optional

In double boiler or microwave, melt four squares of chocolate with milk. Cool to room temperature.

In mixing bowl, beat cream cheese and sugar until smooth. Beat in orange peel and melted chocolate. Fold in whipped cream.

Spread into crust. Arrange strawberries on top. Top with whipped cream or melt one square chocolate and drizzle on top for garnish. Refrigerate at least one hour.

This is one of my family's favorite pies. . . so I usually make two. When I do, I just use a 1 (8-ounce) package of cream cheese.

Strawberry Cheesecake Pie

9-inch graham cracker crust

2 cups sliced fresh strawberries

1/4 cup chopped almonds, toasted

1 tablespoon sugar

8-ounce package cream cheese, softened

2 cups cold milk, divided

3/4-ounce package instant vanilla pudding

In a bowl, combine strawberries, almonds and sugar. Pour into prepared crust. In a mixing bowl, beat cream cheese until smooth; gradually add 1/2 cup milk. Add pudding mix and remaining milk. Beat for 1 minute or until blended; pour over strawberries. Cover and refrigerate for 2 hours or until set.

Strawberry Pie Supreme

9-inch baked pastry shell
1 cup sugar
2 tablespoons cornstarch
2 tablespoons white corn syrup

1 cup water
2 tablespoons strawberry gelatin
Few drops of red food coloring
1 quart fresh strawberries

Mix sugar and cornstarch; add corn syrup and water. Bring to a boil and cook for 6 minutes over medium heat. Add gelatin and coloring; cool mixture.

Wash, stem and drain berries and put in baked pie shell. Pour cooled mixture over berries; refrigerate. Serve with whipped cream.

Angel Pie

1 baked deep dish or two 8 or 9-inch baked pastry shells
2 eggs
1 cup sugar
1 cup strawberries

1 (3-ounce) package strawberry gelatin
1 (12-ounce) can evaporated milk, chilled
Dash of salt

Beat eggs until lemon colored. Add sugar. Stir in strawberries and heat in double boiler, stirring constantly. (Do not boil or over cook.) Add gelatin and stir until dissolved. Cool.

Whip chilled milk and salt until stiff; fold in strawberry mixture. Put in one large or two small baked pastry shells and chill thoroughly.

For variety, use 1 small can crushed pineapple (instead of strawberries) and 1 package lemon gelatin instead of strawberry.

Cranberry Raisin Pie

Pastry for 9-inch double crust pie

1-1/2 cups sugar

1/4 cup all purpose flour

1/4 teaspoon salt

1/2 teaspoon ground cinnamon

1/4 teaspoon ground nutmeg

1 cup orange juice

2-2/3 cups fresh or frozen cranberries

1 cup raisins

Combine sugar, flour, cinnamon, salt and nutmeg in a saucepan. Gradually stir in orange juice until smooth. Stir in cranberries and raisins; bring to a boil. Reduce heat; cook and stir over medium heat until thickened, about 5 minutes. Pour into crust. Cover with top crust. Trim, seal and flute edges. Make slits in top. Bake at 400 degrees for 35-40 minutes or until golden brown and filling is bubbly. Cool on a wire rack. Refrigerate leftovers.

Cranberry Pie

Pastry for 9-inch double crust pie

3 cups cranberries, cut in half

1/2 cup water

1 3/4 cups sugar

5 tablespoons all-purpose flour

1/4 teaspoon salt

1/2 teaspoon almond extract

2 tablespoons butter or margarine

Place cranberries and water in saucepan. Bring slowly to a boil. Mix sugar, flour and salt together. Gradually add to boiling cranberries, stirring constantly. Use a fork to stir the ingredients. Cook on low heat until mixture thickens.

Remove from heat; add almond extract. Cool and pour into pastry-lined pie plate. Dot with butter or margarine.

Add top crust and seal or perhaps cut out holly leaves to make it more elegant. Bake in a 425 degree oven for 35-45 minutes.

Lemon-Cranberry Pie

Pastry for double crust pie
1-1/4 to 1-1/3 cups sugar
2 tablespoons flour
3 cups cranberries
2 lemons, peeled, thinly sliced
and halved (Remove white
membrane)

1 beaten egg white
1 tablespoon water
1 tablespoon coarse sugar

Preheat oven to 375 degrees. In a large mixing bowl combine sugar and flour. Add cranberries and lemon slices. Gently toss to coat.

Transfer fruit mixture to pastry-lined pie plate. Cover with top crust or lattice crust; seal and flute.

Combine egg white and water; brush onto pastry. Sprinkle with coarse sugar.

To prevent over browning, shield the edge of the pie. Bake for 25 minutes with shield then remove and bake for 30 to 35 minutes more or until top is golden brown and filling is bubbly. Cool on a wire rack.

Bumbleberry Pie

Pastry for double crust pie
2 large cooking apples, peeled
and chopped
1 cup chopped fresh rhubarb
1 cup fresh raspberries

1 cup fresh strawberries,
halved
1 cup fresh blueberries
1 cup sugar
1/2 cup flour
1 tablespoon fresh lemon juice

Combine apples and next 7 ingredients in a large bowl. Stir gently to mix. Pour into pastry lined pie plate. Top with top crust, slit and flute edges. Bake at 400 degrees for 25 minutes. Reduce heat to 350 degrees and bake 25 to 30 minutes more, shielding edges of pie to prevent excessive browning.

Note: Substitute frozen rhubarb and berries, thawed and drained for fresh if desired.

85

Sour Cream-Apricot Pie

9-inch deep dish unbaked
pastry shell

1 cup finely chopped dried
apricots

1/4 cup water

3 eggs

1-1/4 cups sugar

1 cup sour cream

1-1/2 teaspoons vanilla

Preheat oven to 400 degrees. Combine apricots and water in small bowl. Let stand until water is absorbed. Beat eggs in bowl. Add sugar gradually, beating until thick. Beat in sour cream and vanilla. Stir in apricots. Spoon into pie shell. Bake for 15 minutes. Reduce oven to 350 degrees. Bake for 25 to 30 minutes longer or until set.

Triple Fruit Pie - 2

Pastry for 9-inch double crust
pie (I suggest crunchy pastry
recipe - see crust section)

1 cup dried apricots, quartered

1 cup rum or orange juice

3/4 cup dried cherries,
snipped

6 to 8 medium pears (4 cups
sliced)

2 tablespoons crystallized
ginger, finely chopped _or_

1/2 teaspoon ground ginger

1 tablespoon finely shredded
lemon peel

1 cup sugar

2 tablespoons quick cooking
tapioca

2 tablespoons flour

In a small saucepan combine apricots, rum or orange juice and cherries. Bring to boil; reduce heat. Simmer gently uncovered until most of the liquid is evaporated and fruit is moist.

Peel, core and slice pears into 1/4-inch slices. In a large mixing bowl, combine apricot mixture, pear slices, ginger, lemon peel, sugar, tapioca and flour.

Place fruit mixture in pastry lined pie pan. Place top crust over filling. Seal and flute. Bake at 350 degrees for 75 minutes or until golden and fruit is tender. Serve warm.

Frosted Orange Pie

9-inch baked pastry shell
3/4 cup sugar
1/2 cup all-purpose flour
1/4 teaspoon salt
1-1/4 cups water
2 egg yolks, lightly beaten
2-3 tablespoons grated orange peel
1/2 teaspoon grated lemon peel
1/2 cup orange juice
2 tablespoons lemon juice

Frosting:
1/2 cup sugar
2 egg whites
2 tablespoons water
1/8 teaspoons cream of tartar
1/8 teaspoon salt
1/2 cup flaked coconut, toasted, optional

In a saucepan, combine sugar, flour, and salt. Gradually add water. Cook and stir over medium-high heat for 2-3 minutes or until thick and bubbly. Remove from heat. Gradually stir 1/2 cup into egg yolks; return to pan. Bring to a gentle boil; cook and stir for 2 minutes.

Remove from heat and stir in orange and lemon peel. Gently stir in juices. Pour into pastry shell. Cool on wire rack for 1 hour. Chill at least 3 hours.

In a heavy saucepan or double boiler, combine sugar, egg whites, water, cream of tartar and salt. Beat on low speed with a mixer for 1 minute. Continue beating on low speed over low heat until frosting reaches 160 degrees, about 8-10 minutes.

With a stand mixer, beat on high for 7 minutes, until frosting forms stiff peaks. Spread over chilled pie. Just before serving, sprinkle with coconut. Store refrigerated.

Florida Orange Meringue Pie

9-inch baked pastry shell
3 eggs
1-1/3 cups sugar
1/4 cup cornstarch
2 cups orange juice

2 tablespoons butter or margarine
1 tablespoon orange juice
6 tablespoons sugar

Preheat the oven to 350 degrees. Separate the egg yolks from egg whites. Place egg whites in a large bowl and set aside for meringue. Place egg yolks in a small bowl. Slightly beat egg yolks. Set aside.

For filling, stir together 1-1/3 cups sugar and cornstarch in a medium saucepan. Gradually stir in the 2 cups orange juice. Cook and stir over medium-high heat until thickened and bubbly. Reduce heat. Cook and stir about 2 minutes more. Remove from heat.

Gradually stir about 1 cup of the hot filling into the slightly beaten egg yolks. Stir the egg yolk mixture into the remaining hot mixture in saucepan. Bring to a gentle boil. Cook and stir for 2 minutes more. Remove from heat. Stir in the butter or margarine. Keep the filling warm while preparing the meringue.

For meringue, add 1 tablespoon orange juice to the egg whites in a bowl. Beat with electric mixer on medium speed for about 1 minute or until soft peaks form. Gradually add the 6 tablespoons sugar, 1 tablespoon at a time, beating on high speed for about 4 minutes more or until mix forms stiff, glossy peaks and sugar is dissolved.

Pour the warm filling into baked pastry shell. Immediately spread meringue over warm filling, sealing to the edge.

Bake pie in the preheated oven for 15 minutes. Cool on a wire rack for 1 hour. Chill in the refrigerator for at least 3 hours or up to 6 hours before serving. Cover the pie for longer storage.

Montana Huckleberry Pie

Pastry for double crust pie
4 cups huckleberries
1 cup sugar

6 tablespoons flour
1-1/2 tablespoons butter or margarine

Combine huckleberries with sugar and flour mixture. Pour filling into pastry-lined 9-inch pie pan. Dot with butter; cover with top crust. Seal, slit and flute edges.

Bake at 425 degrees for 40 to 50 minutes.

Grape Pie

Pastry for double crust pie
5 cups large seedless red and/or green grapes, halved
1/3 cup brown sugar, packed
1 tablespoon port wine or grape juice

1/4 cup flour
1 egg white
1 tablespoon water
Coarse sugar

Preheat oven to 400 degrees. In a large bowl, stir together grapes, brown sugar, flour and port wine or grape juice. Set aside.

Spoon filling into unbaked pastry shell. Shield edges and bake for 25 minutes. Remove shield and bake 25 to 30 minutes more or until filling is bubbly. Cool on wire rack.

Meanwhile, use a 1 to 2 inch leaf cookie cutter to cut out leaves from remaining pastry. Combine egg white and water. Brush leaf cutouts with egg white mixture. Sprinkle with coarse sugar. Place cutouts on a cookie sheet. Bake 7 to 8 minutes or until golden brown. Place leaf cutouts around pie.

Note: You can also make four small pies with same recipe by cutting two 6 to 6-1/2 inch circles from each crust. Line four 4-inch pans with pastry circles. Divide filling and bake about 25 minutes. Place leaf cutout on each pie.

Fresh Fig Pie

Pastry for double crust pie
2/3 cup sugar
2 tablespoons flour
Pinch of salt
2 cups sliced fresh figs, drained

1 tablespoon lemon or lime juice
Slivers of lemon peel
Butter
Milk

Blend dry ingredients. Sprinkle half dry ingredients into pastry lined pie plate. Pour sliced figs over dry mixture. Sprinkle lemon juice and slivers over figs. Add remaining dry mixture.

Dot generously with butter; cover with top crust; seal and flute. Cut slits in pastry; brush with milk. Sprinkle with additional sugar.

Bake at 375 degrees about 12 minutes; reduce heat to 350 degrees and bake until syrup oozes out around top pastry and figs bubble across pie.

Strudel Prune Pie

9-inch unbaked pastry shell
2-3/4 cups cooked pitted prunes, drained
1 egg
1/3 cup white sugar
Dash of salt
1 tablespoon lemon juice

1/2 cup prune liquid
Topping:
1/2 cup brown sugar
1/4 cup sifted flour
1/2 teaspoon cinnamon
3 tablespoons butter

Arrange prunes in pie crust. Beat egg; blend in sugar, salt, lemon juice and prune liquid. Pour over prunes.

Blend brown sugar, flour, cinnamon and butter until crumbly; sprinkle over fruit.

Bake at 450 degrees for 10 minutes, then at 350 degrees for 20 to 30 minutes more until set in center.

Date Pie

3 eggs, separated
1 cup sugar
1 cup graham cracker crumbs
1/2 cup nuts

1/2 cup dates, cut fine
1 teaspoon almond flavoring
Whipped cream

Beat egg whites until stiff. Add 1/2 cup sugar; beat until mixture hold peaks. Set aside.

Beat egg yolks until lemon colored; add remaining sugar and beat until thick. Add graham cracker crumbs to yolk mixture; add nuts, dates and flavoring. Mix well. Fold in egg whites. Bake in greased 9-inch pie plate for 30 minutes at 350 degrees. Top with whipped cream to serve.

Tangerine Pie

9-inch baked pastry shell
1 cup sugar
1/4 cup cornstarch
1/4 teaspoon salt
1-1/2 cups water
3 egg yolks (save whites for meringue)

2 tablespoons margarine
1/3 cup tangerine juice
1-1/2 teaspoons grated tangerine rind
Recipe for meringue

Combine 1/2 cup sugar, cornstarch and salt in top of double boiler; gradually add water. Cook over boiling water, stirring constantly until thickened. Cover and cook 10 minutes longer, stirring occasionally.

Beat together egg yolks and 1/2 cup sugar; blend a little hot mixture into egg yolk mixture. Stir all into remaining hot mixture in double boiler; cook over boiling water 2 minutes, stirring constantly. Remove from water; add margarine, juice and rind. Cool.

Pour into baked shell. Top with meringue. Bake at 350 degrees 15 to 20 minutes.

Hawaiian Fruit Pie

Two (9-inch) baked pastry shells

4 eggs, separated

2 cups milk

1 (4-ounce) package vanilla pudding mix

2 cans salad fruits

2 bananas

1 can cherry pie filling

1/2 cup coconut

4 tablespoons sugar

1 quart marshmallow cream

In saucepan, beat egg yolks; add milk and vanilla pudding mix. Cook until thick. Set aside to cool.

Thoroughly drain salad fruits. When pudding mix is cool, fold in fruits and bananas. Put half of the mixture into each pie shell to form a layer; put half cherry pie filling in a layer on top of pudding in each pie shell. Sprinkle with coconut. Beat egg whites and sugar until stiff; add marshmallow cream while beating. Top each pie with half the marshmallow cream topping mixture. Brown in 350 degree oven.

Fruit Salad Pie

Pastry for double crust pie

1 medium banana

10-ounce package frozen strawberries, thawed and drained (reserve syrup)

20-ounce can pineapple chunks in syrup, drained (reserve syrup)

1 tablespoon lemon juice

1/2 cup sugar

1/4 cup quick-cooking tapioca

1/4 teaspoon salt

2 tablespoons margarine or butter

Topping:

1 cup sour cream

2 tablespoons reserved strawberry syrup

Heat oven to 425 degrees. Slice banana into 2-1/2 quart bowl. Add strawberries, pineapple, lemon juice and 1/4 cup reserved pineapple syrup. Mix sugar, tapioca and salt; stir into fruit mixture. Turn into pastry shell. Dot with margarine. Cover with top crust. Slit and flute edges. Shield edge to prevent excessive browning; remove shield during last 15 minutes of baking.

Bake until crust is brown, 40 to 50 minutes; cool. Serve with Sour Cream Topping. Combine sour cream and 2 tablespoons reserved strawberry syrup.

CREAM PIES

Cream Pie Hints:

- Add a small amount of gelatin to whipped cream to stabilize and make it thicker. Soften 1/2 teaspoon unflavored gelatin in 1 tablespoon cold water; let stand for 5 minutes. Heat in microwave just until melted. Cool until warm. Add gelatin mixture to whipped cream.

- Grated lemon peel can be substituted for grated orange peel.

- One lemon yields about 1/4 cup juice: 1 orange yields about 1/3 cup juice.

- In making custard type pies, bake at a high temperature for about 10 minutes to prevent a soggy crust, then finish baking at a lower temperature.

- To prevent crust from becoming soggy with cream pies, sprinkle crust with powdered sugar.

- To prevent scorching when scalding milk, first rinse pan in water.

- The freshness of eggs can be tested by placing them in a large bowl of cold water. If they float, do not use them.

- Egg whites need to be room temperature for greater volume when whipped.

- For a custard pie, to prevent the crust from bubbling into the filling, prebake the crust at 450 degrees for 5 minutes before you add the custard.

- Frozen or bottled lemon juice can be substituted in equal amounts for fresh lemon juice.

- Equal amounts of skim milk can be substituted for whole milk.

Cream Pie Hints:

- Buttermilk and sour milk can be used interchangeably in most recipes. To make sour milk, place 1 tablespoon white vinegar or lemon juice and enough milk to equal 1 cup. Let stand for 5 minutes.

- Equal amounts of plain yogurt can be substituted for buttermilk.

- Sweetened condensed milk and evaporated milk are very different and cannot be substituted for each other. Evaporated milk can be substituted for milk by adding equal amounts of water. (2 cups milk = 1 cup evaporated milk and 1 cup water.)

- You can substitute 1 cup granulated sugar or 2 cups sifted confectioners sugar for 1 cup brown sugar.

- To substitute tapioca for cornstarch, use 2 tablespoons quick-cooking tapioca for every 1 tablespoon cornstarch. (Using tapioca has several advantages. Most mixtures don't need stirring and can withstand longer cooking times. They freeze well and stay thicker when reheated.)

- When measuring shredded coconut, pack the coconut loosely into your measuring cup . . do not pack!

- Plain yogurt can be substituted in equal amounts for sour cream in baking. Nonfat yogurt does not work well though; it causes a thinner consistency.

Coconut Dream Pie

9-inch baked pastry shell

Filling:

2/3 cup sugar

1/4 cup cornstarch

1/2 teaspoon salt

3 cups milk

4 egg yolks, slightly beaten

2 tablespoons butter or margarine, softened

2 teaspoons vanilla

1 cup flaked coconut

Topping:

1 cup heavy cream

2-ounces white chocolate squares, chopped

1/2 teaspoon vanilla

1 cup flaked coconut (toasted)

To prepare filling, mix sugar, cornstarch and salt in saucepan. Gradually stir in milk. Stir in beaten egg yolks.

Cook over medium heat, stirring constantly until mixture thickens and boils. Boil and stir for one minute. Remove from heat; stir in butter, vanilla and coconut, stirring until butter melts.

Pour filling into a medium bowl. Place plastic wrap directly against surface and cool at room temperature for 30 minutes.

Preheat oven to 325 degrees. Spread 1 cup coconut on a cookie sheet and bake 6-8 minutes, stirring once until toasted. Cool.

Sprinkle crust with 1/3 cup toasted coconut. Pour filling into crust. Spread evenly. Place plastic wrap loosely over pie and refrigerate 3 hours.

Topping:

Measure cream. Transfer 2 tablespoons cream to a small microwaveable bowl. Add white chocolate and microwave on high for 30 seconds. Stir until mixture is smooth. If chocolate doesn't melt completely, microwave 10 seconds more. Cool at room temperature for 15 minutes. Beat remaining cream and vanilla in mixing bowl until thickened. Add chocolate and beat just until stiff. Spread topping over filling. Sprinkle with remaining coconut.

Although this pie takes a little more time to prepare, you will taste the effort!!

Coconut Custard Pie

9-inch unbaked pastry shell
1-1/2 cups milk
1 cup sugar
3/4 cup flaked coconut
2 eggs, beaten

3 tablespoons flour
1 tablespoon butter or margarine, melted
1/4 teaspoon vanilla

In large bowl, combine all ingredients. Pour into pie shell.

Bake in a 350 degree oven for 50 minutes or until a knife inserted near center comes out clean. Cool to room temperature.

Magic Coconut Pie

9-inch unbaked pastry shell
3 eggs
1/2 cup sugar
2 tablespoons melted butter

3/4 cup dark corn syrup
1 4-ounce package coconut cream pudding and pie filling
1/4 cup milk

In mixing bowl, beat eggs until foamy; add sugar, corn syrup and butter. Combine dry pudding mix and milk; add to egg mixture. Blend well.

Pour filling into pie shell and bake in a 375 degree oven for 35 to 40 minutes until deep golden brown and filling is set. Serve cold or warm.

Variation: **Coconut Pecan Pie**

Add: 1/2 cup coconut and 1 cup chopped pecans.

Coconut Cream Cheese Pie

9-inch graham cracker crust

8 ounce package cream cheese, softened

1 cup cream of coconut

1 package (3.4-ounce) cheesecake instant pudding mix

1 package (6-ounces) frozen sweetened flaked coconut, thawed

1 container (8-ounces) frozen whipped topping, thawed

1 cup whipping cream

Sweetened flaked coconut

Beat cheese and cream of coconut at medium speed with an electric mixer until smooth. Add pudding mix, beating until blended. Stir in coconut and fold in whipped topping. Spread cheese mixture evenly into prepared crust. Cover and chill for 2 hours or until set.

Beat whipping cream with an electric mixer until soft peaks form and spread evenly over top of pie. Garnish if desired.

Quick Coconut Cream Pie

9-inch baked pastry shell, or graham cracker crust

1 package (5.1-ounces) instant vanilla pudding mix

1-1/2 cups cold milk

1 carton (8-ounces) frozen whipped topping, thawed, divided

3/4 to 1 cup flaked coconut, toasted, divided

In a mixing bowl, beat pudding and milk on low speed for 2 minutes. Fold in half of the whipped topping and 1/2 to 3/4 cup of the coconut. Pour mixture into crust. Spread with remaining whipped topping and sprinkle with remaining coconut. Chill.

Amazing Coconut Custard Pie

2 cups milk
3/4 cup sugar
1/2 cup buttermilk baking mix
4 eggs

1/4 cup butter or margarine, softened
2 teaspoons vanilla
1-1/3 cups flaked coconut

Place milk, sugar, baking mix, eggs, butter and vanilla in blender container and cover. Blend on low speed 3 minutes.

Pour into greased 9-inch pie plate and sprinkle with coconut.

Bake in the lower third of a 350 degree oven for 45 minutes or until pie is set and top is dark golden brown. Cool completely on wire rack. Refrigerate leftovers.

For Amazing White Chocolate Coconut Custard Pie, prepare as directed except reduce sugar to 1/2 cup. Add 3 squares (1 ounce each) white baking chocolate, melted, to the ingredients in blended container.

Tasty Coconut Pies

2 (9-inch) baked pastry shells
2 (12-ounce cans) evaporated milk
1 cup sugar
5 eggs, separated
1/2 cup butter or margarine

1/4 cup cornstarch
1 cup coconut
1/4 cup sugar
Additional flaked coconut

Preheat oven to 350 degrees. Combine evaporated milk, 1 cup sugar, egg yolks and butter in medium saucepan and mix well. Cook until butter melts, stirring constantly. Stir in cornstarch dissolved in a small amount of water. Cook until thickened, stirring constantly. Fold in 1 cup coconut and spoon into pie shells. Beat egg whites with 1/4 cup sugar in mixer bowl until stiff peaks form. Spread on pies. Sprinkle with additional coconut. Bake until golden brown.

Coconut Cream Meringue Pie

9-inch baked pastry shell
2/3 cup sugar
1/4 cup cornstarch
1/4 teaspoon salt
2 cups milk
3 egg yolks, lightly beaten
(Save whites for meringue)

1 cup flaked coconut, finely chopped
2 tablespoons butter or margarine
1/2 teaspoon vanilla extract
Recipe for meringue

In a saucepan, combine the sugar, cornstarch and salt. Gradually stir in milk until smooth. Bring to a boil; cook and stir for 2 minutes or until thickened. Gradually stir 1 cup hot filling into egg yolks; return mixture to the pan, stirring constantly. Bring to a gentle boil and stir for 2 minutes. Remove from the heat; stir in chopped coconut, butter and vanilla until butter is melted.

Pour hot filling into crust. Spread with meringue, sealing edges to crust. Sprinkle top with flaked coconut. Follow directions for meringue recipe. Serve warm or cool. Refrigerate leftovers.

Luscious Lemon Pie

9-inch baked pastry shell
1 cup sugar
6 tablespoons cornstarch
1 cup milk
6 egg yolks, lightly beaten
1/4 cup butter or margarine

2 tablespoons grated lemon peel
1/2 cup lemon juice
1/2 cup sour cream
1 cup whipping cream, whipped

In a saucepan, combine the sugar and cornstarch. Stir in milk until smooth. Cook and stir over medium heat until thickened and bubbly. Reduce heat; cook and stir 2 more minutes. Remove from the heat. Stir a small amount of hot filling into egg yolks and return mixture to the pan. Bring to a gentle boil; cook and stir for 2 minutes. Remove from the heat and stir in butter and lemon peel. Gently stir in lemon juice. Cool to room temperature. Fold in sour cream and whipped cream. Pour into pastry shell. Chill for at least 1 hour before cutting.

Mom's Lemon Meringue Pie

9-inch baked pastry shell
3 egg yolks
1-1/2 cups milk, scalded
1 cup sugar
2 tablespoons all-purpose flour
1/4 teaspoon salt

1 tablespoon butter or margarine
Juice and grated rind of 1 lemon
1 recipe meringue

Preheat oven to 325 degrees. Beat egg yolks with 1/4 cup scalded milk in medium saucepan. Add mixture of sugar, flour and salt. Mix well. Stir in remaining 1-1/4 cups milk. Bring to a boil then remove from heat. Stir in butter, lemon juice and lemon rind. Spoon into pie shell. Top with meringue. Follow meringue directions.

Lemon-Blueberry Cream Pie

9-inch baked pastry shell
1 cup sugar
3 tablespoons cornstarch
1 cup milk
3 beaten egg yolks
1/4 cup butter or margarine

1 tablespoon finely shredded lemon peel
1/4 cup lemon juice
1 carton (8 ounces) dairy sour cream
2 cups fresh blueberries
Sweetened whipped cream and lemon slices, optional

In a saucepan combine sugar and cornstarch. Add milk, egg yolks, butter or margarine, and lemon peel. Cook and stir over medium heat until thick and bubbly. Cook and stir 2 minutes more.

Remove from heat and stir in lemon juice. Transfer to a bowl. Cover surface with plastic wrap and refrigerate until cool. When cool, stir sour cream and blueberries into mixture; pour into pastry shell.

Cover and chill at least 4 hours. If desired, stir a little lemon peel into sweetened whipped cream. Pipe or spoon on top of pie. Garnish with lemon slices, if desired.

Lemon Chess Pie

9-inch unbaked pastry shell
4 eggs
2 cups sugar
1/4 cup milk
2 teaspoons finely shredded
lemon peel

1/4 cup lemon juice
2 tablespoons butter, melted
1 tablespoon flour
1 tablespoon cornmeal

In a large bowl, beat the eggs with a wire whisk. Add the sugar and milk; beat until combined. Beat in the lemon peel, lemon juice, melted butter, flour and cornmeal. Pour into pastry shell.

Bake in a 375 degree oven for 35 to 40 minutes or until filling is set and top is golden brown. Cool on a wire rack. Serve warm or cover and chill. If chilled, let stand at room temperature for 30 minutes before serving.

Layered Lemon-Blueberry Pie

9-inch graham cracker crust
8 ounce package cream cheese, softened
14 ounce can sweetened condensed milk
1/4 cup powdered sugar
1 package (3.4 ounce) lemon instant pudding mix

2 teaspoons grated lemon rind
1/2 cup fresh lemon juice
1 pint fresh blueberries
2 tablespoons blueberry preserves
1 cup whipping cream
Lemon slices, fresh blueberries

Beat cheese, milk, and powdered sugar at medium speed with an electric mixer until creamy. Add pudding mix, rind, and juice. Beat until blended. Spread half of lemon mix evenly into prepared crust.

Stir together blueberries and preserves; spread evenly over lemon mixture. Spread remaining lemon mixture over blueberry mixture. Cover and chill 2 hours or until set.

Beat whipping cream with an electric mixer until soft peaks form and spread around outer edge of pie forming a 3-inch border. Garnish if desired with lemon slices and fresh blueberries. Chill at least 2 hours.

Lemon Upside-Down Pie

Topping:
1/2 cup flour
1/3 cup sugar
1/4 cup butter

Meringue:
3 egg whites
1/2 teaspoon cream of tartar
1/2 cup sugar
1/2 teaspoon vanilla

Filling:
1-1/2 cups water
1 cup sugar
1/3 cup cornstarch
3 egg yolks
1 tablespoon butter
1/3 cup lemonade concentrate, undiluted
1/2 teaspoon salt
1/2 cup sour cream

Preheat broiler. For topping, combine flour and 1/3 cup sugar in a small bowl. Cut in butter until crumbly. Place in 15x10x1-inch jelly roll pan. Broil 3 to 4 inches from heat, for 3-4 minutes, watching closely and stirring every minute, until golden brown and crunchy. Cool completely. Set aside.

Preheat oven to 275 degrees. Beat egg whites and cream of tartar in a large mixer bowl on medium speed until foamy. Increase speed to high. Beat, gradually adding 1/2 cup sugar, for 3-4 minutes, until stiff peaks form and mixture is glossy. Stir in vanilla. Spread in bottom and up sides of greased 9-inch deep dish pie plate. Bake for 45-55 minutes or until lightly browned. Turn off oven. Cool in oven for 1-2 hours.

Combine water, 1 cup sugar, and cornstarch in a 2-quart saucepan. Cook over medium heat, stirring constantly, for 5-7 minutes, until mixture comes to a boil. Continue cooking 1 minute. Stir in egg yolks; continue cooking 2-3 minutes. Remove from heat and stir in lemonade concentrate, 1 tablespoon butter and salt. Cover and refrigerate 1 hour.

Stir sour cream into cooled filling mixture. Spoon cooled filling mixture into meringue shell; sprinkle with topping. Cover and refrigerate until serving time.

Creamy Lemon Pie

9-inch graham cracker crust
1-3/4 cups cold milk
2 packages (4-serving size each) vanilla instant pudding and pie filling

1 can (6 ounces) frozen lemonade concentrate, thawed
1 tub (8 ounces) whipped topping, thawed

Pour milk into large bowl. Add pudding mixes. Beat with wire whisk 30 seconds. Add concentrate. Beat with wire whisk 30 seconds until thick. Immediately stir in whipped topping. Spoon into crust. Refrigerate 4 hours or until set. Garnish with lemon slices. Store refrigerated.

Lemon Cream Cheese Pie

2 (9-inch) baked pastry shells
1 cup sugar
1/2 cup cornstarch
1-1/2 cups cold water
3 egg yolks, beaten
2/3 cup lemon juice, divided
1/8 teaspoon salt
3 tablespoons butter or margarine

1 can (14-ounces) sweetened condensed milk
1 package (8-ounces) cream cheese, softened
1 package (3.4-ounces) lemon instant pudding mix
Whipped cream
Lemon slices

In a saucepan, combine sugar and cornstarch. Gradually add water, mixing until smooth. Cook and stir over medium-high heat until thickened and clear. Quickly stir in egg yolks. Boil for 1 minute, stirring constantly. Remove from the heat and stir in 1/3 cup lemon juice, salt and butter. Cool for several hours or overnight. In a mixing bowl, blend condensed milk and cream cheese until smooth. Stir in pudding mix and remaining lemon juice. Fold into chilled lemon filling. Divide and spoon into baked pie shells. Refrigerate for several hours. Garnish with whipped cream and lemon slices.

Lemon Supreme Pie

9-inch baked pastry shell
Lemon Filling:
3/4 cup sugar plus 1/2 cup sugar
7 tablespoons cornstarch
1/2 teaspoon salt
1 1/4 cups water
2 tablespoons butter or margarine
2 teaspoons grated lemon peel
4 to 5 drops yellow food coloring, optional
1/2 cup lemon juice
Cream Cheese Filling:
11-ounces cream cheese, softened
3/4 cup confectioners sugar
1 1/2 cups whipped topping
1 tablespoon lemon juice

Combine 3/4 cup sugar, cornstarch and salt in a saucepan. Stir in water and bring to a boil over medium heat. Reduce heat, and add 1/2 cup sugar. Cook and stir until thick and bubbly. Remove from heat. Stir in butter, lemon peel and food coloring. Gently stir in lemon juice. Chill in refrigerator.

Beat cream cheese and sugar until smooth. Fold in whipped topping and lemon juice. Save 1/2 cup of mixture for garnish. Spread remaining mixture into cooled pie shell. Top with cooled lemon filling. Chill at least 3 hours or overnight.

Spoon or pipe reserved cheese mixture onto pie. Store in refrigerator.

Shaker Lemon Pie

Pastry for double crust pie
2 cups sugar
1/3 cup flour
1/4 teaspoon salt
3 eggs, slightly beaten
2/3 cup water
2 tablespoons butter, melted
2-1/2 teaspoons finely shredded orange peel
1 large or 2 small lemons, peeled and thinly sliced - 2/3 cup

In a medium bowl, combine sugar, flour and salt. Stir in eggs, water, butter and orange peel. Gently stir in lemon slices.

(Continued on next page.)

Transfer lemon mixture to pastry-lined pie plate. Cut slits in remaining pastry; place over filling and seal by crimping edges.

Bake in preheated 400 degree oven for 35 to 40 minutes or until top is golden brown. Cool on a wire rack for at least 2 hours. Serve warm or cool.

Lemon Meringue Pie

9-inch baked pastry shell

1 1/2 cups sugar

1/3 cup plus 1 tablespoon cornstarch

1 1/2 cups water

3 egg yolks, slightly beaten (Save egg whites for meringue)

3 tablespoons butter or margarine

2 teaspoons grated lemon peel

1/2 cup lemon juice

Yellow food coloring, optional

Recipe for meringue

Mix sugar and cornstarch in saucepan. Gradually stir in water. Cook over medium heat, stirring constantly until mixture thickens and boils. Boil and stir one minute.

Gradually stir half the hot mixture into egg yolks. Stir back into hot mixture in saucepan. Boil and stir one minute. Remove from heat.

Stir in butter, lemon peel, lemon juice and food color. Pour into pie shell.

Prepare meringue and spoon over hot pie filling. Spread over filling, carefully sealing meringue to edge of crust to prevent weeping.

Bake in a 375 degree oven about 8-12 minutes until delicately brown.

Little Lemon Meringue Pies

1/3 cup flour
1/8 teaspoon salt
1 tablespoon shortening
1 tablespoon cold butter
(no substitutes)
1 teaspoon cold water
Filling:
1/3 cup sugar
1 tablespoon cornstarch

1/8 teaspoon salt
1/2 cup cold water
1 egg yolk, beaten
2 tablespoons lemon juice
1 tablespoon butter
Meringue:
1 egg white
1/8 teaspoon cream of tartar
2 tablespoons sugar

In a bowl, combine flour and salt and cut in shortening and butter until crumbly. Gradually add water, tossing with a fork until dough forms a ball. Divide in half. Roll each portion into a 5-inch circle. Transfer to two 10-ounce custard cups. Press dough 1-1/8 inch up sides of cups. Place on a baking sheet. Bake at 425 degrees for 7-10 minutes or until golden brown.

In a saucepan, combine sugar, cornstarch and salt. Gradually stir in cold water until smooth. Cook and stir over medium heat until thickened and bubbly. Reduce heat and cook and stir 2 minutes more. Remove from the heat. Stir half of the hot filling into egg yolk. Return mixture to the pan. Bring to a gentle boil; cook and stir for 2 minutes. Remove from the heat and stir in lemon juice and butter. Pour into pastry shells.

In a small mixing bowl, beat egg white and cream of tartar on medium speed until soft peaks form. Gradually beat in sugar, 1 tablespoon at a time on high until stiff peaks form. Spread evenly over hot filling, sealing edges to crust. Bake at 350 degrees for 15-20 minutes or until meringue is golden brown. Cool on a wire rack for 1 hour and refrigerate for at least 3 hours before serving.

When you need dessert for just two, this recipe is perfect!

Best Banana Cream Pie

9-inch baked pastry shell
2/3 cup sugar
1/3 cup cornstarch
1/2 teaspoon salt
3 cups milk
4 egg yolks, beaten

2 tablespoons butter or margarine
1 tablespoon vanilla
2-3 bananas, sliced
1 cup whipping cream, optional

Step 1: Mix sugar, cornstarch and salt in saucepan. Gradually stir in milk until smooth. Cook over medium heat, stirring constantly until mixture is hot. Remove from heat.

Step 2: Beat egg yolks in bowl. Gradually stir in about 1 cup of the hot mixture into yolks. Return all of mixture back to saucepan, stirring constantly. Cook mixture until it boils and thickens about 10-12 minutes.

Step 3: Remove from heat and stir in butter and vanilla.

Step 4: Press plastic wrap onto filling. Cool in refrigerator.

Step 5: Slice 2-3 bananas in cooled pie shell. Pour filling over bananas. Top with whipped cream if desired.

Variations:

Coconut Cream

Follow steps 1-3, except decrease vanilla to 2 teaspoons and add 1 cup flaked coconut to mixture and pour into pie shell. Top with meringue if desired. * Save egg whites for meringue.

Tarts: Prepare the macadamia crust recipe and follow tart directions. Fill with coconut cream and enjoy!

Chocolate Cream

Follow steps 1 and 2 increasing sugar to 1-1/2 cups and stir in 2 squares unsweetened chocolate. Follow step 3 except omit butter. Pour mixture into baked pie shell. Top with meringue if desired. * Save egg whites for meringue.

White Chocolate-Banana Cream Pie

40 chocolate wafers

1/3 cup butter or margarine, melted

1/2 cup granulated sugar

1/4 cup cornstarch

1/4 teaspoon salt

2-1/2 cups milk

3 slightly beaten egg yolks

4-ounces white chocolate, finely chopped

1-1/4 teaspoons vanilla

4 medium bananas

1 cup whipping cream

2 tablespoons sifted powdered sugar

Milk chocolate and white chocolate curls, optional

Crush 30 chocolate wafers into fine crumbs (1-1/2 cups). In a bowl combine crumbs and melted butter or margarine and toss to mix well. Spread into a 9-inch pie plate. Press onto bottom and sides to form a firm, even crust; cover and chill.

For filling, in a saucepan combine granulated sugar, cornstarch, and salt. Stir in milk. Cook and stir over medium heat until thick and bubbly. Cook and stir 2 minutes more. Remove from heat and gradually stir 1 cup of hot filling into egg yolks. Pour yolk mix into hot filling in pan. Bring just to boiling. Reduce heat and cook and stir 2 more minutes. Remove from heat. Stir in chopped white chocolate and 1 teaspoon of the vanilla. Stir until chocolate has melted.

Slice 2 bananas onto the chilled crust. Spread half of the filling over all. Layer remaining chocolate wafers on filling. Chop 2 remaining bananas and place on chocolate wafers. Cover with remaining filling. Cover and chill at least 4 hours. Before serving, combine whipping cream, powdered sugar, and remaining 1/4 teaspoon vanilla in a chilled bowl. Beat with an electric mixer on medium speed until stiff peaks form. Spread whipped cream over pie. If desired, top with white and milk chocolate curls.

Banana Cream Pie

9-inch baked pastry shell
3 medium bananas, divided
1 teaspoon lemon juice
1/2 cup sugar
6 tablespoons cornstarch
1/4 teaspoon salt

3 cups fat-free (skim) milk
2 egg yolks
1-1/2 teaspoons vanilla
Nondairy whipped topping (optional)
Cinnamon and powdered sugar (optional)

Slice 2 bananas and toss with lemon juice. Layer in bottom of pie crust. Combine sugar, cornstarch and salt in medium saucepan. Combine milk and egg yolks in a bowl and slowly stir into sugar mixture. Cook over medium heat, stirring constantly until mixture thickens and boils. Boil 1 minute, stirring constantly. Remove from heat, stir in vanilla and pour into pie shell. Immediately cover with plastic wrap. Cool. Just before serving slice remaining banana and garnish pie with banana and whipped topping or cinnamon and powdered sugar, if desired.

Egg Custard Pie

9-inch unbaked pastry shell
4 eggs
1/2 cup sugar
1 teaspoon vanilla

1/4 teaspoon salt
2-1/2 cups milk
Nutmeg (optional)

Preheat oven to 425 degrees.

For crust, prepare as directed, bake for only 5 minutes.

For filling, beat eggs with fork or at low speed of electric mixer until lemon colored. Stir in sugar, vanilla and salt. Stir in milk gradually. Mix well. Pour into partially baked pie crust. Sprinkle with nutmeg, if desired.

Bake at 425 degrees for 15 minutes. Reduce oven temperature to 350 degrees. Bake 20-25 minutes or until knife inserted in center comes out clean. Do not over bake. Cool to room temperature before serving. Refrigerate leftovers.

For Coconut Custard Pie, stir 1/2 cup flake coconut into egg mixture before baking.

Butterscotch Pie with Sugar-Glazed Pecans

9-inch baked pastry shell

Nut Mixture:

3/4 cup coarsely chopped
pecans

1/3 cup sugar

2 tablespoons butter

Filling:

2 packages (3.4 ounce)
instant butterscotch pudding
and pie filling mix

3-1/2 cups milk

1-1/2 cups heavy whipping
cream

Combine pecans, sugar and 2 tablespoons butter in 10-inch skillet. Cook over medium-high heat, shaking pan occasionally, for 3-4 minutes until sugar turns golden. Do not stir. Pour nut mix onto aluminum foil immediately. Cool completely. Break into pieces.

Prepare pudding and pie filling according to package, except use only 3-1/2 cups milk. Refrigerate for at least 10 minutes.

Meanwhile, beat whipping cream in large chilled deep mixer bowl at high speed for 2-3 minutes until stiff peaks form. Gently stir 1 cup whipped cream into chilled filling. Cover and refrigerate remaining whipped cream.

Pour filling mixture into cooled crust. Cover surface with plastic food wrap. Refrigerate 4 hours or overnight.

Remove plastic food wrap. Sprinkle 1/3 cup nuts onto top of pie. Carefully spread remaining whipped cream on top. Sprinkle with remaining nuts.

Butterscotch Pie

9-inch baked pastry shell

1 cup firmly packed light brown sugar

1/2 cup sugar

1/3 cup cornstarch

Pinch of salt

3 egg yolks (save whites for meringue)

1-1/3 cups milk

2/3 cup water

2 tablespoons butter or margarine, melted

1 teaspoon vanilla

1 recipe for meringue

Combine first 4 ingredients in a large heavy saucepan. Combine egg yolks and next 3 ingredients. Gradually stir into brown sugar mixture. Cook over medium heat, stirring constantly, until mixture thickens and boils. Boil, stirring constantly, 1 minute. Remove mixture from heat, and stir in vanilla. Pour into pastry shell and set aside.

Follow directions for the meringue recipe and enjoy.

Chess Pie

10-inch unbaked pastry shell

3 cups sugar

1/2 cup butter or margarine, softened

5 eggs, lightly beaten

3 tablespoons cornmeal

2 teaspoons vanilla

1/8 teaspoon salt

1 cup milk

Preheat oven to 325 degrees.

Combine sugar and butter in a large bowl and beat on low speed with electric mixer until well blended. Beat in eggs, cornmeal, vanilla and salt. Add milk. Beat at low speed until blended. Pour into unbaked pastry shell.

Bake for 1 hour to 1 hour 20 minutes or until filling is set. Cover edge of the pie with foil or shield, if necessary, to prevent over browning. Do not over bake. Cool to room temperature before serving. Refrigerate leftovers.

English Chess Pie

9-inch unbaked pie shell
1 stick butter
1-1/2 cup sugar

3 eggs
1 teaspoon vanilla

Melt butter. Add sugar gradually. Mix well. Cool slightly. Beat eggs until frothy and continue beating while dropping in spoonfuls of the butter-sugar mixture. Add vanilla and pour into pie shell.

Bake at 350 degrees for 40 minutes. Do not substitute margarine for butter.

Shoo-Fly Pie

9-inch unbaked pastry shell
Pie Mixture:
3/4 cup dark molasses
3/4 cup boiling water
3/4 teaspoon baking soda
Crumbs:
1-1/2 cup flour

1/2 teaspoon salt
1/2 cup butter
1/2 teaspoon baking powder
1/4 cup brown sugar
1/4 cup granulated sugar
1/2 teaspoon cinnamon

Mix crumb mixture first. Mix all pie mixture ingredients together. Pour half of crumbs into mixture. Mix well. Pour mixture into unbaked pie shell. Sprinkle remaining crumbs over mixture. Bake at 375 degrees for about 40 minutes. Bottom will be moist, middle will be like soft gingerbread, and top will be light golden.

French Cream Pie

9-inch baked pastry shell
1/3 cup flour
1 cup sugar
1 cup cream or evaporated milk

1 cup milk
2 tablespoons butter or margarine
1 teaspoon vanilla
Cinnamon

In saucepan, blend together flour and sugar. Add cream and milk. Stir until well mixed. Cook on medium heat until thick and remove from heat. Add butter and vanilla. Stir until butter is melted. Set pan in ice water and stir until mixture is cooled to lukewarm. Pour into baked pie shell. Sprinkle with cinnamon.

Peanut Butter Cream Pie

9-inch baked pastry shell (or use cornflake shell recipe - see crust recipes - page 25)
2-1/2 cups milk
1/2 cup sugar
1/2 cup flour
2 teaspoons cornstarch

1/2 teaspoon ground ginger
1/2 teaspoon salt
2 egg yolks, beaten
1/2 teaspoon vanilla
1/2 cup peanut butter
1 recipe meringue

Scald 1-1/2 cups milk. Combine sugar, flour, cornstarch, ginger and salt. Add 1/2 cup milk and blend. Add scalded milk gradually. Cook, stirring, until thick and smooth. Add small amount of hot mixture to beaten egg yolks. Pour all back into mixture and continue to beat and cook 2 minutes. Add vanilla. Combine peanut butter and remaining milk. Add to custard and blend. Cool slightly and pour into crust. Top with meringue; bake for 20 minutes in 325 degree oven until golden brown.

Peanut-Cream Pie Supreme

9-inch baked pastry shell

1/2 cup margarine or butter, softened

1/2 cup sugar

1 egg

1/4 cup semisweet chocolate chips, melted

1/4 teaspoon vanilla extract

1/2 cup finely chopped peanuts

8-ounces cream cheese, softened

1/2 cup creamy peanut butter

1 cup confectioners' sugar

1 egg

1-1/2 cups whipped topping

1/4 cup finely chopped peanuts

Chocolate Curls

Cream margarine and sugar in mixer bowl until light. Beat in 1 egg at medium speed for 2-3 minutes. Blend in chocolate and vanilla. Spread 1 cup of mixture evenly in pie shell and sprinkle with 1/2 cup peanuts. Combine cream cheese, peanut butter, confectioners' sugar, 1 egg and whipped topping in bowl; mix until smooth. Spread in prepared pie shell. Top with remaining chocolate mixture; sprinkle with 1/4 cup peanuts. Garnish with chocolate curls.

Make sure the eggs are fresh and store in refrigerator before and after serving.

Texas Lime Pie

2 graham cracker crusts

3 cans (14-ounces each) sweetened condensed milk

5 egg yolks

2 cups lime juice

Whipped topping, lime slices and fresh mint, optional

In a mixing bowl, beat milk, egg yolks and lime juice on low for 2 minutes or until smooth and slightly thickened. Pour into prepared crusts.

Bake at 350 degrees for 18-22 minutes or until a knife inserted near the center comes out clean. Cool on wire racks for 1 hour. Chill for 6 hours. Garnish with whipped topping, lime and mint if desired.

Peach Blush Chiffon Pie

9-inch baked pastry shell
1 envelope unflavored gelatin
1/4 cup cold water
6-7 ripe peaches
3 eggs, separated
1/2 cup sugar, divided

1/4 teaspoon salt
2 teaspoons lemon juice
Whipped cream and fresh peach slices for garnish, optional

Soften gelatin in water. Set aside. Peel and pit peaches. Puree peaches to make 2 1/2 cups.

Beat egg yolks in small saucepan; add 1/4 cup sugar and salt. Stir in 2 1/2 cups puree. Bring to boil over low heat, stirring constantly. Remove from heat.

Pour peach mixture into large bowl. Add gelatin and lemon juice. Stir until gelatin is dissolved. Chill until mixture mounds.

Beat egg whites until stiff. Add 1/4 cup sugar. Fold into peach mixture then fold into pastry shell. Chill until firm. Garnish with whipped cream and peach slices.

Variation:

Substitute strawberries for peaches for a different treat.

Peach Parfait Pie

9-inch graham cracker pie crust
3-ounce package orange gelatin
1 cup boiling water

1 pint vanilla ice cream, softened
2 cups sliced peaches
Graham cracker crumbs

Dissolve gelatin in boiling water in bowl. Add ice cream, stirring until smooth. Fold in peaches. Spoon into pie shell.

Sprinkle with graham cracker crumbs. Chill until set. May sweeten peaches if desired.

Cherry and Almond Mousse Pie

9-inch baked pastry shell

1-ounce square unsweetened chocolate

14-ounce can sweetened condensed milk

1/4 teaspoon almond extract

8-ounces cream cheese

1 cup cold water

4-ounce package vanilla instant pudding mix

3/4 teaspoon almond extract

1 cup whipping cream, whipped

10-ounce jar red maraschino cherries, drained

1/2 cup chopped toasted almonds

Chocolate curls

Toasted almonds

Melt unsweetened chocolate with 1/2 cup condensed milk in heavy saucepan. Mix well. Stir in 1/4 teaspoon almond extract. Spread in pie shell.

Beat cream cheese in mixing bowl until light. Beat in remaining condensed milk, water, pudding mix and 3/4 teaspoon almond extract gradually. Fold in whipped cream.

Chop cherries, reserving 5 or 6 whole ones for garnish. Fold chopped cherries and 1/2 cup almonds into pie filling. Spoon into prepared pie shell.

Chill for 4 hours or until set. Garnish with reserved cherries, chocolate curls and additional almonds.

Cherry-Nut Pies

2 (9-inch) baked pastry shells

Juice from 2 lemons

14-ounce can sweetened condensed milk

16-ounce can tart pitted cherries, drained

1/3 cup sugar

1 cup chopped pecans

1/2 pint whipping cream, whipped

Food coloring, optional

Mix lemon juice into condensed milk in bowl. Add sugar, pecans and cherries. Mix well. Fold in whipped cream and spoon into pie shells. Chill for 3 hours before serving.

Cool Black Forest Pie

9 or 10-inch baked pastry
shell
4 (1-ounce) squares
unsweetened chocolate
14-ounce can sweetened
condensed milk

1 teaspoon almond extract
1-1/2 cups whipping cream
21-ounce can cherry pie filling
Almonds

Melt chocolate with condensed milk in heavy saucepan over
medium-low heat; remove from heat. Stir in almond extract.
Spoon into large bowl; cool to room temperature. Whip cream in
mixer bowl until soft peaks form. Beat chocolate mixture until
smooth. Fold in whipped cream. Spoon into pie shell. Chill for
4 hours or until set. Spread pie filling over top. Garnish with
almonds.

Raspberry-Port Pie

9-inch baked pastry shell
1 cup Port wine
1 cup water
6-ounce package raspberry
gelatin
10-ounce package frozen
raspberries
1 pint vanilla ice cream,
softened

1 cup whipping cream
2 tablespoons sugar
Salt to taste
1/4 cup ground nuts
Whole raspberries

Bring wine and water to a boil in medium saucepan. Stir in
gelatin until dissolved. Stir in frozen raspberries and ice cream.
Chill until partially set. Reserve 1 cup raspberry mixture.

Chill remaining raspberry mixture until thick. Spoon into pie
shell. Chill until set.

Beat whipping cream in medium mixer bowl until soft peaks
form. Beat in sugar and salt. Fold in reserved raspberry
mixture. Spoon over congealed layer. Chill for 5 hours. Garnish
with nuts and whole raspberries.

O-So-Easy Yogurt Berry Pies

1 package (6 count)
individual graham cracker tart
shells

8-ounces mixed berry yogurt
or flavor of your choice

2 cups whipped topping

Blueberries or raspberries

In a bowl, stir yogurt and whipped topping until combined.
Spoon into tart shells. Cover and freeze for 20 minutes. Top
with berries.

Meringue Berry Pie

1/2 cup sugar, divided

1/4 cup slivered almonds,
toasted and ground

2 tablespoons cornstarch

2 egg whites

1/8 teaspoon cream of tartar

Sauce and Topping:

1/2 cup sugar

1 tablespoon cornstarch

1/3 cup water

1 pint fresh or frozen
raspberries

1 quart vanilla ice cream

2 cups fresh mixed berries

In a small bowl, combine 1/4 cup sugar, almonds and
cornstarch; mix well.

In a small mixing bowl, beat egg whites at high speed until
foamy. Add cream of tartar; continue beating until soft peaks
form. Gradually add remaining sugar; beat until stiff peaks
form. Fold in almond mixture.

Spread over the bottom and sides of a greased 9-inch pie plate.
Bake at 275 degrees for 1 to 1-1/2 hours or until light golden
brown. Turn off oven; do not open door. Let cool in oven for 1
hour. Remove from oven and cool completely.

Meanwhile, for sauce, combine sugar and cornstarch in a
medium saucepan. Gradually stir in water; mix until smooth.
Add raspberries; bring to a boil over medium heat, stirring
constantly. Boil 1 minute or until thickened; set aside. Cool. To
serve, scoop ice cream onto meringue; top with mixed berries
and sauce. Serve immediately. Store leftovers in the freezer.

Spy Pies

2 (9-inch) baked pastry shells
10-ounce package frozen raspberries, strawberries or blueberries
2 egg whites

1 tablespoon lemon juice
1 cup sugar
1 package whipped topping mix, prepared

Mix first 4 ingredients in large mixing bowl. Beat for 15 minutes. Fold in whipped topping and spoon into prepared pie shells. Freeze until serving time.

Raspberry Mallow Pie

1 9-inch graham cracker crust
35 large marshmallows
1/2 cup milk

10-ounce package frozen raspberries
8-ounces frozen whipped topping, thawed

In a large microwave-safe bowl, combine marshmallows and milk. Cook on high in microwave for 1-2 minutes; stir until smooth.

Stir in raspberries. Fold in whipped topping. Pour into crust and refrigerate or freeze.

Berry Fluff Pie

9-inch baked pastry shell
2 (21-ounces each) cans raspberry or strawberry pie filling
14-ounce can sweetened condensed milk

8-ounces crushed pineapple, undrained, optional
12-ounce carton whipped topping, thawed
Fresh berries and mint, optional

Combine pie filling, milk and pineapple if desired in bowl. Fold in whipped topping. Pour into prepared pie shell and chill. Do not freeze. Garnish with fresh berries and mint.

Summer Berry Pie

9-inch baked pastry shell
1-1/2 cups raspberries
1-1/2 cups strawberries, sliced
1 cup blueberries
3/4 cup sugar

3 tablespoons cornstarch
1-1/2 cups water
1 package (4 serving size) strawberry flavored gelatin
8-ounces Cool Whip, thawed

Mix berries in a large bowl. Pour into cooled pastry shell.

Mix sugar and cornstarch in medium saucepan. Gradually stir in water until smooth. Stirring constantly, cook on medium heat until mixture comes to a boil; boil 1 minute. Remove from heat. Stir in gelatin until dissolved. Cool to room temperature. Pour over berries in pastry shell.

Refrigerate 3 hours. Spread whipped topping over pie before serving. Garnish with additional berries, if desired.

Strawberry Margarita Pie

Pretzel crust (See crust section)
1-1/2 cups crushed or pureed strawberries
1/3 cup lime juice

1 can (14-ounces) sweetened condensed milk
8-ounce whipped topping, thawed

Mix condensed milk, strawberries and lime juice in large bowl until well blended. Gently stir in whipped topping. Pour into crust.

Freeze 4 hours or overnight until firm. Let stand at room temperature 15 minutes or until pie can be cut easily. Garnish with additional whipped toping and strawberries. Store leftover pie, covered, in freezer.

Easy Frozen Strawberry Pie

9-inch graham cracker crust
2 egg whites
1 cup sugar

1 cup strawberries
1 pint whipping cream, whipped

Beat first three ingredients on high speed for 10 minutes. Fold in whipped cream. Pour into crust and freeze.

Frozen Strawberry Pie (makes 3 pies)

3 (10-inches each) graham cracker pie crusts

2 packages (8-ounces each) cream cheese softened

12-ounce can frozen pink lemonade concentrate, thawed

2 packages (20-ounces each) frozen unsweetened strawberries, thawed

2 cartons (12-ounces each) frozen whipped topping, thawed

Fresh strawberries and additional whipped topping, optional

Beat cream cheese until smooth in mixing bowl. Gradually beat in lemonade concentrate. Mash berries; add to cream cheese mixture and mix well. Fold in whipped topping.

Spoon into crusts. Freeze until firm. Remove from the freezer 10-15 minutes before serving. Garnish with strawberries and whipped topping if desired.

If you need dessert for a potluck or large gathering, this is the perfect recipe!

Deluxe Strawberry Margarita Pie

9-inch baked pastry shell

3/4 cup finely crushed pretzels

2-ounces white baking chocolate, melted

1/4 cup lime juice

2 tablespoons orange juice

1 teaspoon unflavored gelatin

1 tablespoon Tequila*

1 tablespoon orange flavored liqueur*

1 tablespoon grated lime peel

1 (14-ounce) can sweetened condensed milk

1 cup heavy whipping cream

1 pound quartered strawberries

Lime slices, if desired

Mix pretzels and melted chocolate; press on bottom of crust. Refrigerate while making filling. Mix juices in saucepan, sprinkle gelatin over mixture; let stand 1 minute to soften. Heat over low heat stirring frequently until clear and gelatin is dissolved; cool. Stir in tequila, orange liqueur, lime peel and milk. Beat cream until stiff peaks form; fold into gelatin mixture. Pour into crust. Refrigerate 1 hour or until set. Top with strawberries and garnish with lime slices. * 2 tablespoons orange juice can be substituted for the tequila and orange liqueur.

Cranberry Pie-2

1 shortbread pie crust

8-ounce package cream cheese, softened

1 cup whipping cream

1/4 cup sugar

1/2 teaspoon vanilla

16-ounce can whole berry cranberry sauce

With mixer, beat cheese until fluffy. With mixer in another bowl, beat whipping cream, sugar and vanilla until soft peaks form. Beat cream mixture into cheese until smooth.

Reserve 2 tablespoons whole cranberries from sauce for garnish; fold remaining cranberry sauce into cream and cheese mixture. Spoon into crust.

Freeze 2 hours or until firm. Remove from freezer 15 minutes before serving. Garnish with reserved cranberries or fresh whole cranberries with mint sprig if desired. Return leftovers to freezer.

Sky-Hi Pie

9-inch graham cracker crust

1 package (10-ounce) frozen strawberries

3/4 cup sugar

2 egg whites

2 tablespoons lemon juice

1/8 teaspoon salt

1 cup whipping cream

Put frozen strawberries in large mixing bowl and let thaw. Add the sugar and egg whites, lemon juice and salt. Beat at high speed for 15 minutes. It should be the consistency of angel food cake batter.

Whip 1 cup cream. Fold into strawberry mixture carefully. Pour strawberry mixture into crust and freeze at least 4 hours, preferably overnight. Place a whole strawberry on each piece when serving.

Strawberry Graham Pie

9-inch graham cracker crust

3-ounce package strawberry gelatin

1 cup boiling water

16-ounces sliced frozen strawberries, thawed

1 tablespoon lemon juice

4-ounces cream cheese, softened

1/2 cup confectioners' sugar

1 teaspoon vanilla

Dash salt

1 cup whipping cream, whipped

1/4 cup graham cracker crumbs

Fresh strawberries and mint, optional

In a bowl, dissolve gelatin in boiling water. Stir in strawberries and lemon juice. Refrigerate until partially set, approximately 1-1/2 hours.

In a small mixing bowl, beat the cream cheese, sugar, vanilla and salt until smooth. Fold in whipped cream. Spread half over cooled crust. Cover and refrigerate remaining cream mixture. Pour gelatin mixture over filling; refrigerate until firm. Top with remaining cream mixture. Sprinkle with crumbs. Refrigerate overnight. Garnish with fresh berries and mint if desired.

Red, White & Blueberry Cream Pie

9-inch graham cracker pie crust

1-1/4 cup fresh blueberries, rinsed, drained and divided

1 package (8-ounce) cream cheese, softened

1 can (14-ounce) sweetened condensed milk

1/3 cup lemon juice

1 teaspoon vanilla extract

Sliced fresh strawberries

Place 3/4 cup blueberries on crust. Beat cream cheese in large bowl until fluffy. Gradually beat in sweetened condensed milk until smooth. Stir in lemon juice and vanilla. Spread into crust over blueberries.

Chill 3 hours or until set. Top with remaining 1/2 cup blueberries and strawberries. Refrigerate leftovers.

Delightful Strawberry Pie

3 egg whites
1-1/2 cup sugar, divided
3/4 teaspoon cream of tartar
1/2 cup crushed saltines
(about 15 crackers)
1/2 cup flaked coconut

1/2 cup chopped pecans
2 cups whipping cream
1/2 teaspoon unflavored gelatin
1 quart fresh strawberries, sliced

In mixing bowl, beat egg whites until soft peaks form. Gradually add 1 cup sugar and cream of tartar, beating until stiff peaks form.

Gently fold in crumbs, coconut and pecans. Spread onto the bottom and up the sides of a 9-inch pie plate. Bake for 20-22 minutes or until browned in a 375 degree oven. Cool completely.

In a mixing bowl, beat cream, gelatin and remaining sugar until stiff peaks form. Fold in strawberries; pour into shell. Refrigerate for at least 2 hours before serving.

Strawberry Banana Split Pie

9-inch graham cracker crust, chilled

Filling:
1/2 cup butter or margarine, softened
2 cups confectioners' sugar
1 tablespoon milk
1 teaspoon vanilla
3 large firm bananas, cut into 1/4-inch slices

2 cans (8-ounces each) crushed pineapple, drained
2 quarts fresh strawberries, sliced

Topping:
2 cups whipping cream
1/4 cup confectioners' sugar
1-1/2 cups chopped walnuts

In a mixing bowl, cream butter, sugar, milk and vanilla. Spread over crust; chill 30 minutes. Layer with bananas, pineapple and strawberries. In a small mixing bowl, beat cream until soft peaks form. Add sugar; beat until stiff peaks form. Spread over fruit. Sprinkle with nuts. Chill until serving.

Honey Strawberry Pie

9-inch baked pastry or crumb crust
Filling:
2 pints strawberries, divided

2 cups whipped topping
2 tablespoons honey
1/4 cup slivered almonds, toasted, optional

Slice 1 pint of strawberries; fold into whipped topping. Spoon into pie shell. Cut remaining berries in halves and arrange over top. Drizzle with honey and sprinkle with almonds if desired. Refrigerate for at least 1 hour before serving.

Banana Split Supreme

3/4 cup butter or margarine, divided
2 cups confectioners' sugar
1 cup evaporated milk
3/4 cup semisweet chocolate chips
24 cream-filled chocolate sandwich cookies, crushed
3 to 4 medium firm bananas, cut into 1/2-inch slices

2 quarts vanilla ice cream, softened, divided
20-ounce can crushed pineapple, drained
10-ounce jar maraschino cherries, drained and halved
3/4 cup chopped pecans
Whipped topping, optional

Melt 1/4 cup butter; toss with cookie crumbs. Press into a 13x9x2-inch pan. Freeze for 15 minutes.

Combine 1/2 cup butter, sugar, milk and chocolate chips in a saucepan. Bring to a boil over medium heat; boil and stir for 8 minutes. Remove from the heat and cool completely. Set aside.

Arrange banana slices over crust; spread with 1 quart of ice cream. Top with 1 cup of cooled chocolate mixture Freeze 1 hour.

Refrigerate remaining chocolate mixture. Spread the remaining ice cream over dessert; top with pineapple, cherries and pecans. Cover and freeze for several hours or overnight. Remove from the freezer 10 minutes before serving. Reheat the chocolate mixture. Cut dessert into squares; serve with chocolate mixture and whipped topping if desired.

Jamocha Banana

9-inch prepared pie crust (We suggest Chocolate Granola Crunch Crust - see crust section page 26)

1 large banana, sliced

Jamocha Almond Fudge Ice Cream, softened

1 package whipped topping mix

1 teaspoon instant coffee granules

2 tablespoons hot chocolate mix

Chocolate curls and sliced almonds for garnish, optional

Line bottom of cooled crust with banana slices. Spread ice cream over bananas. Place in freezer. Prepare whipped topping per package directions. Beat in coffee granules and hot chocolate mix. Swirl over ice cream layer. Freeze for 3 hours or until firm. Garnish with chocolate curls and almonds if desired.

Banana Cream Cheese Pie

9-inch graham cracker crust

8-ounces cream cheese, softened

1/2 cup sugar

1 cup mashed ripe bananas (2 to 3 medium)

1 teaspoon lemon juice

8-ounces frozen whipped topping, thawed

Topping:

2 tablespoons sugar

1 teaspoon cornstarch

1-1/4 cups sliced fresh strawberries

5 drops red food coloring, optional

Beat cream cheese and sugar in bowl until smooth. Combine bananas and lemon juice; add to cream cheese mixture. Fold in whipped topping and pour into crust. Cover and refrigerate for 1 hour or until set.

In a saucepan, combine sugar and cornstarch. Stir in strawberries and food coloring if desired. Let stand for 5 minutes. Bring to a boil then reduce heat. Cook and stir for 2 minutes or until thickened. Cool. Drizzle some over pie. Cut into wedges and serve with remaining topping.

Banana Split Pie

9-inch crumb crust (We suggest Crumb-Nut recipe in crust section page 25.)

Filling:

1-1/4 cups sugar

1/3 cup cornstarch

1/3 cup cocoa

1/4 teaspoon salt

2-1/2 cups milk

2 egg yolks, slightly beaten

3 tablespoons butter or margarine

1 teaspoon vanilla extract

2 medium bananas, sliced

Garnishes:

Whipped topping

Chopped peanuts

Additional banana slices

Maraschino cherries

In medium saucepan, stir together sugar, cornstarch, cocoa and salt. Stir together milk and egg yolks. Gradually stir into sugar mixture. Cook over medium heat, stirring constantly, until mix thickens and comes to a boil. Reduce heat to low. Boil, stirring constantly, 3 minutes. Remove from heat and stir in butter and vanilla. Press plastic wrap directly onto filling. Cool about 20 minutes.

Arrange banana slices over bottom of crust. Pour filling over bananas and press plastic wrap onto filling. Refrigerate 3-4 hours. Remove plastic wrap and top pie with whipped topping.

Garnish with chopped peanuts, banana slices and maraschino cherries. Refrigerate leftover pie.

Lemon Icebox Pie

9-inch graham cracker or vanilla wafer crust

1 can sweetened condensed milk

1 tablespoon sugar

2 egg yolks (save whites for meringue)

Juice of 2 lemons

1 recipe for meringue (See crust section)

Mix milk, sugar, and egg yolks well. Add lemon juice. Pour into crust. Top with meringue and bake until golden brown at 350 degrees.

Cranberry-Cream Cheese Pie

10-inch baked pastry shell

1 package (3-ounces) raspberry gelatin

1 cup boiling water

1/2 cup cold water

2 packages (3-ounces) cream cheese, softened

2 tablespoons milk

1 can (16-ounces) whole cranberry sauce

Prepare gelatin using 1 cup boiling water. Stir until dissolved; add 1/2 cup cold water. Cool until thickened. Soften cream cheese with milk and spread into baked pie shell. After gelatin has begun to thicken, whip until fluffy. Stir cranberry sauce to break apart. Fold into gelatin mixture. Pour into cream cheese lined pie shell and refrigerate until set. Serve with whipped cream, if desired.

Light Lemon Mousse Pie

1 chocolate graham cracker pie crust

1 envelope unflavored gelatin

2/3 cup lemon juice

1/4 cup cold water

2 teaspoons grated lemon rind

8 drops yellow food coloring

8-ounces light cream cheese, softened

1 cup confectioners' sugar

16-ounces light whipped topping

Lemon peel, shaved chocolate or whipped topping

Mix gelatin, lemon juice and water in small saucepan; let stand for 2 minutes. Cook over low heat until gelatin dissolves. Stir in lemon rind and food coloring.

Beat cream cheese with confectioners' sugar in small bowl until smooth. Add gelatin mixture gradually, mixing until smooth. Chill for 20 minutes or until slightly thickened.

Fold in 16-ounces whipped topping. Spoon into pie shell and chill until firm. Garnish with strip of lemon peel, shaved chocolate or additional whipped topping.

10-Minute Lemon-Raspberry Pie

9-inch graham cracker crust

12-ounces frozen whipped topping, thawed

14-ounce can sweetened condensed milk

6-ounce can frozen lemonade concentrate, thawed

Scant 1/4 teaspoon liquid yellow food color, optional

12-ounces fresh raspberries (about 3 cups)

Garnish: lemon twist and mint leaves

Spoon 1/2 cup whipped topping into a decorating bag fitted with a medium star tip. Fold top of bag over and seal with a paper clip or tape. Refrigerate until needed.

Put condensed milk, lemonade and food color in a large bowl. Stir until completely blended. Add a large spoonful of whipped topping; mix well. Fold in remaining topping.

Set aside about 1 cup berries for garnish; gently fold remaining berries into the filling. Spoon into crust, smooth top, mounding filling slightly in the middle. Cover loosely with foil and refrigerate at least 6 hours.

About 1 hour before serving, using topping reserved in bag, pipe a border about 1-inch from edge of filling and a dot in the middle. Garnish with reserved berries, the lemon twist and mint. Pretty as a picture.

Lemon-Almond Icebox Pie

9-inch Almond Crumb crust (See recipe in crust section)

1 can sweetened condensed milk

2 egg yolks

1 teaspoon lemon rind

1/2 cup lemon juice

1 cup whipping cream, whipped

1/2 cup chopped almonds, toasted

Mix condensed milk, egg yolks, lemon rind and juice. Pour into cool crust. Top with whipped cream and sprinkle toasted chopped almonds over top. Chill at least 2 hours or overnight before serving. Make sure eggs are fresh and keep in refrigerator.

Frozen Lemon Pie

9-inch baked graham cracker crust

3 eggs, separated

1/2 teaspoon cream of tartar

1/2 cup sugar

1 cup chilled whipping cream

2 teaspoons grated lemon peel

1/4 cup lemon juice

Graham crackers for garnish, if desired

Beat egg whites and cream of tartar in large bowl until foamy. Beat in sugar 1 tablespoon at a time. Continue beating until stiff and glossy. Beat egg yolks until thick and lemon colored. Fold into meringue.

Beat whipping cream in chilled bowl until stiff. Fold whipped cream, lemon peel and juice into egg mixture. Pour into crust and sprinkle with graham cracker crumbs if desired.

Freeze until firm, about 6 hours. Remove from freezer 15 minutes before serving.

Make sure eggs are fresh and keep in refrigerator.

Sour Cream Lemon Pie

9-inch baked pastry shell

1 cup sugar

3-1/2 tablespoons cornstarch

1 tablespoon lemon rind, grated

1/2 cup lemon juice

1 cup milk

3 egg yolks

1/4 cup butter

1 cup sour cream

1 cup whipping cream

Lemon twist for garnish

Combine sugar, cornstarch, lemon rind, juice, egg yolks and milk in heavy saucepan. Cook over medium heat until thick. Stir in butter and cool mixture to room temperature. Stir in sour cream and pour filling into pie shell.

Cover with whipped cream and garnish with lemon twists. Store in refrigerator

Double Layer Lemon Pie

9-inch graham cracker crumb crust or shortbread crumb crust

1/3 cup raspberry or apricot jam

4-ounces cream cheese, softened

1 tablespoon sugar

1 tub (8-ounces) whipped topping, thawed, divided

1-1/2 cups cold milk or half-and-half

2 packages (4-serving size each) lemon instant pudding and pie filling

2 teaspoons grated lemon peel

Spread bottom of crust gently with jam. Mix cream cheese and sugar in large bowl with wire whisk until smooth. Gently stir in 1/2 of the whipped topping and spread on top of jam in crust.

Pour milk into large bowl. Add pudding mixes and lemon peel. Beat with wire whisk for 1 minute or until blended. Mixture will be thick. Gently stir in remaining whipped topping. Spread over cream cheese layer.

Refrigerate 4 hours or until set. Garnish with additional whipped topping. Store leftover pie, covered, in refrigerator.

Cool Lime Pie

9-inch graham cracker crust

8-ounces cream cheese, softened

14-ounces sweetened condensed milk

6-ounces limeade concentrate

4 drops green food coloring, optional

8-ounces frozen whipped topping, thawed, divided

1 kiwi fruit, peeled and sliced

Mandarin oranges and chopped pistachios, optional

In a mixing bowl, beat cream cheese and milk until smooth. Add limeade and food coloring if desired. Fold in half of the whipped topping. Pour into crust.

Cover and refrigerate for 2 hours. Garnish with kiwi, remaining whipped topping and oranges and pistachios if desired.

Key Lime Pies

2 graham cracker crusts
8 large eggs, lightly beaten
2 cups sugar
1/4 cup grated lime rind
2/3 cup Key lime juice
Dash of salt

1 cup unsalted butter or margarine, softened
2 cups whipping cream
1/4 cup sifted powdered sugar
2 teaspoons vanilla extract
Garnish: lime twists

Combine eggs, sugar, lime rind, lime juice and salt in top of a double boiler and bring water to a boil. Reduce heat to low and cook, whisking constantly until thickened. Add butter and cook, whisking constantly, until butter melts and mixture thickens. Pour into graham cracker crusts.

Bake at 300 degrees for 20 minutes or until set. Cool. Cover and chill at least 8 hours.

Beat whipping cream at high speed with an electric mixer until foamy. Gradually add powdered sugar, beating until soft peaks form. Stir in vanilla and spread over filling. Chill. Garnish just before serving.

Pumpkin Ice Cream Pie

1 chocolate crumb crust
3 English toffee candy bars (1.4-ounces each), crushed and divided
3 cups vanilla ice cream, softened, divided

1/2 cup canned or cooked pumpkin
2 tablespoons sugar
1/2 teaspoon ground cinnamon
1/4 teaspoon ground nutmeg

Combine two-thirds of the crushed candy bars and 2 cups ice cream. Spoon into crust; freeze for 1 hour or until firm. In a bowl, combine pumpkin, sugar, cinnamon, nutmeg and remaining ice cream. Spoon over ice cream layer in crust. Sprinkle with remaining crushed candy bars. Cover and freeze for 8 hours or up to 2 months. Remove 10-15 minutes before serving.

Double Layer Pumpkin Pie

1 graham cracker crust
4-ounces cream cheese, softened
1 cup plus 1 tablespoon cold milk
1 tablespoon sugar
8-ounces whipped topping, thawed

16-ounce can pumpkin
2 packages (4-serving size) vanilla flavored instant pudding & pie filling
1 teaspoon ground cinnamon
1/2 teaspoon ground ginger
1/4 teaspoon ground cloves

In a large bowl, mix cream cheese, 1 tablespoon milk and sugar with wire whisk until smooth. Gently stir in 1-1/2 cups whipped topping. Spread on bottom of crust.

In a second bowl, stir pumpkin, pudding mix and spices into remaining milk. Beat with wire whisk until well blended. (Mixture will be thick.) Spread over cream cheese layer.

Refrigerate 4 hours. Serve with remaining whipped topping.

Frozen Pumpkin Pie

Gingersnap Crust, baked (see crust section)
1 cup canned pumpkin
1/4 cup packed brown sugar
1/2 teaspoon salt
1/2 teaspoon ground ginger
1/4 teaspoon ground nutmeg

1/4 teaspoon ground cinnamon
1 container (4-1/2 ounces) frozen whipped topping, thawed
1 pint butter pecan ice cream, softened
2 tablespoons chopped pecans

Mix pumpkin, brown sugar, salt, and spices. Fold in whipped topping. Spread ice cream in crust. Swirl pumpkin mixture over ice cream. Freeze uncovered at least 3 hours. Remove from freezer 15 minutes before serving. Sprinkle with pecans.

Million Dollar Pie

9 or 10-inch baked deep dish
pastry shell

1 (14-ounces) can sweetened
condensed milk

1/4 cup lemon juice

1 (11-ounces) can mandarin
oranges, drained

1 (8-ounces) can crushed
pineapple, drained

1 cup chopped pecans

1 (16-ounces) carton whipped
topping

Mix the milk and juice. Stir in oranges, pineapple and pecans.
Fold in whipped topping. Pour filling into prepared crust. Cover
and refrigerate. Will keep in refrigerator up to 8 days.

* Filling can also be divided into 2 small graham cracker crusts.

Peanut Butter Pie

9-inch baked pastry shell

8-ounces cream cheese

1 cup creamy peanut butter

1 tablespoon softened butter
or margarine

1 teaspoon vanilla

1 cup sugar

1 cup whipped cream

Mix first five ingredients together. Fold in whipped cream.
Spread mixture into cooled pie crust. Cool for at least 30
minutes.

I suggest the chocolate crust recipe for this delicious pie.

Chunky Peanut Butter Pie

9-inch baked pastry shell
4-ounce package vanilla
pudding mix
1-3/4 cup milk

1/2 cup chunky peanut butter
1 cup confectioners' sugar
12-ounces whipped topping

Prepare pudding mix with milk using package directions. Mix peanut butter and sugar in small bowl until crumbly. Layer half the crumb mixture, pudding and remaining crumb mixture in pie shell. top with whipped topping and chill until serving time.

Peanut Butter-Cream Cheese Pie

2 chocolate cookie pie shells or
2 (9-inch) baked pastry shells
1/2 cup peanut butter
1 pound confectioners' sugar

16 -ounces cream cheese,
softened
7-ounces sweetened condensed
milk
32-ounces whipped topping

Combine peanut butter, sugar, cream cheese and condensed milk in food processor. Process until smooth. Combine with half the whipped topping in bowl; mix gently. Spoon into pie shells; top with remaining whipped topping. Freeze until serving time. Drizzle with melted chocolate if desired.

Peanut Butter Jelly Pie

9-inch graham cracker crust

1/2 cup strawberry jelly or jam

8-ounce frozen whipped topping, thawed, divided

1 cup cold milk

1 package (3.4-ounces) instant vanilla pudding mix

1/2 cup peanut butter

Spread 1 cup whipped topping over the bottom of the crust. Drop jelly by tablespoonfuls onto topping; spread carefully.

In a bowl, whisk pudding mix and milk together until thickened. Add peanut butter; mix well. Fold in the remaining whipped topping. Spread over jelly.

Cover and freeze for 4 hours or until firm. Remove from freezer 10 minutes before serving.

Peanut Butter Cookie Ice Cream Pie

9-inch chocolate pie crust

1/2 cup creamy peanut butter

1/4 cup honey

1 quart (2 pints) vanilla ice cream, softened

1 cup peanut butter chip cookies, chopped

1/2 cup chocolate syrup

Whipped cream

Place large bowl in freezer. Mix peanut butter and honey in medium bowl. Place ice cream in bowl from freezer. Add peanut butter mix and cookies. Mix on low speed with electric mixer until blended.

Spoon half of ice cream mixture into crust. Spread chocolate syrup over ice cream mixture in crust. Spoon remaining ice cream mixture over chocolate syrup.

Garnish with whipped cream. Freeze leftovers.

Peanut Butter and Kisses Pie

9-inch baked pastry shell

18 Hershey's Kisses milk chocolates

1 cup (1/2 pint) whipping cream, divided

1 package (6-serving size) vanilla pudding and pie filling mix*

1/2 cup creamy peanut butter

2 cups milk

1 tablespoon powdered sugar

1/4 teaspoon vanilla extract

Additional Hershey's Kisses

Remove wrappers from chocolate pieces. Place chocolates and 2 tablespoons whipping cream in small microwave-safe bowl and microwave on high for 1 minute or until chocolate is melted and mixture is smooth when stirred. Spread chocolate mixture over bottom of pie shell and refrigerate 30 minutes or until set.

In 2-quart saucepan, place pudding mix and peanut butter. Using wire whisk, gradually blend in milk, stirring until smooth. Cook over medium heat, stirring constantly, until pudding thickens and boils. Remove from heat.

Cool 10 minutes, stirring frequently. Pour pudding over chocolate mix in pie crust. Refrigerate several hours or until firm.

In small mixer bowl, beat remaining whipping cream, powdered sugar and vanilla until stiff. Spread over top of pie. Garnish with additional chocolate pieces, if desired. Cover and refrigerate leftover pie.

*Do not use instant pudding mix.

Peanut Butter Chip Banana Pie

9-inch crumb crust of your choice

1/3 cup sugar

1/3 cup cornstarch

1/4 teaspoon salt

2-1/4 cups milk

2 egg yolks, slightly beaten

1-2/3 cups (10-ounce package) peanut butter chips

1 teaspoon vanilla extract

1 small banana, sliced

Whipped topping , additional banana slices, additional peanut butter chips, optional

In medium saucepan, stir together sugar, cornstarch and salt. Stir in milk. Cook over medium heat, stirring constantly, until mixture boils. Boil and stir 1 minute. Remove from heat.

Stir 1/2 cup cooked mixture into egg yolks. Return mixture to saucepan, stirring until blended. Cook over low heat, stirring constantly, 2 minutes. Do not boil. Remove from heat. Immediately add peanut butter chips and vanilla. Stir until chips are melted and mixture is smooth. Cool 10 minutes.

Arrange banana slices over bottom of crust and pour filling over bananas. Press plastic wrap directly onto surface. Refrigerate several hours or overnight. Garnish with whipped topping, banana slices and peanut butter chips, if desired. Cover and refrigerate leftover pie.

Fluffy Grasshopper Pie

9-inch chocolate cookie crust

8-ounces cream cheese, softened

14-ounce can sweetened condensed milk

3 tablespoons bottled lemon juice

1/4 cup green Creme de Menthe liqueur

1/4 cup white Creme de Menthe liqueur

4-ounces whipped topping

Beat cream cheese in mixing bowl until light. Add condensed milk gradually, beating constantly until smooth. Stir in lemon juice and liqueurs.

Fold in whipped topping. Chill for 20 minutes. Spoon into prepared pie shell. Chill or freeze for 4 hours or longer.

Minty Grasshopper Pie

9-inch chocolate pie crust

8-ounce cream cheese, softened

14-ounce can sweetened condensed milk

2-3 drops green food coloring

16 Keebler Grasshopper Fudge Mint Cookies, coarsely crushed

8-ounces frozen whipped topping, thawed

With mixer, beat cream cheese until fluffy; gradually beat in sweetened condensed milk until smooth.Stir in food coloring, then crushed cookies. Fold in whipped topping.Pour into crust. Chill at least 3 hours. Garnish with chocolate shavings or additional cookie pieces. Refrigerate leftovers.

White Christmas Pie

9-inch baked pastry shell

1 envelope unflavored gelatin

1/4 cup cold water

1/4 cup flour

1/2 cup sugar, divided

1/2 teaspoon salt

1-1/2 cups milk

3/4 teaspoon vanilla

1/4 teaspoon almond extract

1 cup whipped cream or whipped topping

3 egg whites

1/4 teaspoon cream of tartar

1 cup coconut

Soften gelatin in water in cup. Mix flour, 1/4 cup sugar and salt in saucepan. Stir in milk gradually. Cook over low heat until thick and bubbly, stirring constantly. Cook for 1 minute longer. Stir in gelatin until dissolved. Beat until smooth. Add flavorings. Fold in whipped cream.

Beat egg white with remaining sugar and cream of tartar in bowl until stiff peaks form. Fold into filling with coconut. Spoon into pie shell. Chill for 2 hours or longer. Let stand at room temperature for several minutes before serving.

Easy Mint Pie

9-inch chocolate pie crust

8-ounce package cream cheese, softened

1/3 cup sugar

12-ounces whipped topping, thawed, divided

3 drops green food coloring

1 cup chopped Keebler Fudge Shoppe Grasshopper Cookies

Mint leaves or chocolate leaves, optional

In large mixing bowl, mix sugar and cream cheese at medium speed until well blended. Fold in 3 cups whipped topping, food coloring and cookies. Spoon into crust.Refrigerate at least 3 hours or until set. Garnish with remaining whipped topping. Decorate with mint leaves or chocolate if desired.

Peppermint Pie

9-inch chocolate pie crust

1 quart peppermint ice cream, softened*

1/2 cup hot fudge sauce

2 cups whipping cream

1/2 cup finely crushed hard peppermint candies

Spoon ice cream into pie crust. Freeze for 1 hour. Drizzle fudge sauce over ice cream; swirl gently with knife. Freeze 2 to 3 hours more. Beat whipping cream until soft peaks form. Fold in candy. Pipe or spoon whipped cream over pie. Freeze 30 minutes. Let stand 5-10 minutes before slicing.

*Tip: 3/4 cup crushed hard peppermint candies and 2 drops of red food coloring stirred into 1 quart softened vanilla ice cream may be substituted.

Creme De Menthe Pie

9-inch chocolate cookie crust

2/3 cup half and half

24 large marshmallows

1/2 pint whipping cream, whipped

1/4 cup creme de menthe

Melt marshmallows with half and half over boiling water. Cool. Stir in creme de menthe. Fold mixture into whipped cream. Pour into crust. Top with a few cookie crumbs or chocolate curls, leaves, etc. Freeze until firm. Let stand at room temperature 30-45 minutes before serving. Best if made 24 hours ahead of serving time.

Cookies 'N' Cream Fluff Pie

9-inch baked pastry shell

2 cups cold milk

1 package (3.4-ounces) instant vanilla pudding mix

8-ounces frozen whipped topping, thawed

15 chocolate cream-filled sandwich cookies, broken into chunks

Additional broken cookies, optional

In a bowl, whisk milk and pudding mix for 2 minutes or until slightly thickened. Fold in whipped topping and cookies. Spoon into pie shell and refrigerate. Top with additional cookies if desired.

Quick and Easy Pie

9-inch baked graham cracker crust

1 cup milk

1 package (3.4 ounce) instant vanilla pudding

1 pint vanilla ice cream

1 package frozen whipped topping or 1/2 pint heavy cream, whipped

1/4 cup graham cracker crumbs

Add milk to vanilla pudding. Add vanilla ice cream and stir until dissolved. Pour into the pie crust and chill until firm. Just before serving, whip cream and drop by teaspoonfuls onto pie. Garnish with graham cracker crumbs. Cut and serve.

Angel Food Pie

9-inch baked pastry shell

1 cup sugar

1/4 cup cornstarch

2 cups boiling water

1/4 teaspoon salt

2 egg whites

1 cup drained crushed pineapple

1 teaspoon lemon juice

1 teaspoon vanilla

Boil sugar, cornstarch, water and salt in double boiler for 15 minutes or until thick. Let cool. Beat egg whites until stiff and fold in pineapple, lemon juice, vanilla and cooled ingredients. Put into pie shell and refrigerate about 2 hours before serving.

Liqueur Pie

2 cups finely crushed chocolate wafers

1/2 cup melted butter or margarine

Grated orange rind to taste

6 egg yolks

1 cup sugar

1-1/2 tablespoons unflavored gelatin

1/4 cup cold water

1/4 cup boiling water

1/3 cup orange liqueur

2 cups whipping cream, whipped

2 squares semisweet chocolate

Mix wafer crumbs, melted butter and orange rind in greased 10-inch springform pan. Spread evenly in pan.

Beat egg yolks and sugar in mixing bowl for 3 minutes. Soften gelatin in cold water in bowl. Stir in boiling water until gelatin dissolves. Add to egg yolk mixture with liqueur; beat at high speed until smooth.

Fold in whipped cream and spoon into pie shell. Grate chocolate over top. Chill for 5 hours or longer.

When ready to serve, place on serving plate and remove side of pan. (May omit orange rind and use other flavor liqueur. May substitute vanilla wafer crumbs for chocolate wafer crumbs, almonds for grated chocolate and use almond liqueur.

Make sure eggs are fresh and store in refrigerator.

Quick Kiwi Pie

1 deep dish graham cracker crust

1 package (8-ounces) frozen whipped topping, thawed

1 can (14-ounces) sweetened condensed milk

1/2 cup lime or lemon juice

3 or 4 kiwi, sliced

Combine lime juice and condensed milk in medium bowl, mixing well. Add whipped topping. Pour into crust evenly. Place kiwi slightly overlapping all around top until covered. Refrigerate for 1 hour before cutting and serving.

Scoops of Ice Cream Pie

2 pints vanilla ice cream, divided

1 cup chocolate wafer crumbs (about 16 wafers)

1/2 cup chopped almonds

1/4 cup butter or margarine, melted

Fresh raspberries

Fresh mint, optional

Soften 1 pint of ice cream. Combine cookie crumbs, nuts and butter. Press onto the bottom and up the sides of a 9-inch pie plate. Spread with the softened ice cream. Cover and freeze until firm.

Scoop remaining ice cream into small balls; pile into crust. cover and freeze. Will keep for up to two months.

Remove from freezer 10 minutes prior to serving. Arrange raspberries between scoops. Garnish with mint if desired.

Marshmallow Pineapple Pie

9-inch graham cracker crust

1 package (16-ounces) large marshmallows

1-1/2 teaspoons lemon extract

20-ounce can crushed pineapple, drained

2 cups milk

2 cups whipping cream, whipped

1/2 cup graham cracker crumbs

Over low heat, melt marshmallows with milk in a heavy saucepan. Remove from heat. Cool; stir occasionally. Add extract; stir.

Fold in whipped cream and pineapple. Spread pineapple mixture into graham cracker crust. Sprinkle crumbs on top and refrigerate.

143

Sunflower Ice Cream Pie

1-1/2 cups crushed cream-filled chocolate sandwich cookies, divided (about 15)

3 tablespoons plus 1/2 cup caramel ice cream topping, divided

2 tablespoons semisweet chocolate chips, melted

2-1/2 to 3 cups vanilla ice cream, softened

1 tablespoon chopped walnuts

Black decorating gel

Set aside 2 tablespoons crushed cookies for garnish. Combine the remaining crushed cookies, 3 tablespoons caramel topping and the melted chocolate chips. Press onto the bottom and up the sides of a greased 9-inch pie plate. Spread ice cream over crust and freeze.

For sunflower, place reserved cookies in a 2-inch circle in center of pie. Top with walnuts. For the petals, drizzle or spread remaining caramel topping over ice cream. Outline petals with decorating gel. Freeze. Remove from freezer 10 minutes before cutting.

Coffee Mallow Pie

9-inch baked pastry shell

1 cup water

1 tablespoon instant coffee granules

4 cups miniature marshmallows

1 cup whipping cream, whipped

1 tablespoon butter

1/2 cup chopped walnuts or pecans, toasted

Additional whipped cream and chocolate curls, optional

Bring water to a boil in a heavy saucepan; stir in coffee granules until dissolved. Reduce heat and add marshmallows and butter. Cook and stir over low heat until marshmallows are melted and mixture is smooth. Set saucepan in ice and whisk mixture constantly until cooled.

Fold in whipped cream and spoon into pastry shell. Sprinkle with nuts. Refrigerate for at least 3 hours before serving. Garnish with whipped cream and chocolate curls.

Rainbow Macaroon Pie

Crust:

3/4 cup pecans, ground

8 soft coconut macaroon cookies (about 2 cups), crumbled

3 tablespoons butter, melted

Filling:

1 pint pistachio almond ice cream, slightly softened

1 pint strawberry frozen yogurt, slightly softened

1 pint vanilla frozen yogurt, slightly softened

Heat oven to 350 degrees. Combine all crust ingredients in medium bowl. Press firmly onto bottom and up sides of ungreased 9-inch pie plate. Bake for 12-15 minutes or until golden brown. Cool completely.

Arrange scoops of ice cream and yogurt in pie shell. Cover with plastic food wrap and freeze at least 1 hour. Let pie stand at room temperature for 10 minutes before serving. Cut into wedges to serve.

Chilly Coconut Pie

9-inch graham cracker crust

3-ounce package cream cheese, softened

2 tablespoons sugar

1/2 cup milk

1/4 teaspoon almond extract

1 cup flaked coconut

8-ounces frozen whipped topping, thawed

In a mixing bowl, beat cream cheese and sugar until smooth. Gradually beat in milk and extract. Fold in coconut and whipped topping. Spoon into crust. Cover and freeze for at least 4 hours. Remove from freezer 30 minutes before serving.

Butterscotch Pecan Sandie Cream Pie

9-inch graham cracker pie crust

1 package (3.4 ounces) instant butterscotch pudding mix

2 cups cold milk

1 carton (16 ounces) frozen whipped topping, thawed, divided

1 cup chopped Pecan Sandie cookies, divided

1/2 cup butterscotch ice cream topping

In a mixing bowl, prepare pudding mix according to package directions using milk. Fold one-third of whipped topping and 1/2 cup cookie pieces into pudding mixture. Spoon filling into pie crust. Spread remaining whipped topping over pudding layer. Sprinkle with remaining cookie pieces. Drizzle with butterscotch topping. Refrigerate 3 hours or until set.

Rum-Butterscotch Pie

18 gingersnaps

2 tablespoons sugar

2 tablespoons melted butter

1 tablespoon rum

2-1/3 cups light cream

2 packages (3.4-ounce each) butterscotch instant pudding

Crush 12 gingersnaps and mix with sugar, butter and 1 tablespoon water. Spread over bottom of 8-inch pie plate. Cut remaining gingersnaps in half and arrange around edge of pie plate. Prepare pudding according to package directions, using combined rum and cream instead of milk. Pour pudding into gingersnap shell and chill for at least 2 hours.

Coffee Cordial Pie

9-inch chocolate cookie or graham cracker crust
1/2 cup water
1 tablespoon instant coffee
32 large jet-puffed marshmallows

1/4 cup coffee liqueur
3 tablespoons Irish whiskey
1-1/2 cups chilled whipping cream

Bake pie crust in 350 degree preheated oven for 8 minutes. Heat water, instant coffee (dry) and marshmallows over low heat, stirring constantly; just until marshmallows are melted.

Refrigerate, stirring occasionally, until mixture mounds slightly when dropped from a spoon (about 20 minutes). If mix becomes too thick, place pan in bowl of warm water and stir mix until it is of proper consistency.

Gradually stir in liqueur and whiskey. Beat whipping cream in chilled 2-1/2 quart bowl until stiff. Fold marshmallow mixture into whipped cream. Pour into crust. Sprinkle with grated semi-sweet chocolate if desired. Refrigerate until set, at least 4 hours.

Alexander Pie: Substitute 1/2 cup milk for water and instant coffee, dark creme de cacao for the coffee liqueur, and brandy for the whiskey.

Cherry Cordial Pie: Substitute 1/2 cup milk for the water and instant coffee and 1/2 cup kirsch for the coffee liqueur and whiskey. Fold few drops red food color into marshmallow-whipped cream mixture if desired

Grasshopper Pie: Substitute 1/2 cup milk for the water and instant coffee, creme de menthe for the coffee liqueur and white creme de cacao for the whiskey. Fold a few drops of green food color into the marshmallow mix if desired.

Creamy Candy Bar Pie

9-inch chocolate cookie crumb
crust

2 cups cold milk

2 (4-ounce) packages
chocolate or vanilla instant
pudding and pie filling

8-ounces whipped topping,
thawed, divided

1 cup chopped candy bars
(1/4-inch pieces), divided

Beat milk and pudding mixes in medium bowl with wire whisk for 1 minute. Stir in half of the whipped topping until thick and well blended. Reserve 1/4 cup of the chopped candy. Stir remaining candy into pudding mixture. Spread into crust.

Spread remaining whipped topping over pudding layer in crust. Sprinkle top with remaining chopped candy. Refrigerate at least 4 hours. Refrigerate leftovers. *Tip for chopping candy: freeze or refrigerate before chopping.*

Buttered Pecan Refrigerator Pie

9-inch graham cracker crust

2 (3.4 ounce) packages
vanilla instant pudding

2 cups milk

1 quart softened butter pecan
ice cream

1 package whipped topping

1 Heath bar

Combine instant pudding and milk. Add ice cream and mix thoroughly. Pour into cracker crumb crust. Chill. Top with whipped topping prepared according to directions. Shave Heath bar over top.

CHOCOLATE LOVERS

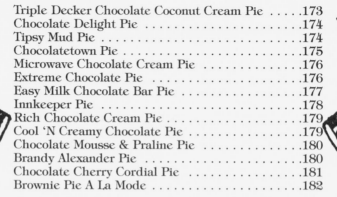

CHOCOLATE LOVERS

Chocolate Tips...

- Equal amounts of melted baking chocolate squares can be substituted for melted chocolate chips . . . it's usually cheaper and tastes the same.

- How to Make Chocolate Sticks:

  Melt a square of baking or white chocolate. Using a pastry brush, brush melted chocolate into thin strips onto clear plastic wrap. Pleat so chocolate wrinkles. Refrigerate until firm. Simply pull the plastic wrap flat so the chocolate breaks into sticks.

- How to Make Perfect Chocolate Curls:

  Starting at the longer end of a solid block of chocolate, use a vegetable peeler and slowly peel off curls. (If you get only shavings try warming the chocolate slightly.)

  To make a block of chocolate, start by melting chocolate chips, chocolate confectionery coating, or solid chocolate candy bars. Pour the melted chocolate onto the back of an inverted cookie sheet and spread to a thin smooth layer. Let cool until firm and pliable but not brittle.

  With a cheese slicer, metal spatula or pancake turner, scrape up a thin layer of chocolate using even pressure, it will curl as you go. The slower you scrape, the wider your curls. Use a toothpick or wooden skewer to carefully lift. Arrange on desserts as desired.

Most Divine Chocolate Pie

9-inch baked pastry shell
Filling:
1 envelope unflavored gelatin
1/2 cup sugar, divided
1/4 teaspoon salt
1 cup milk
3 egg yokes, beaten
3 squares semi-sweet or sweet chocolate

1/2 teaspoon vanilla
3 egg whites
1/4 teaspoon cream of tartar
1 cup heavy cream, whipped
Topping:
1 cup heavy cream, whipped
1/2 square chocolate

Mix gelatin, 1/4 cup sugar and salt in medium saucepan. Blend in milk and beaten egg yolks. Add chocolate. Heat slowly, stirring constantly until chocolate is melted and mixture is slightly thickened. Do not boil. Pour into a large bowl, add vanilla. Stir until smooth. Cool completely.

Beat egg whites and cream of tartar until foamy in medium bowl. Beat in remaining 1/4 cup sugar until stiff.

Beat 1 cup of cream until stiff. Beat cooled chocolate mixture until smooth. Fold in meringue, then whipped cream.

Pour into cooled shell. Cool until firm, about 2-4 hours. Beat 1 cup cream until stiff; mound or pipe on pie. Garnish with shaved chocolate or curls.
• This pie takes a little more time to prepare, but you will taste the effort!!

Easy Chocolate Mallow Pie

9-inch graham cracker pie crust
8-ounce package softened cream cheese
2 cups cold milk, divided

3.9 ounce package instant chocolate pudding mix
1-1/2 cups miniature marshmallows

Beat cream cheese and 1/2 cup milk in bowl until smooth. Add pudding mix and remaining milk; mix well. Stir in marshmallows then pour into crust. Refrigerate until ready to serve. This is ready in 30 minutes or less!

Chocolate-Pecan Chess Pie

9-inch unbaked pastry shell
1 1/4 cups sugar
4 teaspoons cornmeal
4 eggs
1/3 cup half and half or light cream
3 tablespoons butter or margarine, melted and cooled

1 teaspoon vanilla
1/2 cup pecans, toasted and chopped (toasted is optional)
1/2 cup miniature semisweet chocolate pieces

Preheat oven to 450 degrees. Prepare pastry for single crust. Bake about 8 minutes until set and dry, but not brown. Remove from oven and set aside. Reduce oven to 350 degrees.

In a small bowl, combine sugar and cornmeal; set aside.

In a large mixing bowl, beat eggs with electric mixer on medium speed for one minute. Add sugar mixture; mix well. With a wooden spoon, gradually stir in half and half, melted butter or margarine, and vanilla. Stir in pecans.

Sprinkle chocolate pieces into the bottom of pastry shell. Carefully pour the filling into the shell.

Bake in a 350 degree oven for 40-45 minutes until center appears nearly set when shaken. Cool on wire rack. Refrigerate within 2-3 hours.

Chocolate Peppermint Pie

9-inch chocolate cookie crust
1 quart chocolate-chocolate chip ice cream, softened

6-ounces chocolate-covered peppermint candies
1 cup whipping cream, divided

Spoon ice cream into crust. Freeze until firm, about 2 hours. Meanwhile in a small saucepan, heat candies with 3-4 tablespoons of cream; stir until smooth. Cool. Whip the remaining cream; spoon over ice cream. Drizzle with some of the chocolate-peppermint sauce; pass the remaining sauce.

Hot Fudge Mud Pie

8-1/2 ounce package Oreo cookies, finely crushed

1/2 cup melted butter or margarine

1-1/2 pints coffee ice cream, softened

2 (1-ounce) squares unsweetened chocolate

1-1/2 cups sugar

1/2 cup butter or margarine

3/4 cup evaporated milk

1/2 teaspoon vanilla

1/2 teaspoon salt

Almonds

Whipped cream and shaved chocolate

Preheat oven to 375 degrees. Mix cookie crumbs and melted butter in 9-inch pie plate; press evenly over bottom and side of pie pan. Bake for 10 minutes. Cool to room temperature. Spread with ice cream. Freeze for 1-1/2 hours or until firm.

Combine next 6 ingredients in medium saucepan. Bring to a boil, stirring to mix well. Cool slightly . .. . the sauce with be very thin. Pour over servings; sprinkle with almonds and garnish with whipped cream and shaved chocolate.

Creamy German Chocolate Pie

1 graham cracker crust

1-3/4 cups cold milk

2 packages (3.9 ounces each) instant chocolate pudding mix

8-ounces whipped topping, thawed

1/3 cup caramel ice cream topping

3 tablespoons flaked coconut, lightly toasted

3 tablespoons chopped pecans

Combine milk and pudding mixes in large bowl. Beat with a wire whisk for 2 minutes . . . .mixture will be thick. Gently stir in whipped topping. Spoon into pie crust. Refrigerate 4 hours or until set. Before serving, drizzle with caramel ice cream topping and sprinkle with toasted coconut and pecans.

Chocolate Chip Pie

9-inch unbaked deep dish pastry shell

2 eggs

1/2 cup flour

1/2 cup sugar

1/2 cup packed brown sugar

3/4 cup butter or margarine, softened

1 cup semi-sweet chocolate chips

1 cup nuts, chopped

Sweetened whipped cream or ice cream

In a large mixing bowl, beat eggs on high until foamy. Beat in flour, sugars and butter. Stir in chips and nuts. Spoon into pie shell.

Bake at 325 degrees for 55-60 minutes or until knife inserted halfway between outside edge and center comes out clean. Cool on wire rack. Serve warm with whipped cream.

Black Forrest Pie

9-inch unbaked pastry shell

3/4 cup sugar

1/3 cup baking cocoa

2 tablespoons flour

1/3 cup milk

1/4 cup butter or margarine

2 eggs, lightly beaten

21-ounces cherry pie filling, divided

Whipped topping, optional

In a saucepan, combine sugar, cocoa, flour and milk until smooth. Add butter. Bring to a boil; cook and stir for 2 minutes or until thickened. Remove from the heat. Stir a small amount of hot mixture into eggs. Return all to the pan. Fold in half of the pie filling. Pour into pastry shell.

Bake at 350 degrees for 35-40 minutes or until filling is almost set. Cool completely on a wire rack. Just before serving, top with remaining pie filing and whipped topping if desired.

Chocolate Mocha Macadamia Pie

1 shortbread ready crust

1/2 cup light brown sugar, packed

1/3 cup corn syrup

1/4 cup strong brewed coffee

1/4 cup butter or margarine, melted

3 eggs

1/2 teaspoon cinnamon

1/3 cup semi-sweet chocolate chips

1 cup coarsely chopped macadamia nuts

In a mixing bowl, beat brown sugar, corn syrup, coffee, butter, eggs and cinnamon until well blended. Stir in chocolate chips and macadamia nuts.

Pour into pie crust. Bake at 350 degrees for 40 minutes or until set. Cool on wire rack.

Frozen Mocha Pie

1-1/4 cups chocolate wafer crumbs, divided (about 24 wafers)

1/4 cup sugar

1/4 cup butter or margarine, melted

8-ounces cream cheese, softened

14-ounces sweetened condensed milk

2/3 cup chocolate syrup

2 tablespoons instant coffee granules

1 tablespoon hot water

1 cup whipping cream, whipped

Chocolate-covered coffee beans, optional

Combine 1 cup wafer crumbs, butter and sugar together. Press onto the bottom and 1-inch up the sides of a greased 9-inch springform pan. Set aside. (If you're in a hurry, use a chocolate ready crust.)

In a mixing bowl, beat milk, cream cheese and chocolate syrup until smooth. Dissolve coffee granules in hot water; add to cream cheese mixture. Fold in whipped cream. Pour over the crust. Sprinkle with remaining crumbs.

Cover and freeze for approximately 8 hours. Uncover and remove from the freezer 10-15 minutes before serving. Garnish with coffee beans if desired.

Chocolate Cream Pie

9-inch baked pastry shell
1-1/2 cups sugar
1/3 cup flour
3 tablespoons baking cocoa
1/2 teaspoon salt
1-1/2 cup water

12-ounce can evaporated milk
5 beaten egg yolks
1/2 cup butter or margarine
1 teaspoon vanilla
Whipped topping

In large pan, combine the sugar, flour, cocoa, salt, water and evaporated milk. Stir until smooth. Cook and stir over medium heat until thick and bubbly . . . about 2-3 minutes. Reduce heat; cook and stir 2 minutes longer.

Remove from heat; stir 1 cup hot mixture into egg yolks. Return all to the pan and bring to a slow boil stirring continuously.

Remove from heat and add butter and vanilla. Cool slightly. Pour warm filling into pastry shell. Cool for 1 hour then refrigerate until set. Garnish with whipped topping when serving. *This pie can also be topped with meringue. Omit whipped topping. Follow meringue instructions.

Kentucky Derby Pie

9-inch unbaked pastry shell
3 eggs, slightly beaten
3/4 cup light corn syrup
3 tablespoons granulated sugar
3 tablespoons brown sugar
3 tablespoons butter, softened

1 teaspoon vanilla
1/8 teaspoon salt
1/2 cup finely chopped pecans
1/3 cup bourbon
6-ounce package chocolate pieces
1-1/2 cups pecan halves

In a large mixing bowl, combine eggs, corn syrup, sugars, butter, vanilla and salt. Mix well. Stir in chopped pecans and bourbon.

Pat chocolate pieces lightly onto bottom of pastry shell. Pour filling over chocolate pieces. Arrange pecan halves atop filling.

Bake in a 350 degree oven about one hour or until knife inserted near the center comes out clean.

Chocolate Cherry Pie

1 cup flour
2 tablespoons sugar
1/2 teaspoon salt
1/2 cup cold butter or margarine
Filling:
14-ounce can sweetened condensed milk

6-ounces semisweet chocolate chips
1/2 teaspoon salt
21-ounce can cherry pie filling
1/4 to 1/2 teaspoon almond extract
Whipped cream and maraschino cherries, *if desired*

Mix flour, salt and sugar in bowl. Cut in butter until mixture resembles coarse crumbs. Press firmly onto the bottom and sides of a 9-inch pie plate. Bake 15-20 minutes in a 350 degree oven or until golden brown. Cool completely.

In a saucepan, combine chocolate chips, milk and salt. Cook and stir over low heat until chocolate melts. Stir in pie filling and extract. Pour into crust and chill 2 to 3 hours or until firm. Garnish with whipped cream and cherries.

Cocoa Mousse Pie

9-inch graham cracker crust
3-ounce package cream cheese, softened
2/3 cup sugar
1/3 cup baking cocoa
1/4 cup milk

1 teaspoon vanilla
8-ounce carton whipped topping, thawed
Additional whipped topping and baking cocoa, optional

Beat cream cheese, cocoa and sugar together in mixing bowl. Add milk and vanilla; beat until smooth. Fold in the whipped topping. Spoon into crust. Cover and freeze for 20 minutes. When serving top with a dollop of whipped topping and a dusting of cocoa.

Chocolate Mousse Pie

9-inch baked pastry shell

8 (1-ounce) squares semisweet baking chocolate, chopped

1/2 cup water, divided

2 tablespoons butter

3 egg yolks

2 tablespoons sugar

1-1/4 cups whipping cream, whipped

Using a double boiler or microwave, heat chocolate, 1/4 cup water and butter until melted. Cool for about 10 minutes.

In a heavy (small) saucepan, whisk egg yolks, sugar and remaining water together. Cook and stir over low heat 1 to 2 minutes or until mixture reaches about 160 degrees. Remove from heat and add chocolate mixture.

Set saucepan in ice and stir until cooled... about 5 to 10 minutes. Fold in whipped cream. Spoon into pie shell and refrigerate at least 4 hours before serving.

Mocha Mousse Pie

1 chocolate crumb or graham cracker crust

1-1/2 cups semisweet chocolate chips, melted and slightly cooled

2 cups whipping cream

2 tablespoons instant coffee granules

2 tablespoons sugar

1 teaspoon vanilla

Chocolate shavings, optional

In a large microwave-safe bowl, melt chocolate chips; set aside to cool. In a mixing bowl, beat cream, coffee granules, sugar and vanilla on low until coffee and sugar are dissolved. Beat on high just until stiff peaks form. Set aside 1-1/2 cup for topping.

Gradually fold remaining cream mixture into cooled chocolate until well blended. Pour into pie crust. Spread with reserved cream mixture. Refrigerate for 3 hours. Garnish with chocolate shavings if desired. Store in refrigerator.

Chocolate Ribbon Pie

Chocolate cookie crust

8-ounces cream cheese, softened

1/4 cup sugar

2 tablespoons milk

8-ounces whipped topping, thawed and divided

3 cups cold milk

2 packages (4-serving each size) chocolate flavor instant pudding & pie filling

Beat cream cheese, sugar and 2 tablespoons milk in large bowl with electric mixer on medium speed until smooth. Gently stir in 1/2 of the whipped topping. Spread over crust.

Pour 3 cups milk into large bowl. Add pudding mixes. Beat with wire whisk for 2 minutes. Pour over cream cheese layer.

Refrigerate 4 hours or until set. Spread remaining whipped topping over pudding. Garnish with chocolate curls, raspberries and fresh mint leave. Store leftovers in refrigerator.

Chocolate Peanut Butter Truffle Pie

6-ounce chocolate pie crust

2 cups whipping cream, divided

3 tablespoons butter or margarine

1 package (8 ounces) semi-sweet baking chocolate, coarsely chopped

1/2 to 1 teaspoon orange extract

1/3 cup sugar

1/3 cup creamy peanut butter

Warm hot fudge ice cream topping, optional

1/2 cup chopped peanuts

In a medium saucepan over low heat, heat 3/4 cup whipping cream and butter to a simmer. Remove from heat. Add chocolate and orange extract; stir until chocolate is melted. Pour into pie crust and refrigerate 1 hour or until chilled. In a mixing bowl, whip remaining whipping cream, sugar and peanut butter until stiff peaks form. Spread over chocolate filling. Drizzle with hot fudge topping if desired and top with peanuts. Refrigerate at least 30 minutes before serving.

Chocolate-Banana Pie

1 graham cracker crust
1 cup sugar
1/2 cup flour
1/4 teaspoon salt
2 squares (1-ounce each) unsweetened chocolate, grated
2 cups milk

3 egg yolks, slightly beaten
2 tablespoons butter or margarine
1 teaspoon vanilla
2 bananas, sliced
Whipped topping

Combine sugar, flour and salt in saucepan. Add chocolate and milk. Cook over medium heat until thickened, stirring constantly. Cook for 2 minutes longer.

Stir a small amount of hot mixture into egg yolks; stir egg yolks into hot mixture. Cook for 2 minutes, stirring constantly. Remove from heat and add butter and vanilla. Mix well.

Place plastic wrap directly on surface; cool to room temperature. Spoon half the filling into crust. Stir bananas into remaining filling. Spoon over first layer. Cover with whipped topping.

Frosty Chocolate Chip Pie

8-inch baked pastry shell, or crumb crust
1 cup semi-sweet chocolate chips
1/3 cup milk

1 package (3 ounces) cream cheese, softened
2-1/2 cups frozen whipped topping, thawed
Additional whipped topping
Fresh fruit slices

In medium microwave-safe bowl, combine chocolate chips and milk. Microwave on high for 1-1/2 minutes or until hot.

With wire whisk or spoon, beat in cream cheese until well blended and smooth. Cool just to room temperature.

Gently fold 2-1/2 cups whipped topping into chocolate mixture. Spoon into crust. Cover and freeze until firm. Garnish with whipped topping and fresh fruit.

Chocolate Maniac Attack

1 chocolate crumb crust

1 cup semi-sweet chocolate chips

2-1/2 teaspoons instant coffee granules

1 teaspoon hot water

3/4 cup sour cream

1/2 cup sugar

1 teaspoon vanilla

1-1/2 cups whipped cream

1 cup confectioners sugar

1/2 cup baking cocoa

2 tablespoons mini semi-sweet chocolate chips

Melt 1 cup chips in microwave for 1 to 2 minutes or until smooth, stirring every 10 to 20 seconds. Cool for 10 minutes.

In a medium bowl, dissolve coffee granules in water. Add sour cream, granulated sugar and vanilla. Stir until sugar is dissolved. Stir in melted chips until smooth. Spread into crust and refrigerate.

In another medium bowl, beat cream, confectioners sugar and cocoa until stiff peaks form. Spread or pipe over first layer. Sprinkle with mini chips. Freeze for at least 6 hours before serving.

Fudge Pie

1/2 cup margarine

1-1/2 squares baking chocolate

1 cup sugar

1/2 cup flour

2 eggs

1 teaspoon vanilla

1/2 cup nuts, optional

Preheat oven to 375 degrees. In small saucepan over low heat, melt margarine and chocolate. Stir to mix well. Add sugar and flour; mix well. Add eggs; beat just until smooth. Stir in vanilla and nuts. Spoon into 8 or 9-inch pie pan.

Bake 22 to 25 minutes or until pie has a brownie-like gloss and fudgey texture.

Serve with whipped topping, whipped cream or ice cream.

Chocolate-Amaretto Mousse Pie

2 cups semisweet chocolate chips
2 tablespoons butter or margarine
14-ounces sweetened condensed milk
1/4 teaspoon salt
1/4 cup butter or margarine
1/4 cup water
1/2 cup Amaretto
2 cups whipping cream, whipped
Almonds

Line a 9-inch pie plate smoothly with foil. Melt 1 cup chocolate chips with 2 tablespoons butter in saucepan over low heat. Spread quickly in even layer in prepared pie pan. Freeze for 30 minutes.

Combine remaining 1 cup chocolate chips, condensed milk, salt and 1/4 cup butter in saucepan. Cook over low heat until smooth, stirring well. Add water gradually; stir. Cook over medium heat for 5 minutes. Add Amaretto and cook for 5 minutes or until thickened. Stir constantly.

Cool to room temperature. Reserve some of the whipped cream for garnish. Fold remining whipped cream into chocolate mixture.

Lift chocolate pie shell gently from plate and remove foil; return to pie plate. Spoon filling into shell. Garnish with reserved whipped cream and almonds. Chill for 3 hours or until set.

Chocolate Chip Coconut Pie

9-inch unbaked pastry shell
1/4 cup plus 2 tablespoons butter, softened
1 cup sugar
1 teaspoon vanilla
2 eggs
1/2 cup flour
6-ounce package chocolate chips
3/4 cup pecans, chopped
1/2 cup coconut

Combine butter, sugar, vanilla and beat well. Add eggs and flour. Stir in chips, nuts, and coconut. Pour in pie crust. Bake 30-40 minutes in a 350 degree oven.

Heavenly Chocolate Angel Pie

1 cup sugar
1/4 teaspoon cream of tartar
4 egg whites
1/4 cup chopped pecans
1 bar German sweet chocolate
2-1/2 teaspoons water
2 egg yolks

1 tablespoon confectioners'
sugar
2 egg whites, stiffly beaten
8 ounces whipped topping
1/2 cup chopped pecans
Chocolate curls
Whipped topping

Preheat oven to 275 degrees. Sift cream of tartar and sugar together. Beat 4 egg whites in mixer bowl until stiff but not dry. Add sugar mixture gradually, beating until glossy peaks form.

Fold in pecans. Spread 1/4 inch thick over bottom of greased 9-inch pie plate. Spread side of pie plate 1-inch thick.

Bake for 1 hour or until light brown and crisp to the touch. Cool away from drafts; meringue may fall and crack in center.

Microwave chocolate in glass bowl until melted. Stir after 1 minute. Blend in water. Beat in egg yolks one at a time. Add confectioners' sugar; mix well.

Fold in 2 beaten egg whites and 8-ounces whipped topping. Spoon into meringue shell. Sprinkle with chopped pecans.

Freeze until firm. Let stand at room temperature for 20-30 minutes. Garnish with chocolate curls and additional whipped topping.

Make sure eggs are fresh.

Chocolate Custard Pie

9-inch unbaked pastry shell
2 (1-ounce) squares
semisweet chocolate
14-ounce can sweetened
condensed milk

3 eggs, beaten
1-1/2 cups hot water
2 teaspoons vanilla
4-ounces whipped topping

Preheat oven to 425 degrees. Melt chocolate with condensed milk in heavy saucepan over low heat. Remove from heat and gradually stir in eggs. Add hot water and vanilla; mix well.

Spoon into pie shell. Bake 10 minutes then reduce heat to 300 degrees and continue baking for 25 to 30 minutes more or until knife inserted near center comes out clean.

Cool to room temperature. Chill in refrigerator. Spread with whipped topping.

Easy Chocolate Pie

9-inch chocolate wafer pie
shell
2 (4-ounce) packages German
sweet chocolate
1/2 cup milk

8-ounces cream cheese,
softened
2 tablespoons sugar, optional
8-ounces whipped topping

Break chocolate into 8 pieces. Combine 5 pieces with 1/4 cup milk in glass bowl. Microwave on high for 1-1/2 to 2 minutes or until melted; stir until smooth.

Beat in remaining 1/4 cup milk, cream cheese and sugar. Fold in whipped topping. Spoon into pie shell.

Freeze until firm. Let stand for 30 minutes. Melt remaining 3 pieces of chocolate in microwave or heavy saucepan and drizzle over pie.

Chocolate Meringue Pie

3/4 cup sugar
1/4 teaspoon cream of tartar
3 egg whites
1/2 cup chopped walnuts
1 teaspoon vanilla

3/4 cup semisweet chocolate chips
3 tablespoons hot water
1 cup whipping cream, whipped

Preheat oven to 275 degrees. Sift sugar and cream of tartar together. Beat egg whites in mixer bowl until stiff but not dry. Add sugar mixture gradually . . . beating constantly.

Spread in buttered 9-inch pie plate. Sprinkle with walnuts. Bake for 1 hour or until crisp. Cool completely.

Melt chocolate chips in double boiler. Stir in hot water and cook until thickened, stirring constantly. Add vanilla. Cool to room temperature.

Fold in whipped cream and spoon into meringue shell. Chill for 3 hours or longer. Top with additional whipped cream if desired.

Easy Fudge-Pecan Pie

9-inch unbaked pastry shell
1/2 cup margarine
3 tablespoons baking cocoa
3/4 cup hot water
2 cups sugar
1/2 cup flour

1/8 teaspoon salt
1 teaspoon vanilla
3/4 cup evaporated milk
1 cup pecan halves
Whipped topping or ice cream

Melt margarine in small saucepan over low heat. Remove from heat. Blend in baking cocoa and water. Add mixture of sugar, flour and salt. Mix well. Stir in vanilla, evaporated milk and pecans.

Spoon into pie shell. Bake in a 350 degree oven for 50 minutes. Serve warm with whipped topping or ice cream.

Chocolate-Toffee Pie

Crust:
1-1/4 cups finely crushed graham crackers
1/4 cup sugar
5 tablespoons melted margarine
1/2 cup miniature semi-sweet chocolate chips

Filling:
1/4 cup flour
1/8 teaspoon salt
1/3 cup sugar
1-1/2 cups milk

1/2 cup miniature semisweet chocolate chips
1/4 cup almond brickle chips
1 tablespoon margarine
2 egg yolks
1 teaspoon vanilla

Topping:
1 cup whipping cream
1/4 cup confectioners' sugar
1 teaspoon vanilla
1/4 cup almond brickle chips
Additional chocolate chips and almond brickle chips

Crust: Preheat oven to 375 degrees. Mix graham cracker crumbs and sugar in bowl. Stir in melted margarine and chips. Press over bottom and side of 9-inch pie plate. Bake for 6 to 9 minutes or until light brown. Cool to room temperature.

Filling: Mix flour, salt and sugar in saucepan. Stir in milk gradually. Add chocolate chips, almond butter brickle chips and margarine. Cook until thickened, stirring constantly. Reduce heat and cook 2 minutes longer.

Stir in a small amount of hot mixture into egg yolks; stir egg yolks into mixture. Cook for 2 minutes, stirring constantly. Stir in vanilla.

Spoon into pie shell. Chill until serving time.

Topping: Beat whipping cream with confectioners' sugar and remaining 1 teaspoon vanilla in mixer bowl until soft peaks form. Fold in 1/4 cup almond brickle chips. Spread over pie; sprinkle with additional chocolate chips and almond brickle chips.

Frozen Chocolate Cream Pie

9-inch graham cracker crust

1/2 cup plus 4 teaspoons semisweet chocolate chips, divided

5 tablespoons milk, divided

3-ounce package cream cheese, softened

3-1/2 cups whipped topping divided

2 tablespoons sugar

In a microwavable bowl, combine 2 tablespoons milk and 1/2 cup chocolate chips. Microwave uncovered on high for 1-2 minutes or until melted. Stir to blend; set aside.

In another bowl, beat cream cheese and sugar. Stir in chocolate mixture and remaining milk; beat until smooth.

Set aside 1/2 cup whipped topping for garnish. Fold remaining whipped topping into chocolate mixture. Spoon into prepared crust.

Freeze for 4 hours or until firm. Garnish with the reserved whipped topping and remaining chocolate chips.

Candy Bar Pie

1-1/2 cups grated coconut

2 tablespoons margarine

1 teaspoon instant coffee in 2 tablespoons water

1-1/2 milk chocolate candy bars (7-1/2-ounces each) with almonds - divided

4 cups frozen whipped topping

Mix coconut and margarine for crust and press into 8 inch pie plate and bake at 325 degrees for 10 minutes. Cool.

Combine coffee mixture and one candy bar in double boiler until melted and very warm. Let cool and fold in whipped topping.

Fill crust and shave other half of candy bar on top and freeze. Take out of freezer approximately 10 minutes before serving. Do not let this completely thaw or reach room temperature.

Chocolate-Filled Meringues

Meringue:

2 egg whites
1/4 teaspoon cream of tartar
1/4 teaspoon vanilla
Dash salt
1/2 cup sugar

Filling:

8-ounces cream cheese, softened
1 cup confectioners' sugar
1/4 cup baking cocoa
1 cup whipped topping
10-ounces frozen sweetened sliced strawberries, thawed

Place egg whites in a small mixing bowl; let stand at room temperature for 30 minutes. Beat on medium speed until foamy. Add cream of tartar, vanilla and salt. Beat until soft peaks form. Gradually add sugar, 1 tablespoon at a time, beating until stiff peaks form.

Line a baking sheet with parchment paper. Spoon meringue into six mounds on paper. Using the back of a spoon, shape into 3-inch cups. Bake at 300 degrees for 35 minutes. Turn off oven and do not open door; let meringues dry for 1 hour. Cool on a wire rack.

For filling . . . in a mixing bowl, beat cream cheese, confectioners' sugar and cocoa until smooth and fluffy. Fold in whipped topping. Process the strawberries in a blender or food processor until pureed. To serve, spoon filling into meringue shells. Top with strawberry sauce.

Couldn't Be Easier Creamy Chocolate Pie

1 prepared chocolate crumb crust (6-ounces)
1-3/4 cups cold milk

2 packages (4-serving size) chocolate fudge instant pudding and pie filling
1 tub (8-ounces) whipped topping, thawed

Pour milk into large bowl. Add pudding mixes. Beat with wire whisk until well mixed. Mix will be thick. Immediately stir in whipped topping. Spoon into crust. Refrigerate 4 hours or until set. Garnish as desired.

Chocolate Fudge Oatmeal Pie

Crust:

15 crisp oatmeal cookies, crushed (1-1/2 cups)

1/3 cup butter, melted

Filling:

2 eggs, separated

1/2 cup butter, softened

3 (1-ounce) squares unsweetened chocolate, melted

2 tablespoons brandy*

2/3 cup sugar

3 tablespoons flour

Heat oven to 350 degrees. In medium bowl, combine cookie crumbs and 1/3 cup melted butter. Mix well. Press firmly into 9-inch pie plate.

In small mixer bowl, beat egg whites on high speed until soft peaks form. (3 to 4 minutes)

In large mixer bowl, beat egg yolks on medium speed until thick and lemon-colored . . . about 2 to 3 minutes. Add 1/2 cup butter, melted chocolate and brandy. Continue beating until smooth (1 to 2 minutes), Reduce speed to low, add sugar and flour. Beat until smooth (1 to 2 minutes). By hand, gently stir in egg whites. Spoon mixture into crust. Bake for 20 to 25 minutes or until center is set. Serve warm or cool.

* Substitute 2 teaspoons vanilla and 1 tablespoon water.

White Chocolate Hazelnut Pie

6-ounce chocolate pie crust

1-1/4 cups cold milk

2 tablespoons hazelnut flavor instant coffee

2 packages (4-serving size) white chocolate instant pudding and pie filling

1 tub (8-ounces) whipped topping, thawed, divided

Beat milk, flavored instant coffee, pudding mixes and 1/2 of the whipped topping in medium bowl with wire whisk for one minute. Mixture will be thick. Spread in crust. Spread remaining whipped topping over pudding layer in crust.

Enjoy immediately or refrigerate until ready to serve. Garnish as desired.

Chocolate Mallow Pie

1-1/4 cups crushed cream-filled chocolate sandwich cookies (about 14 cookies)

1/4 cup butter or margarine, melted

2 tablespoons sugar

2 packages (one 8-ounce, one 3-ounce) cream cheese, softened

1/2 cup chocolate syrup

1-1/3 cups semisweet chocolate chips, melted

1 carton (8-ounces) frozen whipped topping, thawed

2 cups miniature marshmallows

Chocolate curls, optional

In a bowl, combine the cookie crumbs, butter and sugar. Press onto the bottom and up the sides of a 9-inch pie plate. Bake at 375 degrees for 8-10 minutes or until set. Cool completely on a wire rack.

In a mixing bowl, beat cream cheese and chocolate syrup until blended. Beat in melted chips. Set aside 1/4 cup of whipped topping. Fold marshmallows and remaining whipped topping into chocolate mixture. Spoon into crust. Refrigerate for at least 8 hours or overnight. Garnish with reserved whipped topping and chocolate curls if desired.

Heavenly Chocolate Mousse Pie

6-ounce chocolate pie crust

4 (1-ounce) squares unsweetened chocolate, melted

14-ounce can sweetened condensed milk

1-1/2 teaspoons vanilla

1 cup (1/2 pint) whipping cream, whipped

With mixer, beat chocolate with sweetened condensed milk and vanilla until well blended.

Chill 15 minutes or until cooled; stir until smooth. Fold in whipped cream.

Pour into crust. Chill thoroughly. Garnish as desired. Refrigerate leftovers. *Note:* For more chocolate indulgence, top pie with chocolate shavings or chocolate cookie crumbs, and serve with chocolate-dipped strawberries.

Black Bottom Pie

16 gingersnaps, crushed
5 tablespoons melted butter
2 cups scalded milk
1/2 cup sugar
4 egg yolks, well beaten
1-1/2 tablespoons cornstarch
1-1/2 squares dark chocolate
1 teaspoon vanilla

1 tablespoon unflavored gelatin
2 tablespoons cold water
4 egg whites, beaten stiff
1/2 cup sugar
1/4 teaspoon cream of tartar
2 teaspoons bourbon
1 carton (8-ounces) frozen whipped topping, thawed

Mix gingersnaps and butter and press into 9-inch pie pan. Bake at 375 degrees for 10 minutes. Cool.

For first filling: add egg yolks slowly to hot milk. Combine sugar and cornstarch and stir into milk mixture. Cook in double boiler for 20 minutes stirring occasionally until it coats a spoon.

Remove from heat and take out 1 cup of mixture, add chocolate to the cup of mixture and beat as it cools. Add 1 teaspoon vanilla to chocolate mixture, beat well and pour into pie crust. Chill.

For second filling: Dissolve gelatin in water. Add to remaining custard and cool. Beat 1/2 cup sugar and cream of tartar into egg whites and beat until sugar is dissolved. Add bourbon and fold into custard mixture. Pour over chilled chocolate filling. Cover top with whipped topping. Shave dark chocolate for garnish.

Hot Fudge Brownie-Mint Pie

9-inch unbaked deep-dish pastry shell
1 package (4.6-ounce) chocolate mints

1 package (15.8-ounce) brownie mix
Vanilla ice cream
Hot fudge topping

Chop chocolate mints and set aside 3 tablespoons. Prepare brownie mix according to package directions, stirring remaining chopped mints into brownie batter. Pour into pastry shell.

Bake at 350 degrees for 45 minutes or until done, cool slightly. Serve with ice cream, hot fudge topping, and reserved 3 tablespoons chopped mints.

Chocolate Silk Pie

9-inch baked pastry shell
9-inch baked pastry shell
3/4 cup butter, softened
3/4 cup sugar
3 eggs

1 teaspoon vanilla
3 squares unsweetened chocolate, melted and cooled
1/2 pint whipping cream
2 tablespoons sugar

Cream butter and sugar. Add eggs, one at a time. Beat well and add vanilla and chocolate. Beat until thick. Pour into cooled pie shell. Refrigerate 15 minutes; top with whipped cream to which 2 tablespoons sugar has been added. Chill until serving time.

Triple Decker Chocolate Coconut Cream Pie

9-inch baked pastry shell, cooled
2/3 cup sugar
1/3 cup cornstarch
1/4 teaspoon salt
3 cups milk
3 eggs, slightly beaten

1 tablespoon butter or margarine
2 teaspoons vanilla extract
1/2 cup flaked coconut
3 tablespoons sugar
3 tablespoons cocoa
2 tablespoons milk
Whipped topping

In medium saucepan, stir together 2/3 cup sugar, cornstarch, salt and 3 cups milk. Blend in eggs. Cook over medium heat, stirring constantly, until mixture boils. Boil and stir 1 minute.

Remove from heat and stir in butter and vanilla. Into small bowl, pour 1-1/2 cups cream filling. Stir in coconut. Set aside.

Stir together cocoa, 3 tablespoons sugar and 2 tablespoons milk. Blend into remaining cream filling in saucepan. Return to heat and heat just to boiling, stirring constantly. Remove from heat and pour 1 cup chocolate filling into baked pie crust

Spread coconut filling over chocolate layer. Top with remaining chocolate filling and spread evenly. Cover with plastic wrap and refrigerate until cold. Just before serving, spread with whipped topping.

Microwave Chocolate Cream Pie

9-inch baked pastry shell
1 cup sugar
1/4 cup plain flour
3 egg yolks
2 tablespoons cocoa
2 cups whole milk

2 tablespoons milk chocolate chips
1 teaspoon vanilla extract
Recipe for meringue or whipped topping

Mix sugar, flour and cocoa well in a microwavable bowl. Add 1/2 cup milk and blend. Add 3 well beaten egg yolks to mixture. Mix then add remaining milk. Blend well then stir in chips. Microwave for 4 minutes. Stir thoroughly. Let set another 2 minutes and stir. Then microwave another 2 minutes.

Remove from microwave and stir in 1 teaspoon of vanilla. Pour into baked pie shell. Top with meringue and brown at 350 degrees (see meringues in crust section) or top with whipped topping when pie is cooled.

Extreme Chocolate Pie

1 package (8-ounce) brownie mix
1 cup sugar
3/4 cup butter
6 ounces unsweetened chocolate, melted and cooled
1 teaspoon vanilla
3/4 cup refrigerated or frozen egg product, thawed, or 3/4 cup pasteurized eggs

1 bar (1.45-ounces) dark chocolate, coarsely chopped
Chocolate Whipped Cream:
1/2 cup whipping cream
1 tablespoon sugar
1-1/2 teaspoons unsweetened cocoa powder

Preheat oven to 350 degrees. For crust, prepare brownie mix according to package directions. Spread in the bottom of a greased 9-inch pie plate. Bake 20-25 minutes or until wooden toothpick, inserted near center, comes out clean. Cool on wire rack.

(Continued on next page.)

For filling, in a medium mixing bowl beat sugar and butter with an electric mixer on medium speed about 4 minutes or until fluffy. Stir in melted and cooled chocolate and the vanilla. Gradually add egg product, beating at low speed until combined. Then beat on medium to high speed, scraping sides of bowl about 1 minute or until light and fluffy.

Transfer filling to prepared pie plate. Cover and chill for 4-24 hours. Before serving, sprinkle with chopped chocolate. Serve with Chocolate Whipped Cream.

To make chocolate whipped cream, combine 1/2 cup whipping cream, 1 tablespoon sugar and 1-1/2 teaspoons unsweetened cocoa powder in a small bowl. Beat with chilled beaters on medium speed until soft peaks form. Makes 1 cup whipped cream.

Easy Milk Chocolate Bar Pie

9-inch crumb crust

1/4 cup milk

16 marshmallows or 1-1/2 cups miniature marshmallows

1 milk chocolate bar (7-ounces), broken into pieces

1 cup (1/2 pint) cold whipping cream

Place milk and marshmallows in medium microwave-safe bowl and microwave on high for 1 minute. Stir well. If necessary, microwave at high an additional 15 seconds at a time, stirring after each heating, until marshmallows are melted.

Add chocolate pieces and stir until chocolate is melted and mixture is smooth. Cool completely.

Beat whipping cream until stiff in a small mixer bowl. Fold into chocolate mix. Spoon into crust. Cover and refrigerate until firm, at least 4 hours. Cover and refrigerate leftover pie.

Innkeeper Pie

9-inch unbaked pastry shell

2/3 cup plus 3/4 cup sugar, divided

1/3 cup cocoa

1 cup water

1/3 cup butter or margarine

2-1/2 teaspoons vanilla extract, divided

1 cup all-purpose flour

1 teaspoon baking powder

1/2 teaspoon salt

1/4 cup shortening

1/2 cup milk

1 egg

1/2 cup chopped nuts

Sweetened Whipping Cream:

1 cup (1/2 pint) cold whipping cream

2 tablespoons sugar

1 teaspoon vanilla extract

Heat oven to 350 degrees. In medium saucepan, stir together 2/3 cup sugar and cocoa. Stir in water. Cook over medium heat, stirring occasionally, until mixture boils. Boil and stir 1 minute. Remove from heat. Add butter and 1-1/2 teaspoons vanilla, stirring until butter is melted. Set aside.

In small mixer bowl, stir together flour, 3/4 cup sugar, baking powder and salt. Add shortening, milk and remaining 1 teaspoon vanilla. Beat on medium speed of electric mixer 2 minutes. Add egg and beat 2 minutes.

Spoon batter into prepared pastry crust. Stir chocolate mixture and gently pour over batter. Sprinkle nuts over top.
Bake 55-60 minutes or until wooden pick inserted in cake portion comes out clean. Cool slightly and serve warm with Sweetened Whipped Cream.

To make Sweetened Whipped Cream, combine whipping cream, sugar, and vanilla in a small mixer bowl. Beat until stiff.

Rich Chocolate Cream Pie

9-inch baked pastry shell
1 package (6-serving size)
vanilla pudding and pie filling
mix* (Do not use instant
pudding mix)
3 cups milk

2 cups (12 ounce package)
semi-sweet chocolate chips or
1-3/4 cups (10 ounce
package) semi-sweet chocolate
chunks

Whipped topping, optional

In medium saucepan, combine pudding mix and milk. Cook
over medium heat, stirring constantly, until mixture comes to
full boil.
Remove from heat and immediately add chocolate chips to hot
mixture. Stirring until chips are melted and mixture is smooth.
Pour into baked pie crust.
Place plastic wrap directly onto surface and refrigerate several
hours or overnight. Garnish with whipped topping if desired.

Cool 'N Creamy Chocolate Pie

Graham cracker crust
1 package (3-ounces) cream
cheese, softened
1/4 cup sugar
1 teaspoon vanilla extract

1/2 cup chocolate syrup
1 cup (1/2 pint) cold
whipping cream
Sliced fresh fruit, optional
Chocolate curls, optional

In small mixer bowl, beat cream cheese, sugar and vanilla until
well blended. Gradually add syrup, beating until smooth.

In small mixer bowl, beat whipping cream until stiff. Carefully
fold into chocolate mixture. Pour into crust. Cover and freeze
until firm. Just before serving, garnish with fresh fruit and
chocolate curls, if desired.

Chocolate Mousse & Praline Pie

Graham cracker or cookie crust

1/3 cup butter or margarine

1/4 cup packed light brown sugar

2 tablespoons water

1 tablespoon cornstarch

2/3 cup coarsely chopped pecans

Chocolate Mousse Filling:

1 teaspoon unflavored gelatin

1 tablespoon cold water

2 tablespoons boiling water

1/2 cup sugar

1/4 cup cocoa

1 cup (1/2 pint) cold whipping cream

1 teaspoon vanilla extract

Pecan halves

In small microwave-safe bowl, place butter and microwave at high for 1 minute or until melted. Add brown sugar, water and cornstarch. Stir with wire whisk until smooth.

Microwave on high 1 minute or until mixture comes to full boil. Stir in chopped pecans. Spread mixture on bottom of crust. Place in freezer.

To prepare chocolate mousse filling, sprinkle gelatin over cold water in a small cup. Let stand 1 minute to soften. Add boiling water and stir until gelatin is completely dissolved and mixture is clear. Cool slightly, about 5 minutes. Meanwhile, in small mixer bowl, stir together sugar and cocoa. Add whipping cream and vanilla. Beat on medium speed of electric mixer, scraping bottom of bowl occasionally, until stiff. Add gelatin mixture, beat just until well blended.

Carefully spread filling over pecan layer. Cover and refrigerate 3-4 hours. Garnish with pecan halves. Refrigerate leftover pie.

Brandy Alexander Pie

1 chocolate pie shell

1/3 cup brandy

1 package chocolate instant pudding mix

1 package vanilla instant pudding mix

1-1/2 cup milk

1 tub whipped cream

1/4 cup chocolate liqueur

Chocolate curls for garnish

(Continued on next page)

In a large bowl, prepare pudding. Mix as label directs but mix both packages together and use 1-1/2 cups of milk in total. Stir in chocolate liqueur and brandy. Fold half the whipped cream into the pudding mixture. Spoon into crust. Top with remaining whipped cream and garnish with chocolate curls. Refrigerate at least 1 hour before serving.

Chocolate Cherry Cordial Pie

9-inch baked pastry shell
Filling:
2/3 cup sugar
3 tablespoons flour
3 tablespoons cornstarch
2-1/2 cups milk
3 egg yolks
1 egg
3 tablespoons butter

1 teaspoon almond extract, optional
1 teaspoon vanilla
1-1/2 cups semi-sweet chocolate chips, divided
1 tablespoon water
1 can (17-ounces) pitted cherries, drained and dry
1/2 cup heavy cream
1 tablespoon butter

In a heavy saucepan, mix sugar, flour and cornstarch. Stir in some milk until a thick paste forms. Gradually stir in remaining milk. Cook over medium heat, stirring until thick - about 10 minutes. Beat egg yolks and egg together. Stir 1 cup of hot milk mixture into egg mixture. Pour all back into hot mixture; cook over medium heat stirring constantly until bubbles just appear. Remove from heat and stir in 3 tablespoons butter, vanilla and almond extract. Press plastic wrap directly on filling; cool completely.

In a double boiler, melt 1/2 cup chocolate chips with water. Spread evenly over bottom of baked crust. Arrange cherries evenly over chocolate layer. Pour cooled filling over cherries. Set aside.

Heat cream in a small saucepan until bubbles appear around edge of pan. Remove from heat. Stir in 1 cup chocolate chips until well mixed and glossy. Stir in butter. Pour into bowl; cool until slightly thickened to a glaze consistency. Pour over pie. Smooth over the top. Chill before serving.This decadent pie is well worth the effort. They'll be beggin" for seconds.

Brownie Pie A La Mode

1/2 cup sugar

2 tablespoons butter or margarine

2 tablespoons water

1-1/3 cups semi-sweet chocolate chips

2 eggs

2/3 cup all-purpose flour

1/4 teaspoon baking soda

1/4 teaspoon salt

1 teaspoon vanilla extract

3/4 cup chopped nuts, optional

Favorite flavor ice cream

Fudge Sauce:

1 cup semi-sweet chocolate chips

1/2 cup evaporated milk

1/4 cup sugar

1 tablespoon butter or margarine

Heat oven to 350 degrees. Grease 9-inch pie plate. In medium saucepan, combine sugar, butter and water. Cook over medium heat, stirring occasionally, just until mixture boils.

Remove from heat and immediately add chocolate chips, stirring until melted. Add eggs, beat with spoon until well-blended.

Stir together flour, baking soda and salt. Stir into chocolate mixture. Stir in vanilla and chopped nuts, pour into prepared pie plate.

Bake 25-30 minutes or until almost set. Pie will not test done in center. Cool completely.

Cut into wedges. Serve topped with scoops of ice cream. Drizzle with Fudge Sauce, if desired.

For fudge sauce, combine all ingredients in a medium microwave-safe bowl. Microwave on high 1 to 1-1/2 minutes or until hot. With wire whisk, beat until chips are melted and mixture is smooth. Yield: about 1-1/2 cups sauce.

CHEESECAKES

Tips for the Perfect Cheesecake

There is just something irresistible about cheesecake. And for me they have always been in the same category as pie. Life is just too short not to eat good cheesecake! Even if you are a novice baker, if you follow the instructions carefully, you can make an impressive cheesecake on your very first try.

The techniques for making great and tasty cheesecakes are simple to master. Take the time to read through the techniques and hints that follow and then go bake yourself up a cheesecake and impress your family and friends!

Preparation:

- If all the ingredients are at room temperature, they will mix more easily and the finished cake will have a smoother texture.

- Combine the type of cheese you are using and eggs thoroughly before adding liquids, heavy cream or sour cream. Lumps are next to impossible to remove once the liquid has been added. The paddle attachment of an electric mixer run at medium speed is best for mixing the batter. Regular whipping beaters cause too much air in batter and will lead to cracks in finished cake and your cake will not be as creamy. If you only have whipping beaters make sure to use low speed.

- Gently and slowly fold in whipped cream and beaten egg whites with a wire whisk or rubber spatula. Take special care not to deflate the volume of the whipped ingredients.

- Use only regular cream cheese for your cheesecake unless the recipe says differently.

- Cheesecake crusts are generally made from cookie crumbs mixed with melted butter. . . .but a variety of crumb crusts can be used. If a recipe doesn't have a crust recipe, go to the crust section and select one of the crumb crust recipes.

Tips Continued

- If cracks appear in the surface of your cake too much steam was released too quickly. Baking temperature should always be relatively low. Do not set cake in cold or drafty places to cool. The best place to cool your cheesecake is in a turned off oven. Use a wooden spoon to keep the door slightly open. Shallow cracks usually occur despite all the best efforts. Just accept them as part of your cakes homemade charm or cover with garnish or fruit.

- Another method to help prevent cracks in your cheesecakes is to place a shallow pan of water on the lower rack of the oven while baking.

Step-By-Step:

1. Grease the bottom and sides of 9 or 10-inch springform pan. Combine your crust ingredients according to recipe and press evenly into the bottom or into the bottom and up sides of the pan. Bake according to recipe.

2. Use paddle attachment to beat cream cheese <u>SMOOTH</u> before adding any other ingredients. To make sure the batter has no lumps and no ingredients stuck to the bottom of the bowl, stop the mixer while mixing batter and scrape down the paddle and sides of bowl.

3. Pour batter into the prepared crust and set the pan on a baking sheet. Bake according to recipe. If top is browning too quickly, cover with foil part way through baking.

4. Your finished cheesecake will have a dull, not shiny, finish. The center should be soft but not wobbly.

5. Run a knife around the sides of the cooled cake to loosen it from pan. Release the spring and remove the pan sides. Leave the cake on the pan bottom for easier serving.

6. Decorate or garnish with fresh fruit, whipped cream, sour cream, etc. if desired. . . . and believe me, they taste just as good plain!

<u>IMPORTANT NOTE:</u> In all the following recipes that call for flour, use all-purpose unless specified otherwise. Sugar used is granulated unless otherwise specified.

184

Bavarian Cheesecake

1-3/4 cups graham cracker crumbs

1/2 cup butter, melted

1/4 cup chopped pecans

1/2 teaspoon ground cinnamon

2 packages (8-ounces each) cream cheese, softened

1 container (16-ounces) sour cream

2 large eggs

1 cup sugar

1/4 teaspoon salt

2 teaspoons vanilla extract

1/2 teaspoon almond extract

Combine crumbs, butter, pecans, and cinnamon, stirring well. Reserve 2 tablespoons crumb mixture. Press remaining crumb mix into bottom and 1 inch up sides of a 9-inch springform pan.

Beat cream cheese and next 6 ingredients at medium speed with an electric mixer until smooth. Pour into crust and sprinkle with reserved crumb mix.

Bake at 375 degrees for 1 hour or until set. Cool on a wire rack and chill 4-5 hours. Remove sides of pan.

Chocolate Layer Cheesecake

1 (6-ounce or 9-inch) ready-to-use chocolate flavor crumb crust

2 packages (8-ounces each) cream cheese, softened

1/2 cup sugar

1/2 teaspoon vanilla

2 eggs

3 squares semi-sweet baking chocolate, melted, slightly cooled

Mix cream cheese, sugar and vanilla with electric mixer on medium speed until well blended. Add eggs and mix until blended. Stir melted chocolate into 1 cup of the batter. Pour chocolate batter into crust and top with remaining plain batter.

Bake at 350 degrees for 40 minutes or until center is almost set. Cool. Refrigerate 3 hours or overnight. Garnish as desired. Store refrigerated.

Supreme Cheese Cake

Crust:
3/4 cup flour
1 cup sugar
1/2 teaspoon lemon peel
6 tablespoons butter or margarine
1 egg yolk, beaten
1/4 teaspoon vanilla

Filling:
3 (8-ounce) packages softened cream cheese

1/4 teaspoon lemon peel
1/4 teaspoon vanilla
3 tablespoons sugar
2 tablespoons flour
1/4 teaspoon salt
2 eggs
1 egg yolk
1/4 cup milk
1 can cherry pie filling

Combine flour, sugar and lemon peel. Cut in butter until crumbly. Stir in egg yolk and vanilla. Pat 1/3 of dough onto bottom of a 9x13-inch cake pan. Bake in a 400 degree oven for 7 minutes then let cool. Butter the sides and pat remaining dough onto sides of pan and set aside.

For filling, beat cream cheese, lemon peel and vanilla until fluffy. Stir sugar, flour and salt together. Gradually stir into cream cheese mixture. Add the 2 eggs and egg yolk all at once, beating at low speed just until combined. Stir in milk. Turn into crust lined pan.

Bake at 450 degrees for 10 minutes then reduce heat to 400 degrees and bake 50-55 minutes more until knife inserted in center comes out clean. Cool at least 15 minutes to overnight, then cover top with pie filling.

Chocolate Chip Cheesecake

2 cups finely crushed creme filled chocolate sandwich cookies (about 24 cookies)
1/4 cup melted shortening
3 packages (8 ounces) cream cheese

1 can (14-ounce) sweetened condensed milk
3 eggs
2 teaspoons vanilla
1 cup mini chocolate chips
1 teaspoon flour

(Continued on next page.)

(Chocolate Chip Cheesecake - continued)

Preheat oven to 350 degrees. Combine crumbs and shortening. Press firmly on bottom of 9-inch springform pan.

In large bowl, beat cheese until fluffy. Gradually beat in sweetened condensed milk until mixture is smooth. Beat in eggs and vanilla. Toss 1/2 cup chips with flour to coat and stir into cheese mixture. Pour into prepared pan. Sprinkle remaining chips over top.

Bake 55 minutes or until center is set. Cool completely

New York Style Cheesecake

Crust:
1 cup zwieback crumbs (18 pieces) or graham cracker crumbs

4 tablespoons melted butter

1-1/2 tablespoons sugar

Filling:
5 (8-ounce) packages softened cream cheese

1-1/2 cups sugar

2 teaspoons grated orange zest

1 teaspoon grated lemon zest

3 tablespoons flour

1/2 teaspoon vanilla

5 eggs

2 egg yolks

1/2 cup sour cream

Crust: Mix together crumbs, butter and sugar. Press evenly over bottom of a greased 9-inch springform pan. Bake at 350 degrees for 10 minutes. Cool.

Filling: Beat cream cheese, sugar and zests until creamy. Gradually beat in flour and vanilla. Add eggs and yolks one at a time, beating well after each addition. Add sour cream and beat until smooth. Pour mixture in cool crust. Bake for 25 minutes at 350 degrees. Increase oven temp to 500 degrees. Bake about 4 more minutes until top is golden. Reduce oven temp to 200 degrees. Bake for 30 minutes longer.

Turn off oven, let cake stand in oven with door ajar for 30 minutes. Cool cake slightly. While cake is still warm, gently run knife around edge. When cool remove sides of pan. Chill for 2 hours.

Chocolate Filled Cheesecake

Crust:
1/2 cup softened butter or margarine
1/3 cup sugar
1 cup flour
1 teaspoon vanilla
3/4 cup finely chopped pistachios

Filling:
4 (8-ounce) packages cream cheese, softened
1-1/2 cups sugar
4 eggs
2 teaspoons vanilla
12-ounce package milk chocolate chips

Preheat oven to 350 degrees. Beat together butter and sugar until creamy. Gradually add flour until well blended. Stir in vanilla and pistachios. Press into bottom and up sides of a 9-inch springform pan. Bake for 12 to 15 minutes or until golden. Cool.

For filling, beat cream cheese until fluffy; mix in sugar. Add eggs one at a time, beating just until yellow disappears. Stir in vanilla. Do not over mix.

Pour half of the batter into crust; sprinkle with chocolate chips to within one inch of edge. Pour remaining batter over chips. Bake for 1 hour at 350 degrees. Serve warm with sweetened whipped cream if desired.

Frosted Chocolate Swirl Cheesecake

Crust:
2 cups chocolate wafer crumbs
5 tablespoons melted butter or margarine

Filling:
3 (8-ounce) packages softened cream cheese
1 cup sugar

5 eggs
2 ounces (2 squares) chocolate, melted

Frosting:
6 ounces (6 squares) chocolate melted
1/2 cup sour cream

(Continued on next page)

Preheat oven to 300 degrees. Mix together crumbs and butter or margarine until well blended. Press into a 9-inch springform pan.

To prepare filling beat cream cheese, sugar and eggs until smooth. Spoon half of mixture into crust. Stir melted chocolate into remaining cream cheese mixture. Drizzle over batter in crust and swirl. Bake for 50 minutes. Cool completely. Transfer to serving dish, cover and chill for 2 to 3 hours.

Uncover cheesecake and carefully remove side of pan. For frosting, mix together chocolate and sour cream. Spread over cheesecake and chill until frosting is set.

Chocolate Bliss Cheesecake

1-1/2 cups (about 18) chocolate sandwich cookies, finely crushed

2 tablespoons butter or margarine, melted

3 packages (8-ounces each) cream cheese, softened

3/4 cup sugar

1 teaspoon vanilla

3 eggs

1 package (8 squares) semi-sweet baking chocolate, melted, cooled slightly

Heat oven to 325 degrees. Mix crushed cookies and butter. Press onto bottom of 9-inch springform pan. Bake 10 minutes.

For filling, mix cream cheese, sugar and vanilla with electric mixer on medium speed until well blended. Add eggs, mixing on low speed just until blended. Blend in melted chocolate. Pour over crust.

Bake 55-60 minutes or until center is almost set. Run knife or metal spatula around rim of pan to loosen cake. Cool before removing rim of pan. Refrigerate 4 hours or overnight.

Orange White Chocolate Cheesecake

2 cups vanilla wafer crumbs
6 tablespoons butter, melted
1/4 cup sugar
<u>Filling:</u>
4 packages (8-ounces each)
cream cheese, softened
1 cup sugar
4 eggs
1 cup (8-ounces) sour cream

10 squares (1-ounce each)
white baking chocolate, melted
<u>Topping:</u>
1 cup (8-ounces) sour cream
3 tablespoons sugar
1/2 to 1 teaspoon orange
extract
2 cans (11-ounces each)
mandarin oranges, drained

Combine the first three ingredients and press onto the bottom and 1-1/2 inches up the sides of a greased 10-inch springform pan. Bake at 350 degrees for 10 minutes and cool completely.

In a mixing bowl, beat cream cheese, sugar, eggs and sour cream just until blended, then add chocolate. Pour into crust. Bake at 350 degrees for 1 to 1-1/4 hours or until center is nearly set.

Cool to room temperature, about 2 hours. Combine sour cream, sugar and extract and spread over filling. Bake at 450 degrees for 5-7 minutes or until set. Chill uncovered for one hour. Arrange oranges on cheesecake. Cover and chill at least 4 hours.

Orange Chip Cheesecake

9-inch chocolate crumb crust
12 ounces cream cheese,
softened
1/2 cup sugar
2 eggs
1/2 teaspoon salt
1/2 teaspoon orange extract
3/4 to 1 cup miniature
semisweet chocolate chips

<u>Topping:</u>
1-1/2 cups sour cream (12-ounces)
1/2 teaspoon vanilla extract
2 tablespoons sugar
11-ounce can mandarin
oranges, drained
Additional chocolate chips
(Continued on next page.)

In a mixing bowl, beat cream cheese and sugar until smooth. Add eggs and beat on low speed just until combined. Add salt and orange extract and beat just until blended. Stir in chocolate chips. Pour into crust. Bake at 375 degrees for 20 minutes or until center is almost set. Remove from the oven; increase temperature to 425 degrees.

In a bowl, combine sour cream, sugar and vanilla; spread over cheesecake. Bake 5 minutes longer. Cool on a wire rack for 15 minutes. Refrigerate overnight. Just before serving, garnish with oranges and additional chocolate chips.

Oreo Cheesecake

Crust:
1 cup (about 12) crushed chocolate sandwich cookies

1 tablespoon butter or margarine, melted

Filling:
1 cup sugar

4 packages (8-ounces each) cream cheese, softened

1 teaspoon vanilla

4 eggs

20 chocolate sandwich cookies, coarsely chopped

For crust, mix crushed cookies and butter and press evenly onto bottom of 9-inch springform pan. Bake at 325 degrees for 10 minutes if using a silver springform pan. If using a dark nonstick springform pan, bake at 300 degrees for 10 minutes.

For filling, mix cream cheese, sugar and vanilla with electric mixer on medium speed until well blended. Add eggs, mixing on low speed just until blended. Gently stir in chopped cookies. Pour over crust.Bake at 325 degrees for 1 hour or until center is almost set if using a silver springform pan. If using a dark nonstick springform pan, bake at 300 degrees for 1 hour or until center is almost set. Run knife or metal spatula around rim of pan to loosen cake. Cool before removing rim of pan. Refrigerate 4 hours or overnight. Store leftover cheesecake, covered, in refrigerator.

Quick and Easy Chocolate Cheesecake Pie

1 (9-ounce) packaged graham cracker crumb crust

2 packages (8-ounces each) cream cheese, softened

3/4 cup sugar

2 eggs

1/4 cup cocoa

1-1/2 teaspoons vanilla extract

2 cups frozen non-dairy whipped topping, thawed

Heat oven to 350 degrees. Beat cream cheese and sugar until blended. Beat in eggs until well blended. Add cocoa and vanilla, blending until smooth. Pour into crust.

Bake 30-35 minutes or until almost set in center. Cool completely on wire rack. Cover and refrigerate. Spread whipped topping over top and garnish as desired. Refrigerate leftover pie.

One Bowl Chocolate Swirl Cheesecake

1 (6-ounce or 9-inch) ready-to-use chocolate flavor or graham cracker crumb crust

4 squares semi-sweet baking chocolate

2 packages (8-ounces each) cream cheese, softened, divided

1/2 cup sugar, divided

2 eggs, divided

1/2 teaspoon vanilla

Heat oven to 350 degrees. Microwave chocolate in large microwavable bowl on HIGH 1-1/2 to 2 minutes or until chocolate is almost melted, stirring halfway through heating time. Stir until chocolate is completely melted. Whisk 1 package of cream cheese, 1/4 cup sugar, and 1 egg into the melted chocolate with a wire whisk until well blended. Pour into crust.

Whisk remaining cheese, sugar, egg and vanilla in same bowl until well blended. Spoon plain batter over chocolate batter; use teaspoon to swirl batters together.

Bake 10 minutes or until center is almost set. Cool. Refrigerate 3 hours or overnight. Let stand at room temperature 20 minutes before serving.

Chocolate Chip Cookie Dough Cheesecake

1-3/4 cups crushed chocolate chip cookies or wafer crumbs

1/4 cup sugar

1/3 cup butter or margarine, melted

Filling:

3 packages (8-ounces each) cream cheese, softened

1 cup sugar

3 eggs

1 cup (8-ounces) sour cream

1/2 teaspoon vanilla extract

Cookie Dough:

1/4 cup butter or margarine, softened

1/4 cup sugar

1/4 cup packed brown sugar

1 tablespoon water

1 teaspoon vanilla extract

1/2 cup all-purpose flour

1-1/2 cups miniature semisweet chocolate chips

In a small bowl, combine cookie crumbs and sugar. Stir in butter. Press onto the bottom and 1 inch up the sides of a greased 9-inch springform pan. Set aside.

In a mixing bowl, beat cream cheese and sugar until smooth. Add eggs and beat on low just until combined. Add sour cream and vanilla; beat just until blended. Pour over crust and set aside. In another mixing bowl, cream butter and sugars on medium speed for 3 minutes. Add water and vanilla. Gradually add flour. Stir in 1 cup of chocolate chips. Drop dough by teaspoonfuls over filling, gently pushing dough below surface of filling. It should be completely covered.

Bake at 350 degrees for 45-55 minutes or until center is almost set. Cool on a wire rack for 10 minutes. Carefully run a knife around edge of pan to loosen. Cool 1 hour longer. Refrigerate overnight; remove sides of pan. Sprinkle with remaining chocolate chips.

Cherry Almond Cheesecake

1 cup ground almonds

1/3 cup (about 6 squares) graham cracker crumbs

1/4 cup butter or margarine, melted

3 packages (8-ounces each) cream cheese, softened

1 can (14-ounces) sweetened condensed milk

3 eggs

1 can (21-ounces) cherry pie filling, divided

In a small bowl, combine almonds and cracker crumbs; stir in butter. Press mixture onto the bottom of a greased 9-inch springform pan and set aside.

In a mixing bowl, beat the cream cheese and milk until smooth. Add eggs and beat on low just until combined. Pour into prepared crust. Refrigerate 1/2 cup pie filling for garnish. Drop remaining pie filling by teaspoonfuls onto cream cheese mixture. Cut through batter with a knife to marble the filling. Bake at 325 degrees for 50-55 minutes or until the center is almost set. Cool on a wire rack for 10 minutes.

Carefully run a knife around edge of pan to loosen and cool 1 hour longer. Chill overnight. Remove sides of pan. Cut cheesecake into slices and garnish with reserved pie filling. Refrigerate leftovers.

Lite Black Forest Cheesecake

3/4 cup teddy bear-shaped chocolate graham cracker cookies, crushed

2 packages (8-ounces) reduced fat cream cheese, softened

1-1/2 cups sugar

3/4 cup egg substitute

1 cup (6-ounces) semisweet chocolate morsels, melted

1/4 cup cocoa

1-1/2 teaspoons vanilla extract

1 container (8-ounce) sour cream

1 can (21-ounce) light cherry fruit filling

3/4 cup reduced-fat frozen whipped topping, thawed

(Continued on next page.)

Sprinkle cookie crumbs in bottom of a lightly greased 9-inch springform pan. Beat cream cheese at high speed with an electric mixer until fluffy. Gradually add sugar, beating well. Gradually add egg substitute and next 3 ingredients. Stir in sour cream and pour mixture into prepared pan.

Bake at 300 degrees for 1 hour and 40 minutes. Remove from oven and run a knife around edge of pan to loosen sides. Cool on a wire rack. Cover and chill at least 8 hours. Remove sides of pan and spread cherry fruit filling on cake. Serve with whipped topping.

Tiny Cherry Cheesecakes

1 cup flour
1/3 cup sugar
1/4 cup baking cocoa
1/2 cup cold butter or margarine
2 tablespoons cold water

Filling:
2 packages (8-ounces each) cream cheese, softened
1/4 cup sugar
2 tablespoons milk
1 teaspoon vanilla extract
1 egg
1 can (21-ounces) cherry or strawberry pie filling

In a small bowl, combine flour, sugar and cocoa. Cut in butter until crumbly. Gradually add water, tossing with a fork until dough forms a ball. Shape into 24 balls and place in greased miniature muffin cups; press dough onto the bottom and up the sides of each cup.

In a mixing bowl, beat cream cheese and sugar until smooth. Beat in milk and vanilla. Add egg; beat just until combined. Spoon 1 tablespoonful into each cup.

Bake at 325 degrees for 15-18 minutes or until set. Cool on a wire rack for 30 minutes. Carefully remove from pans to cool completely. Top with pie filling. Store in the refrigerator.

Chocolate Cherry Cheesecake

1/2 cup dried cherries

1/4 cup chocolate liqueur

1 cup crushed shortbread cookies (about 13 cookies)

1/2 cup ground almonds

3 tablespoons butter, melted

1/3 cup sugar

1 package (8-ounces) cream cheese, softened

1 (4-1/2 ounce) round Brie cheese, rind removed and cut up

1 tablespoon flour

1 egg

1 egg yolk

2 tablespoons milk

Preheat oven to 375 degrees. In a small bowl combine dried cherries and chocolate liqueur. Set aside.

For crust, in a medium bowl combine crushed cookies and almonds. Stir in melted butter. Press the crumb mixture onto the bottom and about 2 inches up the sides of a 7-inch springform pan or about 1 inch up the sides of an 8-inch springform pan. Set pan aside.

For filling, in a large mixing bowl beat cream cheese, Brie, sugar and flour with an electric mixer on medium speed until combined. Add egg and egg yolk all at once, beating on low speed just until combined. Stir in milk and undrained cherries.

Pour filling into crust-lined pan. Place on a shallow baking pan in the oven. Bake about 25 minutes or until center appears nearly set when gently shaken.

Cool in pan on a wire rack for 15 minutes. Loosen the crust from sides of pan and cool 30 minutes more. Remove the sides of the pan and cool cheesecake completely. Cover and chill at least 4 hours before serving.

Chocolate Raspberry Cheesecake

1 (6-ounce or 9-inch) chocolate pie crust
2 packages (3 ounce) cream cheese, softened
1 can (14-ounce) can sweetened condensed milk
1 egg
3 tablespoons lemon juice

1 teaspoon vanilla extract
1 cup fresh or frozen raspberries

Chocolate Glaze:
2 squares (1-ounce each) semi-sweet chocolate
1/4 cup whipping cream

Heat oven to 350 degrees. With mixer, beat cream cheese until fluffy. Gradually beat in sweetened condensed milk until smooth. Add egg, lemon juice, and vanilla. Stir well.

Arrange raspberries on bottom of crust. Slowly pour cheese mixture over fruit. Bake 30-35 minutes or until center is almost set. Cool.

For glaze, melt chocolate over low heat in a small saucepan and mix with whipping cream. Cook and stir until thickened and smooth. Remove from heat. Top cheesecake with chocolate glaze and chill. Garnish as desired. Refrigerate leftovers.

Easy Apple Cheesecake

1 (6-ounce) graham cracker pie crust
1 cup apple pie filling
1 teaspoon ground cinnamon
1 package (8-ounces) cream cheese, softened

1/2 cup sugar
1/2 teaspoon vanilla extract
2 eggs
Whipped topping

In a bowl, combine pie filling and cinnamon. Spoon into pie crust. In a mixing bowl, beat cream cheese, sugar and vanilla until light fluffy. Add eggs, one at a time, beating well after each addition. Pour over pie filling. Bake at 350 degrees until cheesecake is set, about 25 minutes. Cool on a wire rack. Garnish with whipped topping if desired.

Caramel Apple Cheesecake

Crust:
1/3 cup margarine
1/3 cup sugar
1 egg
1-1/4 cups flour

Filling:
2 (8-ounce) packages softened cream cheese
2/3 cup sugar, divided

2 tablespoons flour
3 eggs
1/2 cup sour cream
1 cup peeled and chopped apples
3/4 teaspoon cinnamon
1/2 cup caramel topping
1/4 cup chopped pecans

Combine margarine and sugar until light and fluffy. Blend in egg. Add flour; mix well. Spread dough onto bottom and up sides of a 9-inch springform pan. Bake at 450 degrees for 10 minutes. Combine cream cheese, 1/3 cup sugar and flour; mix until well blended. Add eggs one at a time; mix well after each addition. Blend in sour cream.

Toss apples with 1/3 cup sugar and cinnamon. Stir into cream cheese mixture. Pour over crust. Swirl 1/4 cup caramel topping into cream cheese mixture. Bake at 350 degrees for one hour. Loosen cake from rim of pan. Chill. Top cheesecake with remaining caramel topping and pecans.

Apple-of-Your-Eye Cheesecake

Crust:
1 cup graham cracker crumbs
3 tablespoons sugar
1/2 teaspoon ground cinnamon
1/4 cup butter, melted
2 tablespoons finely chopped pecans

Filling:
3 packages (8-ounces each) cream cheese, softened
3/4 cup sugar
3 eggs

3/4 teaspoon vanilla extract

Topping:
2-1/2 cups chopped peeled apples
1 tablespoon lemon juice
1/4 cup sugar
1/2 teaspoon ground cinnamon
6 tablespoons caramel ice cream topping, divided
Sweetened whipped cream
2 tablespoons chopped pecans

(Continued on next page.)

Combine the first five ingredients and press onto the bottom of a lightly greased 9-inch springform pan. Bake at 350 degrees for 10 minutes. Cool. In a mixing bowl, beat cream cheese and sugar until smooth. Add eggs; beat on low just until combined. Stir in vanilla. Pour over crust. Toss apples with lemon juice, sugar and cinnamon. Spoon apples over filling.

Bake at 350 degrees for 55-60 minutes or until center is almost set. Carefully run a knife around edge of pan to loosen. Drizzle with 4 tablespoons caramel topping. Cool for 1 hour. Chill overnight. Remove sides of pan. Just before serving, garnish with whipped cream and drizzle with remaining caramel. Sprinkle with pecans. Store in refrigerator.

Marbled Pumpkin Cheesecake

1-1/4 cups graham cracker crumbs

1/4 cup butter or margarine, melted

1 cup plus 2 tablespoons sugar, divided

1 package (12-ounces) semi-sweet chocolate mini morsels, divided

3 packages (8-ounces each) cream cheese, softened

1/4 cup packed brown sugar

1 can (15-ounces) solid-pack pumpkin

4 eggs

1/2 cup evaporated milk

2 tablespoons cornstarch

3/4 teaspoon ground cinnamon

1/8 teaspoon ground nutmeg

In a medium bowl, combine graham cracker crumbs, butter and 2 tablespoons sugar. Press onto bottom of greased 9-inch springform pan. Sprinkle with 1-1/3 cups morsels. In a medium microwave-safe bowl, microwave remaining morsels on high for 45 seconds. Stir. Microwave at additional 10- to 20-second intervals, stirring until smooth. Cool to room temperature.

In a large mixing bowl, beat cream cheese, brown sugar and remaining sugar until smooth. Beat in pumpkin. Beat in eggs, evaporated milk, cornstarch, cinnamon and nutmeg. Remove 1 cup pumpkin mixture and stir into melted chocolate. Pour remaining pumpkin mixture into crust. Spoon chocolate-pumpkin mixture over top. Swirl with knife to marble. Bake at 325 degrees for 1 hour. Turn oven off and allow cheesecake to stand in oven for 30 minutes. Remove from oven and run knife around the edge of the cheesecake. Refrigerate immediately for 2-3 hours or until firm. Remove side of pan. Garnish as desired.

Blueberry Cheesecake

Crust:
1-1/2 cups finely ground almonds

1/4 cup sugar

3 tablespoons butter or margarine, softened

1 tablespoon flour

Filling:
3 packages (8-ounces each) cream cheese, softened

1-1/4 cups sugar

3 tablespoons all-purpose flour

1/2 teaspoon salt

4 large eggs

1 container (8-ounce) sour cream

1 teaspoon vanilla extract

1 tablespoon grated lemon rind

1-1/2 cups fresh or frozen blueberries

Topping:
1 cup whipping cream

2 teaspoons sugar

2 tablespoons sour cream

Garnishes: blueberries and lemon rind strips, optional

For crust, combine almonds, sugar, butter, and flour in a small bowl. Press mixture into bottom and 1-1/2 inches up sides of a lightly greased 9-inch springform pan. Set aside.

For filling, beat cream cheese at medium speed with an electric mixer until smooth. Combine 1-1/4 cups sugar, 3 tablespoons flour and salt. Add to cream cheese, beating until blended. Add eggs, one at a time, beating well after each addition. Add 8 ounce container sour cream, vanilla, and lemon rind, beating just until blended. Gently stir in blueberries. Pour mixture into prepared crust.

Bake at 300 degrees for 1 hour and 10 minutes or until center is firm. Turn off oven. Let cheesecake stand in oven with door partially ajar for 30 minutes.

Remove cheesecake from oven; cool in pan on wire rack 30 minutes. Cover and chill about 8 hours. Release sides of pan. Beat whipping cream at high speed until foamy; gradually add 2 teaspoons sugar. Beat until stiff peaks form. Fold in 2 tablespoons sour cream; spread over cheesecake and garnish if desired.

(Continued on next page)

Reduced-fat cheesecake: Omit first 4 ingredients and substitute 1 cup graham cracker crumbs, 3 tablespoons melted butter and 1 tablespoon sugar; press into pan. Bake 5 minutes at 350 degrees.

Substitute 16-ounces reduced fat cream cheese and 8-ounces fat-free cream cheese for the 3 packages cream cheese. Reduce 1-1/4 cups sugar to 1 cup. Substitute 2 whole eggs plus 2 egg whites for 4 eggs. Substitute 8-ounce container light sour cream. Omit whipping cream and next 2 ingredients. Substitute mixture of 8-ounce container reduced fat frozen whipped topping and 1/4 cup light sour cream. Proceed as directed. Garnish if desired.

Pumpkin Cheesecake

1-1/2 cups (about 24 squares) graham cracker crumbs

1 tablespoon sugar

5 tablespoons butter or margarine, melted

Filling:

3 packages (8-ounces each) cream cheese, softened

1 cup sugar

1 teaspoon vanilla extract

3 eggs

1 cup cooked or canned pumpkin

1/2 teaspoon ground cinnamon

1/4 teaspoon ground nutmeg

1/4 teaspoon ground allspice

Whipped cream

In a small bowl, combine crumbs and sugar. Stir in the butter. Press onto the bottom and 2 inches up the sides of a greased 9-inch springform pan. Bake at 350 degrees for 5 minutes. Cool on a wire rack.

In a mixing bowl, beat cream cheese, sugar and vanilla until smooth. Add eggs, pumpkin and spices. Beat just until combined. Pour into crust. Bake at 350 degrees for 1 hour or until center is almost set. Cool on a wire rack for 10 minutes.

Carefully run a knife around edge of pan to loosen. Cool 1 hour longer. Refrigerate until completely cooled. It is normal for center of cheesecake to fall. Remove sides of pan just before serving. Garnish with whipped cream.

Cool Lime Cheesecake

Crust:

2-1/4 cups (about 36 squares) graham cracker crumbs

1/3 cup sugar

1/2 cup butter or margarine, melted

Filling:

10-ounces cream cheese, softened

3/4 cup sugar

1 cup (8-ounces) sour cream

3 tablespoons flour

3 eggs

2/3 cup lime juice

1 teaspoon vanilla extract

1 drop green food coloring, optional

Whipped cream

Lime slices

In a bowl, combine crumbs and sugar; stir in butter. Press onto the bottom and 1 inch up the side of a greased 10-inch springform pan. Bake at 375 degrees for 8 minutes. Cool. In a mixing bowl, beat cream cheese and sugar until smooth. Add sour cream and flour and beat well. Beat in eggs on low speed just until combined. Stir in lime juice, vanilla and food coloring if desired just until mixed. Pour into crust. Bake at 325 degrees for 50-55 minutes or until center is almost set. Cool on a wire rack for 1 hour. Refrigerate overnight. Remove sides of pan. Garnish with whipped cream and lime.

Citrus Fruit Cheesecake

Crust:

1 cup graham cracker crumbs

1/3 cup firmly packed brown sugar

1/4 cup butter or margarine, melted

Filling:

4 packages (8-ounces each) cream cheese, softened

1 cup sugar

2 tablespoons flour

1 teaspoon vanilla

1 tablespoon each lemon juice, lime juice and orange juice

1 teaspoon each grated lemon peel, lime peel and orange peel

4 eggs

(Continued on next page)

For crust, mix crumbs, brown sugar and butter; press onto bottom of 9-inch springform pan. Bake at 325 degrees for 10 minutes if using a silver springform pan. If using a dark nonstick springform pan, bake at 300 degrees for 10 minutes.

For filling, mix cream cheese, sugar, flour and vanilla with electric mixer on medium speed until well blended. Blend in juices and peel. Add eggs, mixing on low speed just until blended. Pour over crust.

Bake at 325 degrees for 1 hour and 5 minutes or until center is almost set if using a silver springform pan. If using a dark nonstick springform pan, bake at 300 degrees for 1 hour and 5 minutes or until center is almost set. Run knife or metal spatula around rim of pan to loosen cake; cool before removing rim. Refrigerate 4 hours or overnight. Garnish with shredded lemon peel. Store leftover cheesecake, covered, in refrigerator.

Peach Amaretto Cheesecake

Crust:
3 tablespoons margarine
1/3 cup sugar
1 egg
3/4 cup flour
Filling:
3 (8-ounce) packages softened cream cheese

3/4 cup sugar
3 tablespoons flour
3 eggs
16-ounce can peach halves, drained and pureed
1/4 cup almond flavored liqueur

Combine margarine and sugar until fluffy. Blend in egg; add flour and mix well. Spread dough onto bottom of 9-inch springform pan. Bake at 450 degrees for 10 minutes.

Mix cream cheese, sugar and flour until well blended. Add eggs one at a time, mixing well after each addition. Add peaches and liqueur; mix well. Pour over crust.

Bake at 450 degrees for 10 minutes. Reduce temp to 250 degrees and bake for another hour. Loosen cake from rim of pan; chill. Garnish with peach slices and slivered almonds if desired.

Cappuccino Cheesecake

Crust:
1-1/2 cups finely chopped nuts
2 tablespoons sugar
3 tablespoons margarine, melted

Filling:
4 (8-ounce) packages cream cheese, softened
1 cup sugar
3 tablespoons flour
4 eggs
1 cup sour cream
1 tablespoon instant coffee granules
1/4 teaspoon cinnamon
1/4 cup boiling water

Combine nuts, sugar and margarine; press onto bottom of 9-inch springform pan. Bake at 325 degrees 10 minutes.

Combine cream cheese, sugar and flour, mixing at medium speed on electric mixer until well blended. Add eggs one at a time; mix well after each addition.

Blend in sour cream. Dissolve coffee granules and cinnamon in boiling water. Add to cream cheese mixture; mix well. Pour over crust and bake at 450 degrees for 10 minutes then reduce oven temperature to 250 degrees and continue baking 1 hour.

Loosen cake from rim of pan; cool before removing rim of pan. Chill. Garnish with whipped cream and coffee beans if desired.

Frozen Cheesecake Pie

1 package (21.4 ounces)
no-bake cheesecake with
cherry or strawberry topping
2 tablespoons sugar
6 tablespoons butter or
margarine, melted

1 tablespoon water
1-1/2 cups cold milk
1 tub (8-ounces) whipped
topping, thawed

Mix crumbs, sugar, butter and water thoroughly with fork in 9-inch pie plate until crumbs are well moistened. Press against side of plate first, using finger or large spoon to shape edge. Press remaining crumbs firmly onto bottom using dry measuring cup.

Beat milk and filling mix in medium size bowl with an electric mixer on low speed until blended. Beat on medium speed 3 minutes until thick. Stir in whipped topping until smooth. Swirl fruit topping into mixture with spatula. Spoon into crust.

Freeze 6 hours or overnight until firm. Let stand at room temperature or in refrigerator 15 minutes or until pie can be cut easily. Refrigerate leftovers.

Fluffy Cheesecake Pie

4 cups miniature
marshmallows
1/3 cup orange juice
2 packages (8-ounces each)
cream cheese, softened

1 carton (12-ounces) frozen
whipped topping, thawed
2-1/2 (about 60 wafers) cups
crushed vanilla wafers
1/2 cup butter or margarine,
melted

In a large microwave-safe bowl, combine marshmallows and orange juice. Microwave, uncovered, on high for 1-1/2 minutes. Stir until smooth. In a mixing bowl, beat cream cheese. Add marshmallow mix; beat just until smooth. Fold in whipped topping. Combine wafer crumbs and butter and set aside 3/4 cup for topping. Press remaining crumbs into an ungreased pie pan. Spoon cream cheese filling over crust. Sprinkle with reserved crumbs. Cover and refrigerate for 1 hour or until set. Store in the refrigerator.

Banana Cream Cheesecake

Crust:

1-3/4 cups (about 28 squares) graham cracker crumbs

1/4 cup sugar

1/2 cup butter, melted

Filling:

1 package (8-ounces) cream cheese, softened

1/2 cup sugar

1 carton (8-ounces) frozen whipped topping, thawed, divided

3-4 medium firm bananas, sliced

1-3/4 cups cold milk

1 package (3.4-ounces) instant banana cream pudding mix

In a small bowl, combine cracker crumbs and sugar; stir in butter. Set aside 1/2 cup mixture for topping. Press remaining crumb mixture onto the bottom and up the sides of a greased 9-inch springform pan or 9-inch square baking pan.

Bake at 350 degrees for 5-7 minutes. Cool on a wire rack. In a mixing bowl, beat cream cheese and sugar until smooth. Fold 2 cups of whipped topping into mixture. Arrange half of the banana slices in crust and top with half of the cream cheese mixture. Repeat layers.

In a bowl, beat milk and pudding mix until smooth and fold in remaining whipped topping. Pour over the cream cheese layer. Sprinkle with reserved crumb mix. Refrigerate for 1-2 hours until set.

Mini Fruit-Topped Cheesecakes

1 package (21.4-ounces)
no bake cheesecake with
strawberry or cherry topping
2 tablespoons sugar

1/3 cup butter or margarine,
melted
1-1/2 cups cold milk

Mix crumbs, butter and sugar thoroughly with fork in medium bowl until crumbs are well moistened. Press onto bottoms of 12 paper-lined muffin cups.

Beat milk and filling mix with electric mixer on low speed until blended. Beat on medium speed for 3 minutes until thick. Spoon over crumb mixture in muffin cups.

Refrigerate at least 1 hour or until ready to serve. Just before serving, spoon fruit topping onto cheesecakes. Store leftover cheesecakes in refrigerator.

Raspberry Delight

Crust:
2-1/4 cups flour
2 tablespoons sugar
3/4 cup butter or margarine,
softened

Filling:
1 package (8-ounces) cream
cheese, softened
1 cup confectioners' sugar
1 teaspoon vanilla extract

1/4 teaspoon salt
2 cups whipped topping
Topping:
1 package (6-ounces)
raspberry gelatin
2 cups boiling water·
2 packages (10-ounces each)
sweetened frozen raspberries
Additional whipped topping
and fresh mint, optional

In a bowl, combine flour and sugar; blend in butter until smooth. Press into an ungreased 13x9x2-inch baking pan. Bake at 300 degrees for 20-25 minutes or until set. Crust should not be browned. Cool. In a mixing bowl, beat cream cheese, confectioners' sugar, vanilla and salt until smooth. Fold in whipped topping and spread over crust. For topping, dissolve gelatin in boiling water and stir in fruit. Chill for 20 minutes or until mixture begins to thicken. Spoon over filling. Refrigerate until set. Cut into squares and garnish with whipped topping and mint if desired.

Orange Cream Cheesecake

If you love orange sherbet or orange dreamsicles,
you will love this cheesecake!

Crust:

2 cups graham cracker crumbs

1 teaspoon ground cinnamon

1 teaspoon grated orange peel

1/2 cup butter or margarine, melted

Filling:

1 package (3-ounces) orange gelatin

3 packages (8-ounces each) cream cheese, softened

1-1/4 cups sugar

1 can (5-ounces) evaporated milk

1 teaspoon lemon juice

1/3 cup orange juice concentrate

1 teaspoon vanilla extract

1 carton (8-ounces) frozen whipped topping, thawed

Topping:

2 cups whipped topping

1/4 cup sugar

Garnishes: lemon slices, orange peel strips, etc.

Combine the cracker crumbs, cinnamon, orange peel and butter. Press onto the bottom of a greased 10-inch springform pan. Refrigerate for at least 30 minutes.*

Prepare gelatin according to package directions and set aside 1/2 cup at room temperature. Chill remaining gelatin for 80 minutes or until slightly thickened.

Meanwhile, in a mixing bowl, beat cream cheese and sugar for 2 minutes. Gradually beat in milk and lemon juice. Beat on medium-high speed 2 minutes longer. Gradually beat in orange juice concentrate, vanilla and room-temperature gelatin. Fold in whipped topping. Pour over crust.

In a mixing bowl, beat whipped topping and sugar. Beat in refrigerated gelatin until it forms a thin mixture. Chill for 30 minutes. Gently spoon over filling until pan is full. Refrigerate for 8 hours or overnight. Garnish if desired.

*You can also press crumbs about 1-1/2 inches up side of pan if desired.

Mango Cheesecake

Crust:

15 shortbread cookies, crushed

2 tablespoons butter or margarine, melted

Filling:

1 ripe large mango

2 packages (8-ounces each) 1/3-less-fat cream cheese, softened

1-1/4 cups canned or bottled mango nectar

1/2 cup sugar

2 tablespoons lemon juice

1 envelope (2-1/2 teaspoons) unflavored gelatin

1/4 cup cold water

For crust, combine crumbs and butter until moistened. Press over bottom of 8-inch springform pan.

For filling, Use half of the mango; refrigerate remaining mango. Put the diced mango in food processor and add cream cheese, nectar, sugar and lemon juice. Process until smooth, scraping bowl as needed.

Sprinkle gelatin over water in a microwave-safe cup measure or a small saucepan. Let stand 1 minute. Microwave on high for about 40 seconds or place over low heat and stir 2-3 minutes, until gelatin has completely dissolved and liquid is clear. With processor running, add gelatin and process until well blended. Pour onto crust. Cover tightly and refrigerate at least 5 hours or overnight until firm.

Shortly before serving, remove pan sides and place cake on serving plate. Cut remaining 1/2 mango off seed, peel and thinly slice. Arrange in spoke fashion on top of cake. Dice mango on ends of seed and scatter in middle of the slices.

Cheesecake Supreme

Crust:

1 cup flour
1/4 cup sugar
1 teaspoon grated lemon peel
1/2 cup butter
1 slightly beaten egg yolk
1/4 teaspoon vanilla

Filling:

5 (8-ounces each) packages cream cheese
1/4 teaspoon vanilla
3/4 teaspoon grated lemon peel
3/4 cup sugar
3 tablespoons flour
1/4 teaspoon salt
4 or 5 eggs (1 cup)
2 egg yolks
1/4 cup whipping cream

For crust, combine first three ingredients. Cut in butter until mixture is crumbly. Add egg yolk and vanilla. Blend thoroughly. Pat 1/3 of the dough on the bottom of a 9-inch springform pan (sides removed). Bake in preheated oven at 400 degrees for 8 minutes or until golden brown. Cool. Attach sides to bottom. Butter and pat remaining dough on sides to 1-3/4 inches high.

For filling, soften cream cheese to room temperature. Beat until creamy. Add vanilla and lemon peel. Mix next 3 ingredients, gradually blending into cheese. Add eggs and egg yolks one at a time, beating after each just to blend. Gently stir in whipping cream. Turn into crust-lined pan.

Bake at 450 degrees for 12 minutes. Reduce heat to 350 degrees and continue baking 55 minutes. Remove from oven; cool. Loosen sides with spatula after 1/2 hour. Remove sides at end of 1 hour. Allow to cool 2 hours longer. Glaze with strawberry or pineapple glaze, or any fruit glaze. For simple glaze: Microwave or heat 1 cup any fruit preserves.

TARTS & TURNOVERS

Tips on Making Tartlets

1. To bake tartlet shells, shape the dough into a 2-inch thick log. Cut slices about 1/8-inch thick; press each slice into greased and floured tartlet tins

or

2. Use a floured rolling pin to roll out dough to 1/8-inch thickness. Group together greased and floured tins and cover with dough. Press dough into tins.

3. If tartlets stick to the tins, gently squeeze the bottom of the tin. Loosen shell with a metal cake tester or the tip of a thin knife.

Basic Short Crust Dough For Tarts & Tartlets

1-1/4 cups flour
2 tablespoons sugar
1/2 teaspoon salt

6 tablespoons chilled butter (cut into small pieces)
1 to 3 tablespoons ice water
1/2 teaspoon vanilla

In a large bowl, mix together flour, sugar and salt. Using a pastry blender, cut butter into flour mixture until coarse crumbs form. Add water and vanilla, toss with a fork until soft dough forms. Shape dough into disc shape. Wrap and chill for 30 minutes. On a floured surface, roll dough into a 2-inch thick cylinder. Cut into twenty 1/8-inch thick slices. Press slices into tartlet tins. (You can also use the rolling technique.) Bake shells until golden, 12 to 15 minutes at 375 degrees. Cool completely.

Roll out dough onto floured surface to 1/8-inch thickness. Group together greased and floured tins, cover with dough. Press dough into tins.

If your shells stick to the tart tins, gently squeeze the bottom of the tin or loosen the shell with the tip of a thin knife.

For variety, add 1 teaspoon of grated orange or lemon peel, almond extract or ground nuts.

Tartlets can be filled with sweet or savory fillings, fruits, whipped cream, fruit pie fillings, just let your imagination go wild! For baked fillings use custards, pecan or pumpkin pie filling. The possibilities are endless.

Pressed Tart Crust (for 9-inch crust)

1 cup flour
1/2 cup softened butter or margarine

2 tablespoons brown sugar, packed
1 egg yolk

Mix all ingredients just until dough forms. Press dough evenly in bottom and up sides of ungreased 9-inch tart pan with removable bottom.

If prebaking, bake at 400 degrees for 15 to 20 minutes or until light brown, or follow individual recipe.

Peach Tart

Crust:

1/2 cup blanched sliced almonds

2 cups flour

1/3 cup sugar

1/2 teaspoon salt

3/4 cup (1-1/2 sticks) chilled butter, cut into pieces

1 large egg, lightly beaten

Filling:

1-1/2 cups milk

1 large egg

1/4 cup sugar

2 tablespoons cornstarch

1/4 cup orange liqueur

Topping:

5-6 fresh peaches (1-1/2 pounds)

1 tablespoon fresh lemon juice

3 tablespoons firmly packed light brown sugar

1/4 cup blanched sliced almonds

To prepare crust, in a food processor fitted with metal blade, finely grind nuts. In a large bowl, mix together the flour, sugar, salt, and ground nuts. Cut the butter into flour mixture until coarse crumbs form. Stir in egg until a soft dough forms. Shape into a disk; wrap in plastic wrap; and chill for 4 hours or overnight.

Preheat oven to 425 degrees. On a lightly floured surface, using a floured rolling pin, roll dough into a 12-inch circle. Fit into a 10-inch tart pan with a removable bottom. Trim the edges; press a fork against pan edge; reserve trimmings. Line with foil; fill with pie weights or dried beans.

Roll out trimmings; cut out leaves for decoration. Place on a baking sheet. Bake crust and leaves until lightly browned, 10 to 15 minutes. Remove the foil and weights. Transfer the crust and leaves to a wire rack to cool.

Meanwhile, prepare filling. In a medium saucepan, whisk together milk, egg, sugar, and cornstarch. Cook over medium heat, whisking constantly, until thickened, about 10 minutes. Cool. Whisk in the orange liqueur. Chill for about 1 hour. Pour the filling into the crust.

Preheat broiler. To prepare topping, peel and slice peaches. Dip in lemon juice and pat dry with paper towels. Arrange over filling. Sprinkle with brown sugar. Broil tart until sugar is melted, about 5 minutes. Sprinkle with nuts. Decorate with leaves. Serve warm.

Peaches and Cream Tart

Crust:

1-1/2 cups reduced-fat graham cracker crumbs

6 tablespoons diet margarine

1 teaspoon ground cinnamon

Filling:

1/4 cup sugar

3 tablespoons flour

1 packet unflavored gelatin

1/4 teaspoon salt

1-1/2 cups skim milk

1 egg

1 teaspoon vanilla

1/2 cup frozen fat-free nondairy whipped topping, thawed

2 medium-size freestone peaches, pitted and thinly sliced

2 tablespoons peach jam, melted

For crust, heat oven to 375 degrees. Mix crumbs, margarine and cinnamon in small bowl. Press over bottom and up sides of 9-inch tart pan with removable bottom. Bake 5-7 minutes, until lightly colored. Let cool.

For filling, mix sugar, flour, gelatin and salt in small saucepan. Whisk in milk and egg. Cook over medium heat, stirring, until mixture coats back of spoon, 3 minutes. Do not boil. Remove from heat. Stir in vanilla. Place pan in ice water bath. Refrigerate until mixture mounds when dropped from spoon, 30 minutes. Fold in whipped topping. Spoon into cooled crust. Refrigerate until firm, about 2 hours. Top with peaches. Brush with jam.

Peach Melba Tarts

Baked tart shells

1 package (10-ounces) frozen raspberries, thawed

1-1/2 cups sliced fresh peaches

Vanilla ice cream

Melba Sauce:

1/2 cup reserved syrup

1/4 cup currant jelly

2 teaspoons cornstarch

Bake tart shells. Drain raspberries, reserving syrup.

(Continued on next page.)

Bake tart shells. Drain raspberries, reserving syrup.

Prepare Melba Sauce using 1/2 cup reserved syrup, 1/4 cup currant jelly and 2 teaspoons cornstarch. Mix in 1-quart saucepan over medium heat, stirring constantly, until mixture thickens and boils. Boil and stir 1 minute. Cool.

Mix raspberries and peaches. Divide mixture among tarts and top each tart with ice cream and Melba Sauce.

Peach-Pecan Tart

Clear Orange Glaze:
1 cup sugar
3 tablespoons cornstarch
1/4 teaspoon salt
1 cup orange juice
1/2 cup water
Butter Crust:
1-1/3 cups flour

2/3 cup margarine or butter, softened
1/3 cup packed brown sugar
Filling:
2 packages (3-ounces each) cream cheese, softened
4 cups sliced fresh peaches (4 medium)
1/2 cup chopped pecans

Prepare Clear orange glaze by mixing sugar, cornstarch and salt in 1-quart saucepan. Gradually stir in orange juice and water. Heat to boiling over medium heat, stirring constantly. Boil and stir 1 minute. Cool.

For crust, heat oven to 400 degrees. Mix flour, butter, and brown sugar with a fork until crumbly. Press firmly and evenly against bottom of ungreased 12-inch pizza pan. Bake until light brown, 10-15 minutes.

For filling, beat cream cheese until smooth and spread over crust. Arrange peaches on crust and sprinkle with pecans. Pour glaze over top and refrigerate until set, about 2 hours.

Fresh Peach Cobbler

2 large peaches, peeled and sliced
1-1/2 cups sugar, divided
1/2 cup butter or margarine, melted
1 cup flour

2 teaspoons baking powder
1/4 teaspoon salt
Dash ground nutmeg
3/4 cup milk

In a bowl, combine peaches and 3/4 cup sugar; set aside. Pour butter into an 8-inch square baking pan. In a bowl, combine flour, baking powder, salt, nutmeg and remaining sugar; stir in milk just until combined. Pour mixture over butter. Top with the peaches.

Bake at 375 degrees for 45-50 minutes or until golden brown.

Peach Pizza Pie

1/2 cup butter or margarine, softened
1/4 cup confectioners' sugar
1 cup flour
4-5 cups sliced fresh peaches
Glaze:
2 tablespoons sugar

1 tablespoon cornstarch
1/8 to 1/4 teaspoon ground mace, optional
1/2 cup orange juice
1/2 cup red currant jelly
Whipped cream, optional

In a mixing bowl, cream butter and sugar. Add flour; mix well. Pat into greased 12-inch pizza pan; prick with a fork. Bake at 350 degrees for 10-15 minutes or until golden. Cool completely. Arrange peaches on crust.

In a saucepan, mix sugar, cornstarch and mace. Add orange juice and jelly; cook and stir over medium heat until smooth. Bring to a boil; boil for 2 minutes. Remove from heat and let cool for about 5 minutes. Spoon over peaches.

Chill for 1 hour or until set. Garnish with whipped cream if desired and serve immediately.

Apple-Cream Cheese Tart

Cream Cheese Pastry (See crust section page 15)

1/2 package (8-ounces) cream cheese, softened

1/4 cup sour cream

1 egg yolk

2 tablespoons honey

1/8 teaspoon grated lemon rind

1 large Granny Smith apple, peeled and thinly sliced

1 tablespoon apple jelly

1-1/2 teaspoons water

1/2 cup whipping cream

1-1/2 teaspoons honey

1/8 teaspoon vanilla extract

Roll Cream Cheese Pastry to 1/8-inch thickness on a lightly floured surface; fit into a 7-1/2-inch round tart pan with removable bottom. Trim excess pastry along edges and freeze for 10 minutes. Line pastry with aluminum foil, and fill with pie weights or dried beans

Bake at 400 degrees for 10 minutes. Remove weights and foil, and prick bottom of crust with a fork. Bake for an additional 10 minutes. Cool on a wire rack. Pastry will shrink.

Beat cream cheese with sour cream, egg yolk, honey, and grated lemon rind in a mixing bowl at medium speed with an electric mixer until smooth. Spoon into tart shell, and arrange apple slices on top.

Combine apple jelly and water in a small saucepan and cook over low heat, stirring constantly, until jelly melts. Brush half of jelly mixture over the apples.

Bake at 400 degrees on lower rack of oven for 35 minutes. Cool on a wire rack for 15 minutes. Brush with remaining jelly mixture. Cool.

Beat whipping cream at medium speed until soft peaks form; stir in honey and vanilla. Serve with tart.

Apple-Cinnamon Tart

Pastry for 9-inch Single Crust Pie

3/4 cup red cinnamon candies

2 tablespoons water

2 tablespoons light corn syrup

5 cups thinly sliced pared tart apples (about 5 medium)

2 tablespoons sugar

1 tablespoon margarine or butter

Heat candies, water and corn syrup to boiling and reduce heat. Simmer uncovered until candies are almost dissolved, about 5 minutes. Pour into ungreased round pan, 9x1-1/2 inches. Cool.

Heat oven to 425 degrees. Layer half of the apples, overlapping slices, on candy mixture. Sprinkle with 1 tablespoon sugar. Layer with remaining apples and sprinkle with remaining sugar. Dot with margarine.

Prepare pastry as directed except roll into 10-inch circle. Carefully place over apples. Trim edge of pastry to fit pan. Bake until crust is light golden brown, 40 to 45 minutes. Cool 1 hour. Invert on serving plate. Serve with sweetened whipped cream or ice cream if desired.

Apple Cranberry Tart

Pastry for double crust pie

2 cups fresh or frozen cranberries, coarsely chopped

2 medium tart apples, peeled and coarsely chopped

1-1/4 cups packed brown sugar

2 tablespoons flour

1/2 teaspoon ground cinnamon

1 to 2 tablespoons butter or margarine

Roll half of the pastry into a 13-inch circle. Press onto the bottom and up the sides of an ungreased 11-inch fluted tart pan with removable bottom or press in to the bottom and 1-inch up the sides of a 10-inch springform pan.

In a bowl, combine cranberries, apples, brown sugar, flour and cinnamon; pour into crust. Dot with butter.

(Continued on next page.)

Cut remaining pastry with a 1-inch apple cookie cutter. Place over filling. Place tart pan on a warm baking sheet. Bake at 425 degrees for 35-40 minutes or until filling is hot and bubbly and crust is golden brown. Serve warm.

Almond Apple Tart

Crust:

1/2 (17-1/4-ounce) package frozen puff pastry sheets, thawed

1 (8-ounce) tube or can almond paste

Filling:

2 medium (4 cups) Granny Smith apples, peeled, cored, thinly sliced

1 tablespoon lemon juice

1/4 cup sugar

2 tablespoons flour

1/2 teaspoon ground nutmeg

1 tablespoon butter, melted

Topping:

3 tablespoons sliced almonds

2 tablespoons sugar

Preheat oven to 400 degrees. On lightly floured surface, roll out puff pastry to 11-inch square. Cut off corners to make 11-inch circle. Gently place in 12-inch pizza pan.

On lightly sugared surface, roll out almond paste to 10-inch circle. Place on top of puff pastry.

In large bowl, toss apples with lemon juice to prevent browning. In small bowl combine 1/4 cup sugar, flour and nutmeg. Stir in butter. Toss gently with apple slices. Arrange sugared slices in spoke fashion over almond paste. Bake for 15 minutes.

Meanwhile, combine almonds and 2 tablespoons sugar. Sprinkle evenly over apples. Continue baking for 15 to 20 minutes or until apples are tender and pastry is golden brown. Cut into wedges and serve warm.

Walnut-Apple Pizza

1/2 package active dry yeast (1-1/4 teaspoon)

3/4 cup warm water (105-115 degrees)

1 cup flour

2/3 cup whole wheat flour

1 teaspoon sugar

1 teaspoon salt

1 tablespoon cooking oil

3-ounces Stilton or Blue cheese, crumbled, about 3/4 cup

1 large tart apple, cored and thinly sliced (about 1-1/3 cups)

1/2 cup shredded Monterey Jack cheese (2-ounce)

1/2 cup chopped walnuts

1-1/2 teaspoon snipped fresh rosemary

Stir yeast into warm water. Let stand 5 minutes to dissolve. In a large mixing bowl stir together all-purpose flour, whole wheat flour, sugar, and salt. Make a well in the center of the dry ingredients. Add the yeast mixture and oil. Stir until combined.

Turn out onto a lightly floured surface. Knead gently about 20 times. Place dough in a greased bowl. Cover and let rise in a warm place until doubled in size (about 45 minutes). Punch down.

Preheat oven to 450 degrees. Grease a 12-inch pizza pan. On a lightly floured surface roll dough to a 13-inch circle. Transfer to prepared pizza pan. Build up edges slightly. Bake crust about 10 minutes or until just beginning to brown. Remove from oven.

Sprinkle dough with Stilton or blue cheese. Top with apple slices. Sprinkle with Monterey Jack cheese, walnuts, and rosemary. Bake for 10-12 minutes more or until edges are lightly browned. Makes 12 appetizer servings or 8 main-dish servings.

Easy Apple Dumplings

3 tubes (12-ounces each) refrigerated buttermilk biscuits

15 medium apples, peeled, cored, and halved

2 cups sugar

2 cups water

1 cup butter or margarine, melted

2 teaspoons vanilla extract

1/2 teaspoon ground cinnamon

Flatten biscuits with hands. Wrap each biscuit around an apple half, placing seam side down in two greased 13x9x2-inch baking dishes. Combine sugar, water, butter and vanilla. Pour about 1-2/3 cups into each pan. Sprinkle cinnamon over dumplings.

Bake, uncovered, in a 350 degree oven for 35-40 minutes or until golden brown and apples are tender. Serve immediately. Yield: 30 servings.

Great for a large crowd!

Caramel Apple Pizza

Crust:

1/2 cup butter or margarine, softened

1/4 cup shortening

1 cup packed brown sugar

1-3/4 cups flour

1 cup rolled oats

1 teaspoon salt

1/2 teaspoon baking soda

1/2 cup chopped pecans, optional

Filling:

4-1/2 cups coarsely chopped peeled tart apples

3 tablespoons flour

1 package (14-ounces) caramels

3 tablespoons butter or margarine

Cream first 3 ingredients until fluffy. Mix in flour, oats, salt, baking soda. Stir in pecans. Set aside 2 cups. Press remaining oat mix into bottom of ungreased 15-inch pizza pan. Toss apples with flour; spoon over crust. In saucepan, melt caramels and butter over low heat; drizzle over apples. Top with the reserved oat mix.

Bake at 400 degrees for 25-30 minutes or until browned. Cool before cutting.

Apple-Almond Tart

Crust:
1-1/2 cups flour
2 tablespoons sugar
1/2 teaspoon salt
1/2 cup (1 stick) chilled butter, cut into small pieces
3 tablespoons ice water

Filling:
3/4 cup whole almonds (about 3-ounces)
3 zwieback crackers
1/2 cup sugar
2-3 baking apples (such as Cortland or Granny Smith)
3 tablespoons chilled butter

To prepare crust, in a large bowl, mix together flour, sugar, and salt. Cut butter into flour mixture until coarse crumbs form. Add water, 1 tablespoon at a time, tossing with a fork, until dough forms. Shape dough into a disk, wrap in plastic wrap, and chill in the refrigerator for 1 hour.

Meanwhile, prepare filling. In a food processor fitted with metal blade, process nuts until ground, 10 seconds. Add zwieback crackers and sugar. Process until finely ground, 20 seconds.

Preheat the oven to 425 degrees. Grease a baking sheet. On a lightly floured surface, using a lightly floured rolling pin, roll the dough into a 12-inch circle. Place on the prepared baking sheet. Sprinkle with half the nut mixture to within 1 inch of the edge.

Core and slice apples. Arrange in a circular pattern over the nut mixture. Sprinkle apples with the remaining nut mixture. Dot with butter. Fold up edges of dough over filling and pinch to crimp.

Bake the tart for 25 minutes. Reduce the oven temperature to 375 degrees. Bake until the filling is bubbly and the crust is golden, about 10 minutes. If the pastry browns too quickly, cover with aluminum foil. Transfer the baking sheet to a wire rack to cool for 10 minutes. Serve warm.

Caramelized Quince Skillet Tart

1 recipe Buttery Sweet Pastry
(See crust section page 15)

1/2 cup butter or margarine

6 cups thickly sliced, peeled
quince or cooking apples (5-6
quince or apples)

2/3 cup sugar

Preheat oven to 375 degrees. In a 10-inch ovenproof skillet, melt the butter over medium heat. Stir in the quince or apples and sugar. Cook over medium heat, stirring occasionally, until bubbly. Reduce heat to medium-low. Cook, uncovered, for 20 minutes more or until quince or apples are very tender, stirring occasionally. If using quince, mixture will thicken and turn deep golden brown. Remove from heat.

On a lightly floured surface, roll dough into a 10-inch circle. Cut slits in the pastry. Unroll pastry over quince mixture in skillet, being careful not to stretch pastry. If necessary, fold under edges of pastry.

Bake about 30 minutes or until the pastry is golden brown and filling is bubbly. Cool in skillet on a wire rack for 5 minutes. Invert onto a large serving plate. Carefully lift off the skillet. Allow to stand about 20 minutes more.

Pear Tart

Pastry for 8-or 9-inch single
crust pie

1/2 cup currant jelly, melted

3 cups thinly sliced pared
pears (about 3 medium)

1-2 tablespoons packed brown
sugar

Dairy sour cream or
sweetened whipped cream

Heat oven to 425 degrees. Prepare pastry as directed except roll into 12x10-inch rectangle. Trim edges to make even. Place rectangle on ungreased cookie sheet. Brush 1/2-inch edge around rectangle with water. Fold moistened edges onto rectangle: press lightly with floured fork. Brush half of the currant jelly on rectangle up to folded edges. Arrange pears in rows, overlapping slices on jell-covered pastry. Sprinkle with brown sugar. Bake until pastry is golden brown, 20-25 minutes. Brush remaining currant jelly on pears and pastry edges. Cut into 6 squares. Serve warm or cool topped with sour cream.

Ginger Pear Tart

30 2-inch-wide gingersnaps

1/2 cup broken pecans

1/3 cup margarine or butter, melted

3/4 cup half-and-half or light cream

1 carton (8-ounces) dairy sour cream

1 package (4 serving size) instant vanilla pudding mix

1 tablespoon chopped candied ginger, 2 teaspoons grated ginger root, or 1/4-1/2 teaspoon ground ginger

1 tablespoon apricot brandy (optional)

1 tablespoon margarine or butter

3 tablespoons sugar

1-1/2 pound pears (3 to 5 medium), peeled, cored, and thinly sliced

Mint leaves (optional)

For crust, combine cookies and pecans in a food processor bowl; cover and process until finely crushed. If using a blender, process only one-fourth of the cookies at a time, adding pecans with the last portion. You should have 2-1/2 cups of dry mix.

!n a mixing bowl stir together crumb mixture and 1/3 cup melted margarine or butter. Press firmly onto the bottom and up the sides of a 9-1/2- to 11-inch round tart pan with a removable bottom or a 9-inch pie plate, forming a firm, even crust. Bake in a 350 degree oven for 8 minutes. Cool in pan on a wire rack.

When crust is cool, make filling. In a large mixing bowl gradually stir half-and-half or cream into sour cream. Stir pudding mix, ginger, and apricot brandy using a whisk or rotary beater for 1 to 2 minutes or until thick and smooth. Spread in prepared crust. Cover and chill for several hours or overnight.

In a 10-inch skillet melt the 1 tablespoon butter or margarine and stir in sugar. Add pears; cook, uncovered, over medium heat for 3 to 4 minutes or until just tender, stirring gently. Use a slotted spoon to remove pears; drain on paper towels. Reserve liquid in skillet and boil about 2 minutes or until reduced to 2 tablespoons. Cool pears and liquid.

Before serving, remove the sides of the tart pan. Arrange pear slices in overlapping circles on top of the pudding mix. Brush the pear liquid onto pears and serve immediately. To serve, cut into wedges. Garnish with mint if desired.

Puff Pastry Pear Tart

1 package (8-ounces) cream cheese, at room temperature

1/2 cup sugar

1 egg

1 teaspoon vanilla

1 cup apricot jelly or strained apricot jam

1 teaspoon almond extract

1 box (17-1/4-ounces, 2 sheets pastry) frozen puff pastry, thawed

3/4 cup sliced almonds, toasted

3 ripe pears, such as Bartlett, peeled, cored and thinly sliced

Heat oven to 375 degrees. Beat cream cheese and sugar in medium size bowl with an electric mixer on medium speed until well blended and smooth. On low speed, beat in the egg and vanilla just until blended, scraping down side of bowl with rubber spatula as needed.

Heat jelly in small saucepan over low heat until melted. Stir in almond extract.

On lightly floured surface, roll out one sheet of puff pastry into 15x5-inch rectangle. Fit into 14x4-inch tart pan. Trim off excess dough, prick bottom and sides all over with fork.

Pour cream cheese mixture into tart shell, spreading level. Sprinkle with almonds. Arrange pear slices on top, slightly overlapping. Brush with apricot mixture.

On a lightly floured surface, roll remaining sheet of pastry into a 14x4-inch rectangle. Dust lightly with flour and fold in half lengthwise. With a small sharp knife, cut 8-10 evenly spaced 1/2-inch-long slits along folded edge of pastry.

Brush top edges of pastry in pan with water. Place folded sheet of pastry on top and unfold to fit. Trim pastry if necessary. Crimp edges together to seal. Bake in 375 degree oven for 35-40 minutes or until crust is golden brown. Cool on wire rack for at least 45 minutes. Serve warm.

Almond Pear Tartlets

1 egg, lightly beaten

1/2 cup plus 6 tablespoons sugar, divided

3/4 cup whipping cream

2 tablespoons butter or margarine, melted

1/2 teaspoon almond extract

1 package (10-ounces) frozen puff pastry shells, thawed

2 small ripe pears, peeled and thinly sliced

1/2 teaspoon ground cinnamon

1/8 teaspoon ground ginger

1/2 cup slivered almonds, toasted, optional

In a saucepan, combine the egg, 1/2 cup sugar, cream and butter. Cook and stir until the sauce is thickened and a thermometer reads 160 degrees. Remove from the heat and stir in almond extract. Cover and refrigerate. On an unfloured surface, roll each pastry into a 4-inch circle. Place in an ungreased 15x10x1-inch baking pan. Top each with pear slices. Combine cinnamon, ginger and remaining sugar and sprinkle over pears.

Bake at 400 degrees for 20 minutes or until pastry is golden brown. Sprinkle with almonds if desired. Serve warm with the chilled cream sauce.

Fruit-Topped Lemon Tarts

6 individual graham cracker tart shells

1 can (21-ounces) lemon pie filling

1 can (8-ounce) crushed pineapple, drained

Fruit such as grapes, berries, sliced bananas or kiwi fruit and mandarin oranges or pineapple, cut into chunks

Combine pie filling and crushed pineapple in bowl; mix well. Spoon 1/2 cup into each tart shell. Arrange drained fruit as desired on top of tarts.

Chill until serving time.

Lemon Tarts
Lemon Lover Alert! These tarts could be addictive!!

Crust:

1 1/4 cups flour

1/3 cup sugar

2 teaspoons finely shredded lemon peel

1/2 cup cold butter

1 beaten egg yolk

1 tablespoon water

In medium bowl, mix flour, sugar and lemon peel. Cut in butter until mixture is crumbly.

In small bowl, combine egg yolk and water. Add egg mixture to dry mixture. Mix dough gently just until ball forms. Cover with plastic wrap and chill for 30 to 60 minutes or until easy to handle.

Filling:

(Prepare while pastry is chilling)

2/3 cup sugar

1 tablespoon cornstarch

2 teaspoons finely shredded lemon peel

1/4 cup water

2 tablespoons butter

1/2 cup lemon juice

3 egg yolks, beaten

Powdered sugar and lemon curls for garnish, optional

In medium saucepan, mix sugar and cornstarch. Stir in lemon peel, lemon juice, water and butter. Cook and stir over medium heat until thick and bubbly. Remove from heat.

Beat the egg yolks in small bowl. Slowly stir about half of the hot mixture into the egg yolks. Then return all the egg mixture back to the saucepan stirring constantly. Bring mixture to boil, reduce heat and cook and stir constantly for two more minutes.

Transfer to bowl, cover surface with plastic wrap and chill while pastry shells bake.

Mini-Tarts:

Divide dough into 24 pieces. Press each piece into 2 to 3-inch mini tart or muffin pans. Prick with fork. Place on baking sheet and bake in a 375 degree oven for 12 to 15 minutes or until golden. Cool.. Fill each with about 1 tablespoon filling. Garnish with powdered sugar and lemon curls if desired.

Lemon Meringue Tart

6 egg whites
1 teaspoon vanilla extract
1/8 teaspoon cream of tartar
2 cups sugar, divided
9 egg yolks
1/2 cup lemon juice

1 tablespoon grated lemon peel
4 cups whipping cream
2/3 cup confectioners' sugar
Ground cinnamon

In a mixing bowl, beat egg whites, vanilla and cream of tartar until soft peaks form. Gradually beat in 1 cup sugar, 1 tablespoon at a time, on high speed until stiff glossy peaks form and the sugar is dissolved.

Spread meringue on the bottom and up the sides of a greased 13x9x2-inch baking dish. Bake at 275 degrees for 1 hour. Turn oven off; let stand in oven for 1 hour. Do not open oven door. Remove from the oven and cool on a wire rack.

In the top of a double boiler, combine the egg yolks and remaining sugar. Gradually stir in lemon juice and peel. Cook and stir over simmering water for 15 minutes or until mixture is thickened and reaches 160 degrees. Cover and refrigerate until cool.

In a mixing bowl, beat cream and confectioners' sugar until stiff peaks form. Spread half over meringue; cover with lemon mix. Top with remaining cream mix. Sprinkle with cinnamon. Refrigerate overnight.

Chilly Lemon Tart

Crust:
3/4 cup flour
1/2 cup softened butter or margarine
1/4 cup powdered sugar
Filling:
1 package (2.9-ounces) lemon pudding and pie filling mix, not instant

1/2 cup sugar
2-1/4 cups water
2 egg yolks
1 package (8-ounces) cream cheese
2 cups miniature marshmallows
2 cups whipped topping

(Continued on next page.)

Crust: Beat all crust ingredients on low speed of electric mixer for 1 minute. Beat on medium for 2 minutes or until creamy.

Spread on bottom of ungreased 9-inch springform pan. Bake 12 to 15 minutes at 400 degrees or until golden. Cool.

Filling: In saucepan, mix pudding mix, sugar, water, and egg yolks. Cook, stirring constantly over medium heat until thickened. Remove from heat. Cool slightly. Stir in cream cheese until well blended. Cool completely.

Fold in marshmallows and whipped topping. Spread over crust. Cover and refrigerate at least 3 hours. Store covered in refrigerator.

Lemon Curd Tarts

Pecan Tart Shells:	*Filling:*
1 cup flour	*1 teaspoon unflavored gelatin*
1/2 cup finely chopped pecans	*1 tablespoon cold water*
1/4 cup sugar	*1/2 cup sugar*
1/4 cup butter or margarine, softened	*2 eggs*
1 egg	*2 tablespoons grated lemon peel*
	1/4 cup lemon juice
	2 tablespoons butter or margarine

Preheat oven to 375 degrees. To prepare shells, mix flour, pecans and sugar in medium bowl. Stir in butter and egg until crumbly. Press in bottom and up sides of 24 ungreased mini muffin cups. Bake 10 to 12 minutes until light golden brown. Cool tart shells in pan.

For filling, sprinkle gelatin on cold water in 2-quart saucepan to soften. Beat sugar and eggs in small bowl with electric mixer on medium speed until thick and lemon colored; stir into gelatin mixture. Heat over low heat about 15 minutes, stirring constantly, just until boiling; remove from heat. Stir in lemon peel, lemon juice and butter until butter is melted.

Pour lemon mixture into tart shells. Refrigerate about 1 hour or until set. Store covered in refrigerator.

Crimson Cherry Crunch Tarts

Graham cracker crust
1 egg white, beaten
1 can (21-ounces) cherry pie filling
1 tablespoon lemon juice
1 tablespoon sugar
1 tablespoon light brown sugar
3 tablespoons flour
3 tablespoons quick-cooking oats
2 tablespoons butter or margarine, melted

Preheat oven to 375 degrees. Brush bottoms and sides of crusts with egg white and place on baking sheet.

Bake 2 minutes or until lightly browned. Stir together pie filling and lemon juice and spoon into tart crusts.

Combine remaining ingredients and spoon over pie filling. Bake 20 minutes or until bubbly. Serve warm or at room temperature.

Glazed Cherry Tarts

8 baked tart shells
2 pounds unstemmed dark sweet cherries
1 cup currant jelly
2 packages (3-ounces each) cream cheese, softened
1/4 cup whipped cream

Bake eight 4-inch tart shells and cool. Drop cherries into 3 cups boiling water and reduce heat. Simmer uncovered for 3 minutes. Drain and cool. Remove pits. Heat jelly over low heat until melted. Reserve for later.

Mix cream cheese and whipped cream. Spread 2 tablespoons cheese mixture into bottom of each tart shell. Divide cherries evenly among tart shells. Pour 2 tablespoons jelly over each tart.

Cherry Cheese Pizza

1 cup flour
1/8 teaspoon baking powder
1/4 cup cold butter or margarine
2 tablespoons shortening
3 to 4 tablespoons water
1 package (8-ounces) cream cheese, softened
1/2 cup sugar
2 eggs
1 teaspoon vanilla extract
1/3 cup chopped pecans or almonds

Topping:

2-1/2 cups fresh or frozen pitted tart cherries or 1 can (15 ounces) tart cherries
1/3 cup sugar
2 tablespoons cornstarch
1 tablespoon butter or margarine
1/8 teaspoon almond extract
1/8 teaspoon red food coloring
Whipped cream and fresh mint, optional

In a bowl, combine flour and baking powder; cut in butter and shortening until mixture resembles coarse crumbs. Gradually add water, tossing with a fork until dough forms a ball. Roll out into a 14-inch circle. Place on an ungreased 12-inch pizza pan. Flute edges to form a rim; prick bottom of crust. Bake at 350 degrees for 15 minutes.

In a mixing bowl, beat cream cheese and sugar until smooth. Beat in eggs and vanilla. Stir in nuts. Spread over crust. Bake 10 minutes longer. Cool. Drain cherries, reserving 1/3 cup juice. Set cherries and juice aside. In a saucepan, combine sugar and cornstarch; stir in reserved juice until smooth. Add cherries. Cook and stir over medium heat until mixture comes to a boil. Cook and stir 2 minutes longer. Remove from heat; stir in butter, extract and food coloring. Cool to room temperature; spread over cream cheese layer. Garnish with whipped cream and mint if desired.

Summer-Fresh Strawberry Pastries

1 cup cake flour

1/2 cup confectioners' sugar

1/4 teaspoon ground nutmeg

1/2 cup (1 stick) chilled butter, cut into small pieces

1/4 teaspoon almond extract or vanilla extract

1/4 cup ground almonds (about 1-ounce)

Filling:

5-ounces cream cheese, softened

3 tablespoons sugar

3 tablespoons sour cream

3 tablespoons heavy cream

3 tablespoons seedless strawberry jam

Topping:

2 cups fresh strawberry halves

3-ounces (3 squares) semisweet chocolate, melted

Spray 12 standard size muffin-pan cups with vegetable cooking spray.

In a medium bowl, mix together flour, confectioners' sugar, and nutmeg. Cut butter into flour mixture until coarse crumbs form. Stir in almond extract and nuts. Shape dough into a disk, wrap in plastic wrap, and chill for 30 minutes.

Preheat oven to 400 degrees. On a floured surface, using a floured rolling pin, roll dough to a 1/8-inch thickness. Cut out twelve 4-inch circles. Fit circles into prepared pan. Fold overhang under to form a stand-up edge; flute with fingers.

Bake pastry shells until golden, 10 minutes. Transfer pan to a wire rack to cool completely. Remove shells from pan.

To prepare filling, beat cream cheese and sugar at medium speed until light and fluffy. Beat in sour cream, cream, and jam. Spoon filling into shells.

Arrange strawberries over filling. Drizzle melted chocolate on top. If desired, brush bottoms of shells with 1 ounce (1 square) melted semisweet chocolate.

Coconut Berry Tart

Coconut Pastry:

1 cup flour

3/4 cup shredded coconut

6 tablespoons butter or margarine, softened

2 tablespoons sugar

1 egg yolk

Filling:

1 package (8-ounce) cream cheese, softened

3/4 cup marshmallow creme

3-1/2 cups assorted berries (blueberries, raspberries, strawberries, blackberries)

1/2 cup cut-up peeled kiwi fruit

1/4 cup apricot preserves

1 tablespoon water

Preheat oven to 350 degrees. To prepare pastry, mix all ingredients with fork or hands just until blended. Press firmly on bottom of ungreased 12-inch pizza pan to within 1/2 inch of edge of pan. Prick thoroughly with fork. Bake 20 to 25 minutes or until golden brown. Cool completely.

Mix cream cheese and marshmallow creme with spoon until smooth. Spread over baked crust. Arrange berries and kiwi fruit on top.

Heat preserves and water over low heat, stirring occasionally, until preserves are melted. Cool slightly and spoon over fruit. Store covered in refrigerator.

Strawberry Delight Tart

Crust:
1-1/2 cups flour
3/4 cup butter, melted
3/4 cup chopped pecans
Topping:
2 cups powdered sugar
8-ounces cream cheese, softened
8-ounce carton whipped topping
3 cups fresh sliced strawberries

Glaze:
1 cup sugar
1/4 cup flour
3 tablespoons strawberry flavored gelatin
1 cup water

Whipped topping, optional

Crust: Combine flour and butter; stir in pecans. Pat into tart or pizza pan. Bake at 350 degrees for 20 minutes or until golden. Cool.

Topping: Beat powdered sugar and cream cheese with mixer until combined. Add the whipped topping; beat until smooth. Spread over crust. Arrange strawberries on top. Chill while preparing glaze.

Glaze: In a medium saucepan combine all glaze ingredients. Cook and stir over medium heat until thickened. Cook and stir for 1 more minute. Remove from heat, cover and cool. Spoon cooled glaze over berries. Cover and chill in refrigerator before serving.

Garnish with whipped topping if desired.

Variations: For Peach Delight substitute fresh peaches for berries and peach flavored gelatin for strawberry favored gelatin.

Blackberry Pudding Tarts

1 package (10-ounces) frozen tart shells

2 quarts fresh blackberries or 2 packages (16-ounce) frozen blackberries, thawed

1 cup water

1-3/4 cups sugar, divided

1/2 cup self-rising flour

1/4 cup butter or margarine

2-1/8 teaspoons vanilla extract, divided

1 cup whipping cream

Garnish:

Fresh blackberries

Mint sprigs

Bake tart shells according to package directions; let cool completely.

Bring the blackberries and 1 cup of water to boil over medium heat. Reduce heat to simmer for 5 minutes or until blackberries are soft.

Mash blackberries with a fork; pour through a wire-mesh strainer into a 4-cup liquid measuring cup, using the back of a spoon to squeeze out 2 cups juice. Discard pulp and seeds. (Boil juice to reduce amount to 2 cups, if necessary.)

Combine 1-1/2 cups sugar and flour in a saucepan; gradually add blackberry juice, whisking constantly until smooth. Bring to a boil over medium heat, whisking constantly. Reduce heat, and simmer 3 minutes or until thickened. Remove from heat. Stir in butter and 2 teaspoons vanilla.

Spoon filling into prepared tart shells. Cool completely

Beat whipping cream at high speed with an electric mixer until foamy; gradually add remaining 1/4 cup sugar, beating until stiff peaks form. Fold in remaining 1/8 teaspoon vanilla. Dollop whipped cream over tarts and garnish, if desired.

Walnut-Cranberry Tartlets

Crust:

2 cups flour

1/3 cup sugar

1/8 teaspoon salt

6 tablespoons (3/4 stick) butter, softened

2-3 tablespoons ice water

Filling:

1 cup firmly packed brown sugar

1/2 cup light corn syrup

1/3 cup butter, melted and cooled

4 large eggs

2 tablespoons dark molasses

1 teaspoon vanilla extract

1/8 teaspoon salt

2 cups fresh or frozen cranberries

2 cups coarsely chopped walnuts, toasted (8-ounces)

Preheat oven to 350 degrees. Grease 24 mini muffin-pan cups or 24 tartlet tins. Dust with flour; tap out excess.

In a medium bowl, mix together flour, sugar, and salt. Cut butter into flour mixture until fine crumbs form. Add water, 1 tablespoon at a time, tossing with a fork until a soft dough forms. Shape dough into a disk, wrap in plastic wrap, and chill for 30 minutes.

On a floured surface, roll dough into a 2-inch-thick cylinder. Cut into 1/8-inch-thick slices. Press into prepared cups or tins. Trim dough and make decorative edge, if desired.

To prepare filling, mix together brown sugar, corn syrup, butter, eggs, molasses, vanilla, and salt. Stir in cranberries and nuts. Spoon filling into prepared cups or tins.

Bake tartlets until pastry is golden and cranberries are tender, 20 minutes. Transfer cups or tins to wire racks to cool completely. Using the tip of a knife, loosen tartlets; remove from pan.

Dainty Raspberry-Almond Turnovers

1 cup flour
1/4 teaspoon salt
1/2 cup (1 stick) chilled
butter, cut into small pieces
1 package (3-ounces) chilled
cream cheese, cut into small
pieces

Filling and Garnish:

1 cup raspberry jam or
preserves
1/4 cup coarsely chopped
almonds, toasted (about 1
ounce)
1 large egg, lightly beaten
Confectioners' sugar
Fresh raspberries

In a medium bowl, mix together flour and salt. Cut butter and cream cheese into flour mixture until a soft dough forms. Shape dough into a disk, wrap in plastic wrap, and chill for 3 hours.

Preheat oven to 350 degrees. Spray a baking sheet with vegetable cooking spray.

To prepare filling, mix together jam and nuts.

On a floured surface, divide dough in half. Let rest for 10 minutes. Using a floured rolling pin, roll each dough half into a 16-inch square.

Using a 4-inch round or fancy cookie cutter, cut out 8 circles. Repeat with remaining dough half. Brush edges of each circle with beaten egg.

Place 1 heaping tablespoonful of filling in the center of each circle. Fold pastry over filling. Press edges together to seal. Place turnovers on prepared baking sheet.

Bake turnovers until light golden brown, 20 minutes. Transfer to a wire rack to cool completely. Dust turnovers with confectioners' sugar. Serve with fresh raspberries.

Blueberry-Pecan Cobbler

Recipe for double crust pie
Filling:
4 pints fresh or frozen blueberries
1-1/2 cups sugar
1/2 cup flour
1/2 teaspoon ground cinnamon

1/3 cup water
2 tablespoons lemon juice
1 teaspoon vanilla extract
1/2 cup chopped pecans, toasted
Vanilla ice cream
Garnish:
Fresh mint sprigs

Bring first 7 ingredients of filling to a boil in a saucepan over medium heat, stirring until sugar melts. Reduce heat to low; cook, stirring occasionally, 10 minutes. Spoon half of blueberry mixture into a lightly greased 8-inch square pan.

Roll 1 pie crust to 1/8-inch thickness on a lightly floured surface; cut into an 8-inch square. Place over blueberry mixture; sprinkle with pecans. Bake at 475 degrees for 10 minutes.

Spoon remaining blueberry mixture over baked crust. Roll remaining piecrust to 1/8-inch thickness; cut into 1-inch strips. Arrange in lattice design over blueberry mixture.Bake at 475 degrees for 10 minutes or until golden. Serve with vanilla ice cream, and garnish if desired.

Cranberry Torte

1-1/4 cups graham cracker crumbs (about 20 squares)
1/4 cup finely chopped pecans
1-1/4 cups sugar, divided
6 tablespoons butter or margarine, melted
1-1/2 cups ground fresh or frozen cranberries
1 tablespoon orange juice concentrate

1 teaspoon vanilla extract
1/8 teaspoon salt
1 cup whipping cream
Topping:
1/2 cup sugar
1 tablespoon cornstarch
3/4 cup fresh or frozen cranberries
2/3 cup water

In a bowl, combine cracker crumbs, pecans, 1/4 cup sugar and butter. Press onto the bottom and 1 inch up the sides of a 9-inch

(Continued on next page.)

(Cranberry Torte - continued.)

springform pan. Bake at 375 degrees for 8-10 minutes or until lightly browned. In a bowl, combine the cranberries, orange juice concentrate, vanilla, salt and remaining sugar. In a mixing bowl, beat cream until soft peaks form. Fold into the cranberry mixture. Pour into the crust. Freeze until firm. For topping, combine sugar and cornstarch in a saucepan. Stir in cranberries and water until blended. Bring to a boil. Reduce heat; cook and stir until berries pop and mixture is thickened, about 5 minutes. Cool. Let torte stand at room temperature for 10 minutes before slicing. Serve with topping.

Brunch Berry Pizza

1 cup flour
1/4 cup confectioners' sugar
1/2 cup cold butter or margarine
1/2 cup chopped pecans
1 package (8-ounces) cream cheese, softened
1 egg
1/3 cup sugar

Topping:
1-3/4 cups frozen mixed berries, thawed
1/2 cup sugar
2 tablespoons cornstarch
1/4 cup water
2-1/2 cups fresh strawberries, sliced
2 cups fresh blackberries
2 cups fresh raspberries
1 cup fresh blueberries

In a bowl, combine flour and confectioners' sugar. Cut in butter until crumbly. Stir in pecans. Press into an ungreased 12-inch pizza pan. Bake in a 350 degree oven for 12-14 minutes or until crust is set and edges are lightly browned. Meanwhile, in a mixing bowl, beat cream cheese, egg and sugar until smooth. Spread over crust. Bake 8-10 minutes longer or until set. Cool to room temperature.

For topping, process mixed berries and sugar in a blender or food processor until blended. In a saucepan, combine cornstarch and water until smooth. Add mixed berry mixture. Bring to a boil; cook and stir for 2 minutes or until thickened. Set saucepan in ice water for 15 minutes, stirring mixture several times. Spread berry mixture over the cream cheese layer. Arrange fresh fruit on top. Refrigerate for at least 2 hours or overnight before slicing.

Blackberry Turnovers

1-3/4 cups flour
1/4 cup sugar
1/2 teaspoon salt
2/3 cup chilled solid vegetable shortening, cut into small pieces
2 tablespoons chilled butter
2 tablespoons water

Filling:
2 teaspoons cornstarch
1 tablespoon water
1 package (16-ounces) frozen, thawed blackberries
1 tablespoon sugar
3/4 teaspoon ground cinnamon

Glaze and Garnish:
1 large egg, lightly beaten
Fresh blackberries
Sprigs of fresh mint

In a large bowl, mix together flour, sugar, and salt. Cut shortening and butter into flour mixture until coarse crumbs form.

Stir in water, 1 tablespoon at a time, tossing with a fork until a soft dough forms. Shape into a disk, wrap in plastic wrap, and chill for 1 hour.

To prepare filling, dissolve cornstarch in water. In a medium saucepan, heat blackberries, sugar, and cinnamon over medium heat, stirring occasionally, until mixture boils. Add cornstarch mixture, stirring constantly until thickened. Remove from heat. Cool completely.

Preheat oven to 400 degrees. Grease a baking sheet. On a floured surface, using a floured rolling pin, roll dough to a 1/8-inch thickness. Cut out six 6-inch circles. Gather trimmings, roll to a 1/8-inch thickness, and cut out pastry leaves.

Spoon filling evenly into center of each circle. Fold dough over filling. Press edges to seal. Place turnovers on prepared baking sheet. Brush with some beaten egg. Place pastry leaves on top of turnovers. Brush with remaining egg.

Bake turnovers until golden, 30 minutes. Transfer baking sheet to a wire rack to cool. Garnish with blackberries and mint sprigs.

Pineapple Cheese Torte

Crust:
1 cup flour
1/4 cup confectioners' sugar
1/4 cup finely chopped almonds
1/3 cup butter or margarine, softened

Filling:
2 packages (8-ounces each) cream cheese, softened
1/2 cup sugar

2 eggs
2/3 cup unsweetened pineapple juice

Pineapple Topping:
1/4 cup flour
1/4 cup sugar
1 can (20-ounces) crushed pineapple, juice drained and reserved
1/2 cup whipping cream
Fresh strawberries, optional

Combine crust ingredients and pat into the bottom of a 11x7x2-inch baking dish. Bake at 350 degrees for 20 minutes.

Beat cream cheese in a mixing bowl until fluffy; beat in sugar and eggs. Stir juice into mixture. Pour filling over hot crust.

Bake at 350 degrees for 25 minutes or until the center is set. Cool completely.

Topping: Combine flour and sugar in a saucepan. Stir in 1 cup of reserved pineapple juice. Bring to a boil, stirring constantly. Boil and stir 1 minute. Remove from heat and fold in pineapple. Cool completely.

Whip cream until stiff peaks form and fold into topping. Spread carefully over dessert. Refrigerate at least 6 hours or overnight.

Garnish with strawberries if desired.

Pineapple Cobbler

1 cup sugar
1/3 cup biscuit/baking mix
1 teaspoon grated lemon peel
4 cups fresh pineapple chunks
Topping:
3/4 cup biscuit/baking mix

2/3 cup sugar
1 egg, beaten
1/4 cup butter or margarine, melted
Vanilla ice cream, optional

In a bowl, combine sugar, biscuit mix and lemon peel; stir in pineapple. Pour into a greased 9-inch square baking dish.

Combine biscuit mix, sugar and egg; sprinkle over the top. Drizzle with butter. Bake in a 350 degree oven for 40-45 minutes or until browned.

Serve warm or cold with ice cream if desired.

Giant Pineapple Turnover

Dough for 9-inch pastry
1 medium tart apple, peeled and coarsely chopped
1 can (8-ounces) crushed pineapple, well drained
3/4 cup sugar

1/3 cup finely chopped celery
1/3 cup raisins
1/3 cup chopped walnuts
1/4 cup flour
Ice cream, optional

Roll pastry to 10 to 11-inch circle. In a bowl, combine apple, pineapple, sugar, celery, raisins, walnuts and flour; toss gently. Spoon filling onto half of crust, leaving 1 inch around edge. Fold pastry over filling; seal edge well. Cut slits in top.

Bake in a 400 degree oven for 30-35 minutes or until crust is golden brown and filling is bubbly. Cool on a wire rack. Cut into wedges. Serve with ice cream if desired.

English Almond Tart

1-1/3 cups flour

1/2 cup sugar

1 tablespoon grated lemon zest

1/2 teaspoon salt

1/4 cup (1/2 stick) chilled butter, cut into small pieces

1 large egg, lightly beaten

Filling:

2/3 cup raspberry jam or preserves

3 large eggs

1/2 cup sugar

1 cup ground almonds (4-ounces)

1/3 cup flour

1/2 cup sliced almonds (2-ounces)

In a medium bowl, mix together flour, sugar, lemon zest, and salt. Cut butter into flour mixture until coarse crumbs form. Add egg; mix just until a smooth dough forms. Shape dough into a disk, wrap in plastic wrap, and chill for 1 hour.

On a floured surface, using a floured rolling pin, roll dough into an 11-inch circle. Fit dough into a 9-inch tart pan with removable bottom; trim excess. Make a decorative edge. Chill for 30 minutes.

Preheat oven to 350 degrees. To prepare filling, spread jam evenly over crust. Beat together eggs and sugar at medium speed until very light.

Sprinkle ground nuts and flour over egg mixture; beat at low speed just until smooth. Pour evenly over jam in crust. Sprinkle with sliced nuts.

Bake tart until top is golden brown and set, 30 to 35 minutes. Transfer pan to a wire rack to cool completely. Carefully remove sides of pan.

Pecan Tart with Praline Cream

Recipe for single crust pie
3/4 cup sugar
3/4 cup light corn syrup
1/4 cup butter or margarine
3 large eggs, lightly beaten

1 teaspoon vanilla extract
1/4 teaspoon salt
1 cup pecan halves
1/4 cup semisweet chocolate morsels
Praline Cream (recipe below)

Roll piecrust into a 12-inch circle on a lightly floured surface. Fit into a 10-inch tart pan with removable bottom; trim excess pastry. Prick bottom with a fork, and line with aluminum foil; fill with pie weights or dried beans.

Bake at 450 degrees for 5 minutes. Carefully remove weights and foil; bake 2 additional minutes. Set aside.

Combine sugar, corn syrup and butter in a saucepan over medium heat, stirring constantly, until sugar dissolves and butter melts. Cool slightly. Stir in eggs, vanilla and salt. Pour mixture into prepared piecrust. Top with pecan halves.

Bake at 325 degrees for 55 minutes or until set.

Place chocolate morsels in a small but heavy-duty zip-top plastic bag and seal. Submerge in hot water until chocolate melts. Snip a tiny hole in one corner of bag and drizzle chocolate over tart.

Serve with Praline Cream.

Praline Cream:
1 cup whipping cream
2 teaspoons praline liqueur

1 teaspoon vanilla extract
1/4 cup sifted powdered sugar

Combine first 3 ingredients in a small bowl; beat at medium speed with an electric mixer until it becomes foamy. Add powdered sugar, 1 tablespoon at a time, beating until soft peaks form. Yield: 2 cups

Extra-Special Almond Tart

1-3/4 cups plus 2 tablespoons flour

3/4 teaspoon salt

1/3 cup chilled butter, cut into small pieces

3-4 tablespoons ice water

1 tablespoon lemon juice

Filling:

1 cup blanched slivered almonds (about 4-ounces)

1 cup sugar

3/4 teaspoon ground cardamom

3/4 teaspoon ground cinnamon

1 large potato (10-ounces) peeled, cooked, cooled, and cubed

1/4 teaspoon almond extract

1 large egg

Glaze:

1 large egg

1 tablespoon water

In a medium bowl, mix together flour and salt. Cut butter into flour mix until coarse crumbs form. Add water and lemon juice, 1 tablespoon at a time, tossing with a fork until a soft dough forms. Shape dough into a disk, wrap in plastic wrap, and chill for 30 minutes.

On a floured surface, using a floured rolling pin, roll two-thirds of dough into an 11-inch circle. Press dough into bottom and up sides of a 9-inch tart pan with a removable bottom. Trim overhang; fold edge under. Chill for 10 minutes.

Meanwhile, prepare filling. In a blender or food processor fitted with the metal blade, process nuts, sugar, cardamom, and cinnamon until finely ground. Add potato and almond extract; process until smooth. Add egg; process until combined.

On a floured surface, using a floured rolling pin, roll remaining dough into a 10-inch circle. Cut into eight 1/2-inch strips.

Preheat oven to 350 degrees. Spread filling evenly in prepared crust; smooth top. Arrange dough strips on top of filling in a lattice pattern. Trim ends; pinch to seal.

To prepare glaze, mix together egg and water. Brush pastry edge and lattice with glaze.

Bake tart until golden and a toothpick inserted in the center comes out clean, 45 minutes. Transfer pan to a wire rack to cool completely.

Tempting Tangerine Tart

1-1/4 cups flour
1 tablespoon sugar
1 teaspoon grated lemon peel
1/2 cup (1 stick) chilled butter, cut into small pieces
1 large egg, lightly beaten

Filling:

8 small tangerines
1/3 cup sugar
1/2 cup (1 stick) butter, cut into small pieces
4 large egg yolks
2 large eggs

Topping and Garnish:

4 cans (11-ounces each) mandarin orange segments, drained and patted dry
Candied orange peel strips
Sprigs of fresh mint

In a large bowl, mix together flour, sugar, and lemon peel. Cut butter into flour mixture until coarse crumbs form. Add egg, 1 tablespoon at a time, tossing with a fork until a soft dough forms. Shape into a disk, wrap in plastic wrap, and chill for 45 minutes.

To prepare filling, squeeze juice from tangerines; strain juice. Grate peel from 4 tangerines.

In a medium saucepan, cook tangerine juice, sugar, and tangerine peel over medium heat until sugar dissolves. Stir in butter, egg yolks, and eggs. Reduce heat to low; cook filling, stirring constantly, until thickened, 15 minutes. Chill completely.

Preheat oven to 375 degrees. Press dough into bottom and up sides of a 14 x 4-inch tart pan with a removable bottom. Prick several times with a fork. Line with aluminum foil; fill with pie weights or dried beans.

Bake crust for 20 minutes. Remove foil and weights. Bake until golden, 15 minutes more. Transfer pan to a wire rack to cool completely. Remove sides of pan.

Pour filling into prepared crust; smooth top. Arrange orange segments over filling. Garnish with orange peel strips and mint sprigs.

Fabulous Fruit Tart

8-ounces cream cheese,
softened
1 1/2 cups milk

1 box (3.4 oz.) instant vanilla
pudding mix
1 cup whipped topping

We suggest that you prepare the sugar dough crust for this recipe on page 21. Roll out to fit a 12-inch greased and floured pizza or tart pan.

Filling: Mix cream cheese and milk until smooth. Add pudding mix. Fold in whipped topping.

Spread into cooled crust. Arrange fruit of your choice on top. I have used raspberries, blueberries, kiwi, strawberries and mandarin orange slices. Use your imagination and see what yummy combinations you come up with!

Holiday Cheese Tarts

2 packages (4-ounces)
Graham Cracker pie crusts
1 package (8-ounces) cream
cheese, softened
1 can (14-ounces) sweetened
condensed milk, not
evaporated milk

1/3 cup lemon juice
1 teaspoon vanilla extract
Assorted fruit (strawberries,
blueberries, bananas, orange
segments, raspberries, kiwi,
cherries, grapes, pineapple)
1/4 cup apple jelly, melted
(optional)

With mixer, beat cheese until fluffy. Gradually beat in sweetened condensed milk until smooth. Stir in lemon juice and vanilla. Spoon into crusts. Chill 2 hours or until set.

Just before serving, top tarts with fruit and brush with jelly if desired. Refrigerate leftovers.

Vanilla Cream Fruit Tart

3/4 cup butter or margarine, softened

1/2 cup confectioners' sugar

1-1/2 cups flour

1 package (10-ounces) vanilla chips, melted and cooled

1/4 cup whipping cream

1 package (8-ounces) cream cheese, softened

1 pint fresh strawberries, sliced

1 cup fresh blueberries

1 cup fresh raspberries

1/2 cup pineapple juice

1/4 cup sugar

1 tablespoon cornstarch

1/2 teaspoon lemon juice

In a mixing bowl, cream butter and confectioners' sugar. Beat in flour (mixture will be crumbly). Pat into the bottom of a greased 12-inch pizza pan. Bake at 300 degrees for 25-28 minutes or until lightly browned. Cool. In another mixing bowl, beat melted chips and cream. Add cream cheese and beat until smooth. Spread over crust. Chill for 30 minutes. Arrange berries over filling. In a saucepan, combine pineapple juice, sugar, cornstarch and lemon juice; bring to a boil over medium heat. Boil for 2 minutes or until thickened, stirring constantly. Cool; brush over fruit. Chill 1 hour before serving. Store in the refrigerator.

Summer Fruit Tart

Crust:

4 large eggs

1/2 cup sugar

3/4 cup plus 1 tablespoon flour

Filling, Topping, and Glaze:

1 package (8-ounces) cream cheese, softened

1-2 tablespoons almond liqueur, or 1-2 teaspoons vanilla extract

1/2 cup heavy cream

2 tablespoons sugar

3-4 fresh peaches or nectarines

3/4 cup fresh raspberries

1/4 cup fresh blueberries

2 tablespoons apple jello

Preheat oven to 375 degrees. Grease and lightly flour a 12-inch tart pan.

(Continued on next page.)

(Summer Fruit Tart - continued.)

Crust: Beat together eggs and sugar until blended. Place mixture in the top of a double boiler set over simmering (not boiling) water and heat until just warm.

Remove from double broiler. At high speed, beat egg mixture until tripled. Fold in flour. Spread batter in prepared pan. Bake cake until golden, 20 to 25 minutes. Transfer pan to a wire rack to cool slightly. Turn cake out onto rack to cool completely.

Filling: In a medium bowl, beat together cream cheese and almond liqueur until combined. Beat cream and sugar at high speed until still peaks form.Gently fold whipped cream into cream cheese mixture. Using a flat knife, spread into the center of cooled cake base. Using a sharp knife, thinly slice peaches. Arrange peach slices on top of tart. Add berries in a decorative pattern in center of tart.

Glaze: In a small saucepan, cook jelly over low heat until just warm. Using a pastry brush, spread over top of fruit to preserve color and give dessert a glossy shine.

Norene's Fried Pies

Crust:
3 cups flour
1/2 cup shortening
1 egg
1 cup water
1 tablespoon salt

Filling:
2 (6-ounce) packages dried apricots
3 cups water
1/2 cup cornstarch
1 cup sugar

Crust: Mix ingredients together. Roll dough to 1/4-inch on floured board. Cut into 6-inch rounds or desired size.

Filling: Cook apricots in water about 30 minutes or until softened. Mix cornstarch and sugar together and add to cooked apricots. Stir to thicken.

Place 2 tablespoons of mixture in center of each round. Fold over, press edges together and crimp with a fork to seal. Deep fry in hot oil. Drain on paper towels. These can also be baked. Bake at 375 degrees for 35 to 40 minutes. **Optional:** Before baking brush with egg white and sprinkle with sugar.

White Chocolate-Raspberry Tart

1-1/4 cups flour
1 tablespoon sugar
1/4 teaspoon salt
1/2 cup (1 stick) chilled
butter, cut into small pieces
1 large egg, lightly beaten

Filling:
3-ounces white chocolate,
coarsely chopped
1 cup heavy cream
2-1/2 cups fresh or frozen,
thawed, and drained
raspberries or strawberries

In a medium bowl, mix together flour, sugar, and salt. Using a pastry blender or 2 knives, cut butter into flour mixture until coarse crumbs form. Add egg, 1 tablespoon at a time, tossing with a fork until a soft dough forms. Shape dough into a disk, wrap in plastic wrap, and chill for 1 hour.

Preheat oven to 375 degrees. On a floured surface, using a floured rolling pin, roll dough into an 11-inch circle. Fit into a 9-inch tart pan with a removable bottom. Trim overhang, fold edges under. Prick bottom and sides of dough with a fork. Line dough with aluminum foil; fill with pie weights or dried beans.

Bake crust for 10 minutes. Remove foil and weights. Bake until golden, 10 to 15 minutes more. Transfer pan to a wire rack to cool completely. Remove sides of pan.

To prepare filling, in the top of a double boiler set over simmering (not boiling) water, heat chocolate and 1/4 cup cream, stirring constantly, until melted and smooth. Remove from over water; cool slightly.

Beat remaining cream at medium speed until just thickened. Add chocolate mixture, beating until soft peaks form. Spoon filling into crust. Arrange berries on top of filling.

Creamy Chocolate Tarts

2/3 cup semi-sweet chocolate chips

1/4 cup milk

1 tablespoon sugar

1/2 teaspoon vanilla extract

1/2 cup cold whipping cream

6 (4-ounce) single serving graham crusts

Sweetened whipped cream

Sliced fresh fruit, maraschino cherries or fresh mint

In small microwave-safe bowl, place chocolate chips, milk and sugar. Microwave on high power for 1 minute or until milk is hot and chips melt when stirred. Using whisk or rotary beater, beat until mixture is smooth and stir in vanilla. Cool to room temperature.

In small mixer bowl, beat whipping cream until stiff, carefully fold chocolate mixture into whipped cream until blended. Spoon or pipe into crusts. Cover and refrigerate until set. Top with sweetened whipped cream. Garnish as desired.

Chocolate Peanut Butter Pizza

1/2 cup shortening

1/2 cup peanut butter

1/2 cup packed brown sugar

1/2 cup sugar

2 eggs, lightly beaten

1/2 teaspoon vanilla extract

1-1/2 cups flour

2 cups miniature marshmallows

1 cup (6-ounces) semisweet chocolate chips

In a mixing bowl, cream first four ingredients. Beat in eggs and vanilla. Stir in flour and mix well. Pat into a greased 12-inch pizza pan.

Bake at 375 degrees for 12 minutes. Sprinkle with marshmallows and chocolate chips. Return to the oven for 4-6 minutes or until lightly browned.

Mandarin-Chocolate Tarts

1-3/4 cups flour

1/4 cup unsweetened cocoa powder

1/4 cup sugar

1 teaspoon salt

2/3 cup (1-1/4 sticks) chilled butter, cut into small pieces

3 tablespoons ice water

Filling:

2 cups heavy cream

1/3 cup sugar

2 large eggs

4 large egg yolks

2 teaspoons vanilla extract

Topping and Garnish:

2 cans (4-ounces each) mandarin orange segments, drained

2 tablespoons sugar

Sprigs of fresh mint

In a medium bowl, mix together flour, cocoa powder, sugar, and salt. Cut butter into flour mixture until coarse crumbs form. Add ice water, 1 tablespoon at a time, tossing with a fork until a dough forms. Shape into a disk, wrap in plastic wrap, and chill for 1 hour.

Divide dough into five equal pieces. On a floured surface, roll each piece to a 1/8-inch thickness. Fit dough into five 4-inch tart pans with removable bottoms. Trim even with pan edges.

Preheat oven to 350 degrees. Line crusts with aluminum foil. Fill with pie weights or dried beans. Place tart pans on a baking sheet. Bake crusts until just set, 8 to 10 minutes. Transfer baking sheet to a wire rack to cool completely. Remove foil and weights.

To prepare filling, in a saucepan, cook cream, sugar, eggs, and egg yolks over medium heat until thickened, 10 minutes. Stir in vanilla. Strain filling through a fine sieve. Pour into prepared crusts.

Preheat oven to 300 degrees. Bake tarts until filling is set, 20 to 25 minutes. Transfer baking sheet to a wire rack to cool.

Preheat broiler. For topping, place oranges on top of tarts. Sprinkle with sugar. Place baking sheet under broiler until sugar bubbles, 2 to 3 minutes. Transfer baking sheet to rack to cool completely. Garnish with mint. Makes 5 individual tarts.

White Chocolate Fruit Tart

Crust:
3/4 cup butter, softened
1/2 cup confectioners' sugar
1-1/2 cups flour

Filling:
1 package (10-ounces) white chocolate baking chips, melted
1/4 cup whipping cream
1 package (8-ounces) cream cheese, softened

1 can (20-ounces) pineapple chunks, undrained
1 pint fresh strawberries, sliced
1 can (11-ounces) mandarin oranges, drained
2 kiwi fruit, peeled and sliced

Glaze:
3 tablespoons sugar
2 teaspoons cornstarch
1/2 teaspoon lemon juice

In a mixing bowl, cream butter and sugar. Gradually add flour; mix well. Press into ungreased 11-inch tart pan or 12-inch pizza pan with sides.

Bake at 300 degrees for 25-30 minutes or until lightly browned. Cool.

In a mixing bowl, beat chips and cream. Add cream cheese and beat until smooth. Spread over crust. Chill 30 minutes. Drain pineapple, reserve 1/2 cup juice. Arrange fruit over filling.

In a saucepan, combine glaze ingredients with juice. Boil 2 minutes or until thick over medium heat, stirring constantly. Cool. Brush over fruit. Chill 1 hour before serving. Store in refrigerator.

Tiny Shortbread Tarts

1 cup butter or margarine, softened
1/2 cup confectioners' sugar

2 cups flour
1 can (21-ounces) raspberry, cherry or strawberry pie filling

In mixing bowl, cream butter and sugar. Add flour and mix well. Shape into 1-inch balls and press onto the bottom and up the sides of greased miniature muffin cups. Bake at 300 degrees for 17-22 minutes. Cool for 15 minutes, then carefully remove from pans. Spoon 1 teaspoon of pie filling into each tart cup.

Honey Mousse Tart

1-1/4 cups flour
2 tablespoons sugar
1 teaspoon grated lemon peel
1/4 teaspoon salt
1/2 cup (1 stick) chilled butter, cut into small pieces
1 large egg, lightly beaten
1-3 tablespoons ice water

Filling:
1 teaspoon unflavored gelatin
2 teaspoons orange juice
1/4 cup honey, at room temperature
1-1/2 cups heavy cream

Garnish:
1/4 cup honey, at room temperature

In a large bowl, mix together flour, sugar, lemon peel, and salt. Cut butter into flour mixture until coarse crumbs form. Add egg and ice water, 1 tablespoon at a time, tossing with a fork until a soft dough forms. Shape dough into a disk, wrap in plastic wrap, and chill for 1 hour.

Preheat oven to 375 degrees. On a floured surface, using a floured rolling pin, roll dough into an 11-inch circle. Fit dough into bottom and up sides of a 9-inch tart pan with a removable bottom. Trim overhang. Prick dough with a fork. Line with aluminum foil; fill with pie weights or dried beans.

Bake crust for 10 minutes. Remove foil and weights. Bake until golden, 10 to 15 minutes more. Transfer pan to a wire rack to cool completely. To prepare filling, sprinkle gelatin over juice. let stand until softened, 5 to 10 minutes.

In a small saucepan, heat honey over low heat, stirring until melted. Add gelatin mixture, stirring until gelatin has dissolved. Place pan in a medium bowl of ice water. Stir honey mixture until cool and slightly thickened, 5 minutes.

Beat cream at medium speed until soft peaks form. Fold honey mixture into cream mix. Chill for 4 hours.

Just before serving, stir filling until fluffy and spoon into prepared shell.

To prepare garnish, in a small saucepan, melt honey over low heat. Remove sides of pan. Swirl honey over filling.

Apple Dumplings

Dough:

cup shortening

cups flour

teaspoon salt

egg, beaten

tablespoon vinegar

tablespoons water

Filling:

5-6 medium apples, peeled and sliced

1 tablespoon butter or margarine

2 tablespoons cinnamon sugar to each square of dough

Syrup:

2-1/2 cups sugar

1-1/4 cups water

1-1/2 cubes butter or margarine

Nutmeg

Cut shortening, flour and salt together. Mix egg, vinegar, water; stir into flour mixture. Form a ball; divide and roll dough on floured surface. Cut dough in to ten 6-inch squares, add sliced apples to dough, plus 1 tablespoon margarine and 2 tablespoons cinnamon sugar. Fold over dough or bring corners together and pinch. Bake 30 minutes at 350 degrees. Cook syrup until dissolved. Pour over and around dumplings and bake 15-20 minutes longer.

Variation: Core a whole apple and fill with nuts or raisins, butter and spice mixture. Wrap with dough square and bake according to recipe. Pinch four corners of dough together and fan four edges down to form leaf shapes as illustrated below.

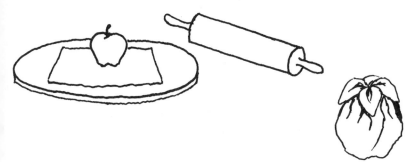

275

Pear Beehive Dumplings

Dough:
1 cup shortening
3 cups flour
1 teaspoon salt
1 egg, beaten
1 tablespoon vinegar
5 tablespoons water

Filling:
6 to 8 pears
Nuts or raisins

1 teaspoon lemon peel
1 tablespoon butter or margarine
2 tablespoons cinnamon sugar to each square of dough

Syrup:
2-1/2 cups sugar
1-1/4 cups water
1-1/2 cubes butter or margarine
Nutmeg

Cut the top off the pear and set aside. Partially core pear (down to about 1/2-inch from bottom of pear. Fill with nuts or raisins butter, lemon peel and spice mixture. Place top back on.

Cut shortening, flour and salt together. Mix egg, vinegar, water stir into flour mixture. Form a ball; divide and roll dough on floured surface. Cut dough into six to eight 12 inch strips. Star at bottom of pear and twist dough around pear, overlapping slightly. To attach a new strip of dough, moisten and crimp to previous strip. Cut decorative leaves for top or use mint leaves after baking and cooling.

Bake 30 minutes at 350 degrees. Cook syrup until dissolved Pour around dumplings and bake 15-20 minutes longer.

Easy Variation:

Filling: 5-6 medium pears, peeled and sliced
1 teaspoon lemon peel
1 tablespoon butter or margarine
2 tablespoons cinnamon sugar to each square of dough

Cut dough into 10 squares; add sliced pears to dough, plus margarine, lemon peel and 2 tablespoons cinnamon sugar. Fold over dough or bring corners together and pinch.

Nut Pies

Sweet Potato Pecan Pie

1 graham cracker pie crust or 9-inch unbaked pastry shell

1 pound yams or sweet potatoes, cooked and peeled

1/4 cup butter or margarine

14-ounce can sweetened condensed milk (Do not use evaporated!)

1 teaspoon each ground cinnamon, grated orange rind and vanilla extract

1/2 teaspoon ground nutmeg

1/4 teaspoon salt

1 egg

Pecan Topping:

1 egg

2 tablespoons each dark corn syrup and firmly packed brown sugar

1 tablespoon melted butter

1/2 teaspoon maple flavoring

1 cup chopped pecans

Preheat oven to 425 degrees. With mixer, beat hot yams and butter until smooth. Add remaining ingredients except crust and pecan topping. Mix well. Pour into crust.

Bake 20 minutes. Meanwhile, prepare pecan topping.

Beat together all ingredients for topping except for the nuts. Stir in nuts. Spoon topping on pie.

Bake 25 minutes longer or until set. Cool. Serve warm or at room temperature. Garnish with orange zest twist if desired. Refrigerate leftovers.

Butter-Nut Pie

4 egg whites, stiffly beaten

1 cup sugar

1 teaspoon baking powder

Pinch of salt

1 cup graham cracker crumbs

1 cup nuts, chopped fine

2 tablespoons melted butter

Whipped cream, optional

Add sugar gradually to beaten egg whites. Fold in remaining ingredients. Pour into a greased 9-inch pie plate. Bake 30 minutes at 350 degrees. Cool. Top with whipped cream if desired.

Coconut Pecan Pie

9-inch unbaked pastry shell
3 eggs
1/2 cup packed light brown sugar
1 cup cream of coconut
1 cup pecan pieces or halves

2 tablespoons melted butter or margarine
1 teaspoon vinegar
1 teaspoon vanilla
Whipped cream
Chopped pecans

Preheat oven to 350 degrees. Beat eggs in medium bowl. Add sugar; stir until sugar dissolves. Add next 5 ingredients; mix well. Spoon into pie shell.

Bake for 30 to 35 minutes or until center is puffed. Cool on wire rack. Chill until serving time. Spoon whipped cream onto servings; sprinkle with chopped pecans. Add 1/2 cup coconut for Double Coconut-Pecan Pie.

Cranberry Pecan Pie

9-inch unbaked pastry shell
3/4 cup firmly packed brown sugar
3/4 cup dark corn syrup
1/4 cup butter, melted

3 eggs
1/8 teaspoon salt
1 cup dried cranberries
1 cup pecan halves

Heat oven to 350 degrees. In large mixer bowl, combine brown sugar, corn syrup, butter, eggs and salt. Beat until well mixed (about 1 to 2 minutes) by hand; stir in cranberries and pecans.

Pour filling into pie shell. Bake for 50 to 55 minutes or until filling is set. Serve with sugared cranberries, if desired.

Chunky Pecan Pie

1-1/2 cups flour

1/2 cup plus 2 tablespoons butter or margarine, softened, divided

1/4 cup packed brown sugar

3 eggs

3/4 cup corn syrup

3/4 cup sugar

1 teaspoon vanilla extract

11-1/2-ounces semi-sweet chocolate chips

1-1/2 cups pecans, coarsely chopped

In a small mixing bowl, beat flour, 1/2 cup butter and brown sugar until crumbly. Press into greased 9 or 10-inch pie pan. Bake at 350 degrees for 12-15 minutes or until lightly browned.

In a medium bowl, beat eggs, corn syrup, sugar, vanilla and remaining butter with a wire whisk. Stir in chocolate chips and pecans. Pour evenly over baked crust. Bake for 35-45 minutes or until set. Cool in pan on wire rack.

Chocolate Chip Pecan Pie

10-inch unbaked pastry shell

4 eggs

1 cup sugar

1 cup light corn syrup

1 teaspoon vanilla

1/2 cup butter or margarine, melted

1 cup chopped pecans

1/2 cup semisweet chocolate chips

Vanilla ice cream, optional

In a mixing bowl, beat eggs, sugar, vanilla and corn syrup. Add butter, mixing well. Stir in pecans and chocolate chips.

Pour into pie shell. Bake at 350 degrees for 50-55 minutes or until set. Top with ice cream for a special treat.

Triple Decker Fudgey Pecan Pie

9-inch unbaked pastry shell

4-ounces German sweet chocolate

1/4 cup butter or margarine

14-ounce can sweetened condensed milk

1/2 cup water

2 eggs, beaten

1 teaspoon vanilla

1/4 teaspoon salt

1/2 cup chopped pecans

Filling:

1 cup cold milk

1 package (3.9-ounces) instant chocolate pudding mix

1 cup whipped topping

Topping:

1 cup whipping cream

1 tablespoon confectioners' sugar

1 teaspoon vanilla

Line unpricked pastry shell with a double thickness of heavy-duty foil. Bake for 5 minutes in a 450 degree oven. Remove foil and set shell aside. Reduce heat to 375 degrees.

In a heavy saucepan, melt chocolate and butter. Remove from heat; stir in milk and water. Add a small amount of melted chocolate mixture to eggs; return all to the pan. Stir in vanilla and salt. Pour into shell; sprinkle with nuts. Cover edges with pie shield and bake for 35 minutes or until a knife inserted near the center comes out clean. Remove to a wire rack and cool completely.

In a mixing bowl, beat milk and pudding mix until smooth. Fold in whipped topping. Spread over nut layer. Cover and refrigerate.

In a mixing bowl, beat cream until soft peaks form. Add sugar and vanilla, beating until stiff peaks form. Spread over pudding layer. Refrigerate until set, about 4 hours.

Picnic Pecan Pie

9-inch unbaked pastry shell
3 eggs
1 cup dark corn syrup
1/2 cup sugar

2 tablespoons butter or
margarine, melted
1 teaspoon vanilla
1/8 teaspoon salt
1 cup chopped pecans

Beat eggs lightly in a bowl. Stir in sugar, corn syrup, vanilla, butter and salt. Add pecans; mix well. Pour into pie shell.

Cover edges with pie shield and bake at 350 degrees for 40 minutes or until a knife inserted in middle comes out clean. Keep leftovers refrigerated.

Maple Walnut Pie

9-inch unbaked pastry shell
1 egg white, beaten
3/4 cup maple syrup
1/4 cup butter or margarine, melted
2 eggs, beaten

1/2 cup packed light brown sugar
3/4 cup chopped banana
1 tablespoon instant coffee granules
3/4 cup chopped walnuts

Brush egg white on surface of pie crust; bake at 375 degrees for 5 minutes. Mix remaining ingredients in bowl until blended; pour into crust. Bake at 350 degrees until toothpick inserted near center comes out clean. . . . about 45-50 minutes. Cool on wire rack.

Toffee Pecan Pie

2 cups flour
1/2 cup confectioners' sugar
1 cup cold butter or margarine, softened
14-ounce can sweetened condensed milk

1 egg
1 teaspoon vanilla
Pinch of salt
6-ounces toffee chips
1 cup chopped pecans

In a mixing bowl, combine flour and confectioners' sugar. Cut in butter until it resembles coarse meal. Press firmly into 10-inch pie plate. Bake at 350 degrees for 15 minutes.

Meanwhile, in another bowl, beat egg, vanilla, salt and milk together. Stir in toffee chips and pecans; spread evenly over baked crust. Bake for another 20-25 minutes or until lightly browned. Cool, then refrigerate.

Butterscotch Pecan Pie

1/2 cup cold butter or margarine
1 cup flour
3/4 cup chopped pecans, divided
8-ounces cream cheese, softened

1 cup confectioners' sugar
8-ounces frozen whipped topping, thawed, divided
3-1/2 cups milk
2 packages (3.4 or 3.5-ounces each) instant butterscotch or vanilla pudding mix

Cut the butter and flour together in a bowl until crumbly. Stir in 1/2 cup chopped pecans. Press into an ungreased pie plate. Bake at 350 degrees for 20 minutes or until lightly browned. Cool.

In a mixing bowl, beat cream cheese and sugar until fluffy. Fold in 1 cup whipped topping; spread over crust. Combine milk and pudding mix until smooth; pour over cream cheese layer. Refrigerate for 15-20 minutes or until set. Top with remaining whipped topping and pecans. Refrigerate for 1-2 hours before serving.

Almond Pie

2 cups flour
1/2 cup confectioners' sugar
1 cup cold butter (Must use butter!!)

Filling:
2 cups sugar

1 cup chopped almonds
2 tablespoons flour
4 eggs, beaten
1/2 cup <u>butter,</u> melted
1/3 cup light corn syrup
1/2 teaspoon almond extract

Combine flour and confectioners' sugar. Cut in butter until mixture resembles coarse crumbs. Press into a greased 10-inch pie plate. Bake at 350 degrees for 10-15 minutes or until lightly browned.

In a bowl, combine sugar, almonds and flour. Stir in remaining filling ingredients. Pour over crust then bake 25-30 minutes or until center is almost set. Cool on wire rack then refrigerate.

Pecan Apple Pie (makes 2 pies)

2 (9-inch) unbaked pastry shells
1 cup sugar
1/3 cup flour
2 teaspoons ground cinnamon
1/4 teaspoon salt
12 cups thinly sliced peeled, tart apples - about 10 apples

Topping:
1 cup packed brown sugar
1/2 cup flour
1/2 cup quick-cooking oats
1/2 cup cold butter or margarine
1/2 to 1 cup chopped pecans
1/2 cup caramel ice cream topping

In large bowl, combine sugar, flour, cinnamon and salt; add apples and toss to coat. Pour into pastry shells.

For topping, combine brown sugar, flour and oats; cut in butter until crumbly. Sprinkle over apples. Cover edges with pie shield and bake at 375 degrees for 55 minutes until bubbly. Sprinkle with pecans, drizzle with caramel topping. Cool on wire racks.

Pecan Pumpkin Pie

30-ounce can pumpkin pie mix

1 cup sugar

1 (5-ounce) can evaporated milk

3 eggs

2 teaspoons ground cinnamon

1/2 teaspoon salt

1 package (18-1/4 ounces) yellow cake mix

1-1/2 cups chopped pecans

1 cup butter or margarine, melted

Caramel Sauce:

1 cup butter or margarine

2 cups packed brown sugar

1 cup whipping cream

Topping:

2 cups whipping cream

3 tablespoons confectioners' sugar

1-1/2 teaspoons vanilla

Line two 9-inch pie plates with waxed paper or parchment paper. Coat the paper with nonstick cooking spray. Set aside.

In a mixing bowl, combine pumpkin, sugar and milk. Beat in eggs, cinnamon and salt. Pour into prepared pans. Sprinkle with dry cake mix. Drizzle with butter. Sprinkle with pecans and press down lightly. Bake at 350 degrees for 50-60 minutes or until golden brown. Cool for 2 hours on wire racks. Carefully run a knife around edge of pan to loosen. Invert pies onto serving plates; remove waxed paper. Chill.

In a heavy saucepan, melt butter over low heat. Add brown sugar and cream. Cook and stir until sugar is dissolved. For topping, in a mixing bowl, beat cream until foamy. Beat in confectioners' sugar and vanilla until soft peaks form.

Cut the pie into slices; drizzle with caramel sauce and garnish with topping.

284

Sweet 'n' Spicy Pecan Pie

9-inch unbaked pastry shell
3 eggs
1 cup dark corn syrup
1/2 cup dark brown sugar
1/4 cup butter or margarine, melted

1 tablespoon Tabasco brand Pepper Sauce
1-1/2 cup pecans, coarsely chopped
Whipped cream, optional

Preheat oven to 425 degrees. Beat eggs lightly in large bowl. Stir in corn syrup, brown sugar, butter and Tabasco sauce. Mix well. Place pecans in prepared pie crust and pour filling over pecans. Bake 15 minutes.

Reduce oven to 350 degrees. Bake pie for 40 minutes or until knife inserted 1 inch from edge comes out clean. Cool pie on wire rack. Serve with whipped cream.

Peanut Supreme Pie

9-inch unbaked pastry shell

Peanut Layer:
1/2 cup chopped peanuts
1/2 cup creamy peanut butter
1/2 cup confectioners' sugar
1/2 cup half-and-half

Filling:
1 can (14 ounces) sweetened condensed milk
1/2 cup creamy peanut butter
1 cup milk
1 package (6-serving size) vanilla instant pudding and pie filling mix (not sugar free)

Topping:
3/4 cup chopped peanuts

For peanut layer, combine 1/2 cup nuts, peanut butter, confectioners' sugar and half-and-half in medium bowl. Stir until well blended. Pour into unbaked crust. Bake at 400 degrees for 20-25 minutes or until crust is golden brown. Do not over bake. Cool completely.

For filling, combine sweetened condensed milk and peanut butter in large bowl. Beat at low speed of electric mixer until well blended. Add milk slowly. Add pudding mix. Increase speed to medium. Beat 2 minutes. Pour over cooled peanut layer. For topping, sprinkle 3/4 cut nuts over filling. Refrigerate 1 hour or more.

Pumpkin Pecan Pie

9-inch unbaked pastry shell
1 tablespoon butter, melted
1-1/4 cups chopped pecans
3 eggs
3/4 cup brown sugar
1/4 cup light corn syrup

1/2 teaspoon each salt, nutmeg, and cinnamon
1 cup hot milk or Half and Half
1-1/2 cups cooked, mashed pumpkin
Pecan halves, optional

Brush pastry shell with melted butter. Sprinkle with chopped pecans. Beat eggs, brown sugar and syrup for 5 minutes. Add salt and spices. Stir in hot milk and pumpkin. Pour into pie shell.

Bake in a 350 degree oven for 50 to 55 minutes. Arrange pecan halves around edge and 3 in center, optional.

Butterscotch-Caramel Praline Pies

Two (9-inch) baked pastry shells
1/2 cup butter*
1 can (7-ounce) coconut
1 cup chopped pecans
16-ounces whipped topping

8-ounces cream cheese, softened
1 can (14-ounces) sweetened condensed milk
1 jar butterscotch-caramel ice cream topping

Melt butter in heavy saucepan over low heat. Stir in coconut and pecans. Cook until coconut is light brown, stirring constantly. Cool to room temperature.

Beat cream cheese and condensed milk in mixer bowl until smooth. Fold in whipped topping. Layer whipped topping mix, coconut mix and ice cream topping 1/2 at a time into pie shells. Chill until serving time.

* Do not substitute margarine for butter

English Pie

Two (9-inch) unbaked pastry shells
2 cups sugar
4 eggs, separated
1/8 pound butter
1 cup pecans
1 teaspoon cloves, allspice and cinnamon, mixed1 cup seedless raisins

Cream sugar, egg yolks and butter together. Add spices, pecans and raisins. Fold in beaten egg whites. Pour into two unbaked pie shells. Bake at 375 degrees for 30 minutes.

Quick Southern Pecan Pie

9-inch unbaked pastry shell
1 cup sugar
1/2 cup corn syrup
1/4 cup melted butter
3 eggs, well beaten
1 cup pecans

Mix sugar, syrup and butter. Add eggs and pecans. Pour mixture into crust. Bake at 400 degrees for 10 minutes, then for 30-35 minutes at 350 degrees. Serve either cold or hot. Top with unsweetened whipped cream, if desired.

Molasses Pecan Pie

8-inch unbaked pastry shell
3 eggs, slightly beaten
3/4 cup molasses
3/4 cup light corn syrup
2 tablespoons butter or margarine, melted
1/8 teaspoons salt
1 teaspoons vanilla
1 tablespoon flour
1 cup pecans

Combine eggs, molasses, corn syrup, melted butter, salt and vanilla in mixing bowl. Make a paste of a small amount of mixture and flour. Stir into remaining mixture. Add pecans. Pour into pastry shell.

Bake at 325 degrees for 1 hour or until firm.

Magical Macadamia Pie
This crustless pie makes a wonderfully cool summer treat!

1 cup graham cracker crumbs plus 2 tablespoons for garnish

1 cup coarsely chopped macadamia nuts

1/3 cup flaked coconut

5 egg whites

1/4 teaspoon salt

1 teaspoon cream of tartar

1-1/4 cups sugar - divided

1 teaspoon vanilla

1 cup whipping cream

Preheat oven to 350 degrees. Grease bottom, sides and rim o 9-inch pie pan. Mix together 1 cup crumbs, nuts and coconut.

Beat egg whites, salt and cream of tartar on high until foamy Gradually beat in 1 cup sugar until stiff peaks form; beat in vanilla. Fold egg whites into coconut mixture. Spoon evenly int pie pan. Bake until golden and firm about 30 minutes. Coo completely.

Beat whipping cream with remaining 1/4 cup sugar until sof peaks form. Spread over cool pie or for a very pretty pie, use a star tip and pipe a rosette border around the edge of the pie and a lattice pattern over top. Sprinkle with remaining crumbs.

Nutty Chocolate Pie

9-inch unbaked pastry shell

1 cup semi-sweet chocolate morsels

2 cups assorted unsalted nuts -cashews, pecans, peanuts, macadamias etc.

3 eggs, lightly beaten

1/2 cup light brown sugar, firmly packed

1/2 cup light corn syrup

2 tablespoons melted butter

1 teaspoon vanilla

Sprinkle chocolate morsels evenly over bottom of unbaked pie shell. Top with nuts. Lightly whisk eggs with light brown sugar, corn syrup, butter and vanilla. Pour mixture slowly over the nuts. Bake in preheated 375 degree oven for 40 to 50 minutes or until golden brown. Cool at least 30 minutes before slicing.

LOW-FAT & UNUSUAL PIES

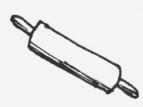

Pumpkin Chiffon Pie

Reduced-fat graham cracker crust

2-3/4 cups cold skim milk

2 packages (1.5-ounces each) instant sugar-free vanilla pudding mix

15-ounce can solid pack pumpkin

1 teaspoon ground cinnamon

1/2 teaspoon ground ginger

1/4 teaspoon ground cloves

Light frozen whipped topping and additional cinnamon, optional

In a mixing bowl, combine milk and pudding mix. Beat for 1 minute . . . mixture will be thick. Add pumpkin and spices; beat 1 minute longer. Pour into pie crust. Cover and refrigerate for 2 hours or until firm. If desired, garnish with whipped topping and sprinkle with cinnamon.

Sugar Free Pumpkin Pie

9-inch unbaked pastry shell

1 can (16-ounces) pumpkin

1 can (12-ounces) evaporated skim milk

3 eggs

5-1/2 teaspoons sugar substitute

1/4 teaspoon salt

1 teaspoon ground cinnamon

1/2 teaspoon ground ginger

1/4 teaspoon ground nutmeg

1/8 teaspoon ground cloves

Beat first 3 ingredients in a medium bowl, then beat in remaining ingredients. Pour mix into pastry shell.

Bake at 425 degrees for 15 minutes. Reduce heat to 350 degrees and bake until knife inserted near center comes out clean, about 40 minutes. Cool on wire rack.

Pumpkin Cloud Pie

Graham cracker pie crust

1 package (8-ounce) fat free cream cheese

3/4 cup fat free whipped topping

1 teaspoon coconut extract

2 cups (15-ounce can) pumpkin

1 package (4 serving) sugar-free instant butterscotch pudding mix

2/3 cup nonfat dry milk

3/4 cup water

1 teaspoon pumpkin pie spice

2 tablespoons flaked coconut

2 tablespoons (1/2-ounce) chopped pecans

In a bowl, stir cream cheese until soft. Add 1/2 cup whipped topping and coconut extract. Mix gently to combine. Set aside.

In a large bowl, combine pumpkin, dry pudding mix, dry milk powder and water. Mix well using a wire whisk. Blend in pumpkin pie spice and remaining 1/4 cup whipped topping.

Spread half of mix into piecrust. Evenly spread cream cheese mixture over pumpkin layer and spread remaining pumpkin mixture over cream cheese mix. Sprinkle coconut and pecans evenly over top. Refrigerate for at least 2 hours.

Pecan-Pumpkin Crumble Pie

Graham cracker pie crust

2/3 cup nonfat dry milk powder

3/4 cup water

2 cups (15-ounces) pumpkin

1/2 cup sugar substitute

2 teaspoons pumpkin pie spice

2 eggs or equivalent in egg substitute

6 tablespoons graham cracker crumbs

1/4 cup (1-ounce) chopped pecans

2 tablespoons brown sugar substitute

(Continued on next page)

Pecan-Pumpkin Crumble Pie - *continued)*

Preheat oven to 375 degrees. In a large bowl, combine milk powder and water. Add pumpkin, sugar substitute, pumpkin pie spice and eggs. Mix well to combine. Spread mixture into piecrust. Bake for 30 minutes.

In a small bowl, combine graham cracker crumbs, pecans and brown sugar substitute. Evenly sprinkle mix over top of pie. Continue baking for 20-25 minutes or until knife inserted near center comes out clean. Place pie plate on wire rack and cool completely.

Chocolate Layer Pie

Reduced fat graham cracker pie crust

1-1/2 cups plus 3 tablespoons cold skim milk

2 (4-serving size) packages chocolate flavored fat free instant pudding and pie filling

1 tablespoon sugar

4-ounces reduced fat cream cheese, softened

1-1/2 cups frozen nondairy light whipped topping thawed

2 teaspoons grated semi-sweet or milk chocolate, optional

Combine 1-1/2 cups milk and pudding mix; with mixer, beat 1 minute (mixture will be very thick). Spoon into crust

With mixer, beat cream cheese, sugar and remaining 3 tablespoons milk until smooth. Fold in whipped topping. Spread over chocolate mixture in crust.

Top with grated chocolate. Chill at least 3 hours. Refrigerate leftovers.(35% less grams of fat than recipe made with full-fat ingredients.)

Low Fat Chocolate Chip Pie

Crust:
1/2 cup Grape Nuts cereal
2-1/2 tablespoons sugar
1/2 teaspoon butter flavor sprinkles

Filling:
1 cup reduced fat egg product
1-1/3 cups sugar
1/3 cup flour

1-1/2 tablespoons butter flavor sprinkles
1 teaspoon vanilla extract
1/4 teaspoon almond extract
1/3 cup fat free sour cream
1/3 cup semi sweet chocolate chips
Mini chocolate chips, optional

Sprinkle cereal evenly over bottom of 9-inch pie plate sprayed with nonstick cooking spray. Sprinkle evenly with 2-1/2 tablespoons sugar and 1/2 teaspoon butter flavor sprinkles. Set aside. In medium bowl, using mixer, combine egg product, sugar, flour, butter flavor sprinkles, extracts and sour cream. Cream until smooth. Gently pour slowly over cereal crust, trying not to disturb crust. Evenly sprinkle the chocolate chips on top of filling until all chips are used. These will gradually sink into filling. Sprinkle mini chips on top for garnish. Bake at 325 degrees for 50 minutes.

Chocolate Cherry Cream Pie

Chocolate pie crust

1 package (4 serving) sugar-free cook-and-serve chocolate pudding mix

1 package (4 serving) sugar-free strawberry gelatin

1-1/2 cups water

2 cups (16-ounces) tart red cherries, packed in water

1 teaspoon almond extract

1 package (4 serving) sugar-free instant chocolate pudding mix

2/3 cup nonfat dry milk powder

1/2 cup fat free whipped topping

2 tablespoon slivered almonds

(Continued on next page)

In a saucepan, combine pudding mix, gelatin, and 1/2 cup water. Stir in undrained cherries. Cook over medium heat until mix thickens and starts to boil, stirring often, being careful not to crush cherries. Remove from heat. Stir in almond extract. Let set for 5 minutes.

Spoon cherry mixture into pie crust. Refrigerate for at least 30 minutes.

Meanwhile, in a bowl, combine instant pudding, milk powder and remaining 1 cup water. Mix well. Blend in fat free whipped topping. Spread mix evenly over cherry filling. Sprinkle almonds over top. Refrigerate for at least 1 hour.

Lower Cal Marbled Cheesecake

1 cup (about 35 wafers) reduced-fat chocolate wafer crumbs

2 tablespoons margarine, melted

3 packages (8-ounces each) cream cheese, softened

1-1/4 cups sugar

1 tablespoon all-purpose flour

Egg substitute equivalent to

2 eggs (see package)

1 cup (8-ounces) light sour cream

2 teaspoons vanilla extract

2 squares (1-ounce each) semisweet chocolate, melted and cooled

Fresh raspberries and chocolate curls, optional

Combine wafer crumbs and margarine. Press onto the bottom of a greased 9-inch springform pan. Set aside.

In a mixing bowl, beat cream cheese and sugar until smooth. Add flour and beat well. Beat in egg substitute, sour cream and vanilla just until blended. Remove 1-1/2 cups batter to a small bowl and stir in chocolate until well blended. Pour half of remaining plain batter over crust. Top with half of chocolate batter and repeat layers. Cut through batter with a knife to swirl the chocolate.

Bake at 325 degrees for 55-60 minutes or until center is almost set. Cool on a wire rack for 1 hour. Cover and refrigerate for at least 4 hours. Top of cake will crack.

Remove sides of pan. Garnish with raspberries and chocolate curls if desired.

Mint Chocolate Sundae Pie

Chocolate pie crust

2 cups sugar-free and fat-free vanilla ice cream

6-8 drops green food coloring

1 teaspoon mint extract

1 package (4 serving) sugar-free chocolate cook-and-serve pudding mix

2/3 cup nonfat dry milk powder

2/3 cup water

1/2 cup (1-ounce) miniature marshmallows

1/2 cup fat free whipped topping

1 tablespoon (1/4 ounce) miniature chocolate chips

Place ice cream in large bowl and let set for 10 minutes to soften. Add 4-6 drops green food coloring and 1/2 teaspoon mint extract. Mix well until mix is combined. Spread mix into pie crust. Cover and place in freezer while preparing chocolate sauce.

Combine pudding mix, milk powder, and water in a medium saucepan. Cook over medium heat until mix thickens and starts to boil, stirring constantly. Remove from heat. Stir in marshmallows. Mix well until mixture is smooth. Cool for 10 minutes. Drizzle chocolate sauce evenly over top of ice cream mixture.

In a small bowl, combine whipped topping, remaining 1/2 teaspoon mint extract, and remaining food coloring. Top pie with whipped topping and sprinkle with chocolate chips.

Cover and freeze for at least 4 hours. Let set at room temperature for at least 15 minutes before serving.

Chocolate Banana Meringue Pie

9-inch baked pastry shell

1 package (4 serving) sugar-free chocolate cook-and-serve pudding mix

2/3 cup nonfat dry milk powder

1-1/2 cups water

1-1/2 teaspoons rum extract

1/4 cup chopped pecans

2 cups (2 medium) sliced bananas

6 egg whites

6 tablespoons sugar substitute

1 tablespoon miniature chocolate chips

In a saucepan, combine pudding mix, milk powder, and water. Cook over medium heat until mix thickens and starts to boil, stirring constantly. Remove from heat. Stir in 1 teaspoon rum extract and pecans. Let set 5 minutes.

Meanwhile, layer bananas in bottom of pie crust. Evenly spoon partially cooled pudding mix over bananas. Beat egg whites with an electric mixer until soft peaks form. Add remaining 1/2 teaspoon rum extract and sugar substitute. Continue beating until stiff peaks form. Spread meringue mix evenly over filling, being sure to seal completely to edges of piecrust. Evenly sprinkle chocolate chips over top.

Bake for 15 minutes at 350 degrees or until meringue starts to turn golden brown. Allow pie to cool for 15 minutes. Refrigerate for at least 1 hour.

Sugarless Apple Pie

9-inch unbaked pastry shell

6 cups sliced peeled tart apples (about 4 large)

1/3 cup apple juice concentrate

2 tablespoons quick-cooking tapioca

1 teaspoon ground cinnamon

1/4 cup finely chopped walnuts

In a large bowl, combine the apples and next three ingredients; let stand for 15 minutes. Stir and pour into pastry shell. Sprinkle with nuts.

Bake at 425 degrees for 15 minutes. Reduce heat to 350 degrees. Bake 40 -50 minutes longer or until apples are tender.

Sugar Free Apple Pie

Pastry for double crust pie

5 apples, peeled, cored and thinly sliced

1 large can concentrated apple juice (frozen)

1/4 cup tapioca

1 teaspoon cinnamon

Combine juice concentrate, tapioca and cinnamon. Cook over medium heat, stirring constantly until mix comes to a boil. Add apples and simmer for 15 minutes. Pour into unbaked pie shell and cover with top crust. Bake at 375 degrees for 30 minutes or until lightly browned.

Low Calorie Coconut Apple Pie

Graham cracker pie crust

1 package (4 serving) sugar-free vanilla cook-and-serve pudding mix

1-1/3 cups water

1-1/2 teaspoons coconut extract

1 teaspoon apple pie spice

1/4 cup raisins

3 cups cored, unpeeled, and diced cooking apples

3/4 cup fat free whipped topping

2 tablespoons flaked coconut

In a saucepan, combine pudding mix and water. Add 1 teaspoon coconut extract and apple pie spice. Stir in apples and raisins. Cook over medium heat until mix thickens and apples become soft, stirring constantly. Remove from heat. Allow to cool for 10 minutes.

Spread partially cooled mixture evenly into pie crust. Refrigerate for at least 1 hour. In a small bowl, combine fat free whipped topping and remaining 1/2 teaspoon coconut extract. Spread mix evenly over filling. Evenly sprinkle coconut over top.

Apple Pizza Pie

9-inch unbaked pastry shell

3 cups (6 small) cored, unpeeled, and sliced apples

1/4 cup brown sugar substitute

1 teaspoon apple pie spice

1/4 cup (1-ounce) chopped pecans

3/4 cup (3-ounces) shredded reduced-fat Cheddar cheese

Preheat oven to 450 degrees. Place pie crust in center of 12-inch pizza pan. Press pie crust to fit pan. Evenly sprinkle apples over crust.

In a small bowl, combine brown sugar substitute, apple pie spice, and pecans. Sprinkle mixture evenly over apples. Top with Cheddar cheese. Bake for 10-12 minutes.

Apple Raisin Meringue Pie

9-inch unbaked pastry shell

1 package (4 serving) sugar-free vanilla cook-and-serve pudding mix

1 cup unsweetened apple juice

1/2 cup water

2 cups (4 small) cored, unpeeled, and diced cooking apples

1/4 cup raisins

1 teaspoon apple pie spice

6 egg whites

1 teaspoon vanilla extract

6 tablespoons sugar substitute

Preheat oven to 450 degrees. Place crust in a 9-inch plate. Flute edges and prick bottom and sides with fork. Bake for 9-11 minutes or until lightly browned.

In a saucepan, combine pudding mix, apple juice, water. Add fruit and apple pie spice. Cook over medium heat until apples are soft, stirring often. Pour hot apple mix into partially cooled pie crust. Continue baking for 10 minutes.

In a medium bowl, beat egg whites with an electric mixer until soft peaks form. Add vanilla extract and sugar substitute. Continue beating until stiff peaks form. Spread meringue evenly over hot apple filling, being sure to seal edges.

Bake at 450 degrees for 5-6 minutes or until lightly browned.

Sour Cream Apple Walnut Pie

Graham cracker pie crust

1 package (4 serving) sugar-free vanilla cook-and-serve pudding mix

1 cup unsweetened apple juice

1 teaspoon apple pie spice

2 cups cored, peeled, and diced cooking apples

1/4 cup chopped walnuts

1/2 cup no fat sour cream

6 tablespoons graham cracker crumbs

In a saucepan, combine pudding mix and apple juice. Cook over medium heat until mix thickens and starts to boil, stirring constantly. Remove from heat. Stir in apple pie spice. Add apples and walnuts. Mix well to combine. Fold in sour cream. Spread mix into pie crust. Evenly sprinkle graham cracker crumbs over top.

Bake for 30 minutes at 375 degrees. Cool completely.

Low Calorie Cherry Tarts

1 package (6 single serve) graham cracker crusts

2 cups (one 16-ounce can) tart red cherries, packed in water, drained, and 1/2 cup liquid reserved

3/4 cup water

1 package (4 serving) sugar-free cherry gelatin

1 package (4 serving) sugar-free vanilla pie mix

1/2 cup fat free whipped topping

1 teaspoon vanilla extract

1 tablespoon unsweetened cocoa

1 tablespoon (1/4-ounce) mini chocolate chips

In a saucepan, combine reserved cherry liquid, water, dry gelatin, and pudding mix. Stir in cherries. Cook over medium heat until mixture thickens and starts to boil, stirring constantly, being careful not to crush the cherries. Remove from heat. Cool for 10 minutes.

Evenly spoon cherry mix into graham cracker crusts. Refrigerate for at least 1 hour. In a small bowl, combine whipped topping, vanilla extract and cocoa. Evenly spoon mixture over filling. Sprinkle with 1/2 teaspoon chocolate chips over each tart.

Tart Cherry Pie

9-inch baked pastry shell

2 cans (16-ounces each) pitted tart cherries

1 package (8-ounce) cook and serve sugar-free vanilla pudding mix

1 (3-ounce) package sugar-free cherry gelatin

Artificial sweetener equivalent to 4 teaspoons sugar

Drain cherries, reserving juice; set cherries aside. In a saucepan, combine cherry juice and dry pudding mix. Cook and stir until mixture comes to a boil and is thickened and bubbly.

Remove from the heat; stir in gelatin powder and sweetener until dissolved. Stir in the cherries; transfer to pastry shell. Cool completely. Store in the refrigerator.

Low Calorie Peach Tarts

1 package (6 single serve) graham cracker crusts

1 package (4 serving) sugar-free vanilla cook and serve pudding mix

1 package (4 serving) sugar-free lemon gelatin

3 cups (6 medium) peeled and coarsely chopped fresh peaches

1/2 cup water

1/4 teaspoon ground nutmeg

6 tablespoons lite whipped topping

In a medium saucepan, combine pudding mix and gelatin. Place 1 cup peaches and water in a blender container. Cover and process until mix is smooth. Pour mixture into saucepan with pudding and gelatin. Stir in remaining 2 cups peaches. Cook over medium heat until mix thickens and starts to boil, stirring constantly. Remove from heat.

Stir in nutmeg. Evenly spoon hot mixture into graham cracker crusts. Refrigerate for at least 2 hours. When serving, top each with 1 tablespoon lite whipped topping. If desired, lightly sprinkle additional nutmeg over whipped topping

Peach Custard Pie

9-inch unbaked pastry shell

3 cups (6 medium) peeled and sliced fresh peaches

1/2 cup sugar substitute

6 tablespoons flour

1/2 teaspoon ground nutmeg

2/3 cup nonfat dry milk powder

1 cup water

1/4 cup sliced blanched almonds

Preheat oven to 350 degrees. Evenly arrange peaches in pie crust. In a small bowl, combine sugar substitute, flour, nutmeg, and dry milk powder. Add water. Mix well to combine. Spread mix evenly over peaches. Sprinkle almonds evenly over top.

Bake for 50-60 minutes or until filling is set. Place pie plate on a wire rack and allow to cool completely.

Peach Banana Cream Pie

Graham cracker pie crust

1 cup (1 medium) diced banana

1 package (4 serving) sugar-free banana cream pudding mix

2/3 cup nonfat dry milk powder

1/4 cups water

3/4 cup lite whipped topping

6 tablespoons peach spreadable fruit

2 tablespoons (1/2-ounce) chopped pecans

Layer banana in bottom of pie crust. In a bowl, combine pudding mix, milk powder, and water. Mix well. Blend in 1/4 cup whipped topping and spreadable fruit. Spread pudding mix evenly over banana. Refrigerate for 5 minutes. Spread remaining whipped topping over pie. Evenly sprinkle pecans over top. Refrigerate for at least 1 hour.

Peach Crumb Pie

9-inch unbaked pastry shell

4 cups (two 16-ounce cans) peaches, drained, and 1 cup liquid reserved

1/4 cup water

1 package (4 serving) sugar-free vanilla cook-and-serve pudding mix

1 package (4 serving) sugar-free lemon gelatin

6 tablespoons reduced fat baking mix

2 tablespoons sugar substitute

2 teaspoons reduced-calorie margarine

1 tablespoon chopped pecans

Preheat oven to 375 degrees. In a saucepan, combine peach liquid, water, pudding mix, and gelatin. Mix well to combine. Coarsely chop peaches. Stir peaches into pudding mix. Cook over medium heat until mixture thickens and starts to boil, stirring often.

Spoon hot peach mixture into crust. In a medium bowl, combine baking mix, sugar substitute and margarine. Mix well using a fork until mix becomes crumbly. Stir in pecans. Evenly sprinkle crumb mixture over peach filling. Bake for 50-55 minutes.

Rocky Road Pistachio Pie

Chocolate pie crust

1 package (4 serving) sugar-free instant pistachio pudding mix

2/3 cup nonfat dry milk powder

1 cup (8-ounces) crushed pineapple, drained, and 1/4 cup liquid reserved

1 cup water

3/4 cup fat free whipped topping

2 tablespoons (1/2-ounce) miniature chocolate chips

1 teaspoon coconut extract

1 tablespoon flaked coconut

In a bowl, combine pudding mix and milk powder. Add pineapple liquid and water. Mix well. Blend in 1/4 cup whipped topping, chocolate chips, and half of crushed pineapple. Spread mix into pie crust.

In a small bowl, combine remaining 1/2 cup whipped topping, remaining pineapple, and coconut extract. Frost pie with whipped topping mix. Sprinkle coconut evenly over the top. Refrigerate for at least 30 minutes.

Fluffy Pistachio Pie

1/2 cup reduced-fat margarine
softened
1 cup flour
1/2 cup confectioners' sugar
1/2 cup chopped walnuts

First Layer:

8-ounces fat-free cream cheese,
softened
8-ounces nonfat sour cream
8-ounces frozen light whipped
topping, thawed

Second Layer:

3 cups cold skim milk
2 packages (1-ounce each)
sugar-free fat-free instant
pistachio pudding mix

Topping:

1 (8-ounce) carton frozen
light whipped topping, thawed
2 tablespoons ground
walnuts*

In a mixing bowl, cream the margarine. Add flour and sugar; blend until crumbly. Stir in walnuts. Press onto the bottom and up the sides of a 10-inch pie pan coated with nonstick cooking spray. Bake at 375 degrees for 10-12 minutes or until set. Cool.

In a mixing bowl, beat cream cheese and sour cream. Fold in whipped topping. spread over crust. In another mixing bowl, combine milk and pudding mixes; beat on low speed for 2 minutes. Spread over first layer. Carefully spread whipped topping over second layer. Sprinkle with walnuts. chill at least 1 hour.

• Chopped pistachios can be substituted for the walnuts.

Pear Pistachio Pie

1 (6-ounce) shortbread pie
crust
2 cups (16-ounces) pear
halves, drained, and 1/2 cup
liquid reserved
1 package (4 serving) sugar-
free instant vanilla pudding
mix
1 package (4 serving) sugar-
free cherry gelatin

1-1/3 cups nonfat dry milk
powder
1-2/3 cups water
3/4 cup fat free whipped
topping
1 package (4 serving) sugar-
free instant pistachio pudding
mix
4 maraschino cherries, halved

(Continued on next page.)

310

Coarsely chop pears. Evenly arrange in bottom of piecrust.

In a bowl, combine vanilla pudding mix, gelatin, and 2/3 cup milk powder. Add reserved pear liquid and 2/3 cup water. Mix well. Blend in 1/4 cup whipped topping. Spread mix evenly over pears. Refrigerate while preparing topping.

Combine pistachio pudding mix, remaining 2/3 cup milk powder and remaining 1 cup water. Mix well. Blend in remaining 1/2 cup whipped topping. Spread topping mixture evenly over cherry layer. Garnish with maraschino cherry halves. Refrigerate for at least 1 hour.

Strawberry-Pear Tarts

1 package (6 single serve) graham cracker crusts

1 package (4 serving) sugar-free instant vanilla pudding mix

2/3 cup nonfat dry milk powder

1 cup water

1 cup (8-ounces) sliced pears, drained, and 1/4 cup liquid reserved

1 package (4 serving) sugar-free strawberry gelatin

2 teaspoons cornstarch

1 cup sliced fresh strawberries

Combine pudding mix, milk powder, and water. Mix well. Fold in pears. Evenly spoon mixture into graham cracker crusts. Refrigerate while preparing topping.

In a saucepan, combine gelatin, cornstarch, reserved 1/4 cup pear liquid, and strawberries. Cook over medium heat until mixture thickens and starts to boil, stirring constantly. Remove from heat. Cool for 10 minutes. Evenly spoon mixture over pears in graham cracker crusts. Refrigerate for at least 30 minutes.

Low Fat Strawberry Cream Cheese Pie

Crust:
2 large flour tortillas

1/2 teaspoon butter flavor sprinkles

Butter flavored nonstick cooking spray

Filling:
1 envelope unflavored gelatin

1/2 cup hot water

1 (16-ounce) package frozen strawberries with sugar

12-ounce carton fat free cream cheese

1/3 cup sugar

Topping:
1/2 envelope unflavored gelatin

1/2 cup hot water

1-1/2 cups fat free sour cream

1/3 cup sugar

1/2 teaspoon vanilla extract

For crust, preheat oven to 350 degrees. Place 1 tortilla in deep 9-1/2-inch pie plate sprayed with nonstick cooking spray. Spray tortilla lightly with butter spray and sprinkle with butter flavor sprinkles. Place second tortilla on top and lightly spray with butter spray. Spray outside bottom of another empty pie plate and set it down inside and on top of tortillas for baking. Bake for 13 minutes. Remove and cool. Remove extra pie plate. Cool thoroughly before adding filling.

For filling, stir gelatin into hot water until dissolved. Combine with remaining ingredients in food processor and mix. Pour into prepared crust.

For topping, stir gelatin into hot water until dissolved. Combine with remaining ingredients and mix with electric mixer. Pour gently over filling. Chill several hours or overnight.

Sugar Free Strawberry Pie

Graham cracker crust

1 small package sugar-free vanilla pudding, cooked variety

1 small package sugar-free strawberry gelatin

2 cups water

1 teaspoon vanilla3 packages (individual serving size) artificial sweetener

2 cups sliced fresh strawberries

Combine pudding mix, gelatin, water and vanilla. Cook and stir until thickened. Set aside to cool.

Prepare strawberries and sprinkle with sweetener. When pudding mix has cooled, fold in the strawberry mix and pour into crust.

Refrigerate for an hour or overnight before serving. Top with whipped topping.

Fruit and Berry Pie

1 (6-ounce) graham cracker pie crust

1 cup (1 medium) sliced banana

2 cups sliced fresh strawberries

1 package (4 serving) sugar-free vanilla cook-and-serve pudding mix

1 package (4 serving) sugar-free strawberry gelatin

1 cup (8-ounces) crushed pineapple, undrained

1-1/4 cups water

1/2 cup lite whipped topping

Layer banana and strawberries in bottom of pie crust. In a saucepan, combine pudding mix, gelatin, undrained pineapple and water. Cook over medium heat until mixture thickens and starts to boil, stirring constantly.

Spoon mixture evenly over top of fruit. Refrigerate for at least 2 hours. Cut into 8 servings. Top each piece with 1 tablespoon lite whipped topping.

Low Fat Strawberry and Banana Pie

Crust:
1 cup all purpose flour
3/4 teaspoon lite salt
1/3 cup light corn syrup
2 tablespoons skim milk

Filling:
1 pint fresh strawberries
3/4 cup water

1/2 cup sugar
2-1/2 tablespoons cornstarch
1 large banana or 2 small ones
Red food coloring

Topping:
1 envelope whipped topping
1/2 cup cold skim milk
1 teaspoon vanilla

Spray a 9-inch pie pan with nonfat cooking spray. Mix all the crust ingredients until moistened. Form into a ball and roll out on a floured surface to fit pie pan. Do not overwork the dough. Prick bottom of crust and bake at 475 degrees for 10 minutes or until golden brown.

For filling, wash, hull and slice strawberries in half. Place in saucepan with water and 1/2 teaspoon food coloring. Bring to boil. When it reaches a full boil, add sugar and cornstarch that has been mixed together. Stir until thickened and clear. Remove from heat, refrigerate.

When cooled, slice banana and layer in bottom of baked cooled crust. Pour strawberry filling over bananas and return to refrigerator until time to serve. Whip topping ingredients together. Spread over pie.

Strawberry Cream Pie

Shortbread pie crust
2 packages (4 serving) sugar-free instant vanilla pudding mix
1-1/3 cup nonfat dry milk powder
2-1/3 cups diet clear soda
1/3 cup fat free whipped topping

1 teaspoon coconut extract
2 cups medium-sized fresh strawberries, halved
6 tablespoons strawberry spreadable fruit
2 tablespoons flaked coconut

(Continued on next page.)

(Strawberry Cream Pie - *continued*)

In a large bowl, combine pudding mixes, milk powder, and soda. Mix well. Blend in whipped topping and coconut extract. Spread mix into pie crust. Refrigerate for 5 minutes.

Evenly arrange strawberry halves, cut-side down, over pudding mixture. Place spreadable fruit in a small glass dish. Microwave on high for 45 seconds. Evenly spoon warm spreadable fruit over strawberries. Refrigerate for at least 1 hour. Just before serving, evenly sprinkle coconut over top.

Low-Cal Strawberry Daiquiri Pie

Graham cracker pie crust

2 cups fresh whole strawberries

1/2 cup diet clear soda

1 package (4 serving) sugar-free instant vanilla pudding mix

1 package (4 serving) sugar-free strawberry gelatin

2/3 cup nonfat dry milk powder

2 tablespoons lemon juice

2 tablespoons lime juice

1 cup lite whipped topping

1 teaspoon rum extract

Reserve 4 whole strawberries. In a blender container, combine remaining strawberries and soda. Cover and process on blend for 15 seconds or until mix is smooth.

In a large bowl, combine pudding mix, gelatin, and milk powder. Add blended strawberry mixture, lemon, and lime juice. Mix well. Blend in 1/2 cup whipped topping and rum extract. Spread mixture into pie crust. Drop remaining 1/2 cup whipped topping by tablespoon to form 8 mounds.

Cut reserved strawberries in half and garnish each mound with a half. Refrigerate for at least 1 hour.

Rhubarb Custard Pie

9-inch unbaked pastry shell

1 package (4 serving) sugar-free vanilla cook-and-serve pudding mix

3/4 cup water

3 cups diced fresh or frozen rhubarb

6 tablespoons reduced fat baking mix

2 tablespoons sugar substitute

1 tablespoon plus 1 teaspoon reduced calorie margarine

Preheat oven to 450 degrees. Place crust in a 9-inch pie plate. Flute edges, prick bottom and sides with fork. Bake 9-11 minutes or until lightly browned.

In a saucepan, combine pudding mix, water, and rhubarb. Cook over medium heat until thickened and rhubarb is soft. Stir often. Spoon hot mix into crust. In a medium bowl, combine baking mix and sugar substitute. Add margarine, mix with a fork until crumbly. Evenly sprinkle mix over filling.

Bake 15 minutes; lower heat to 350 and bake for another 30 minutes.

Rhubarb Meringue Pie

9-inch unbaked pastry shell

1 package (4 serving) sugar-free vanilla cook-and-serve pudding mix

1 package (4 serving) sugar-free strawberry gelatin

3/4 cup water

3 cups finely diced fresh or frozen rhubarb

1-1/2 teaspoons coconut extract

6 egg whites

6 tablespoons sugar substitute

2 tablespoons flaked coconut

Preheat oven to 450 degrees. Place crust in a 9-inch pie plate. Flute edges and prick bottom and sides with fork. Bake 9-11 minutes or until lightly browned. Lower heat to 350 degrees.

(Continued on next page.)

(Rhubarb Meringue Pie - *continued*)

In a saucepan, combine pudding mix, gelatin, and water. Stir in rhubarb. Cook over medium heat until rhubarb becomes soft and mixture starts to boil, stirring often. Stir in 1 teaspoon coconut extract. Pour hot mixture into cooled pie crust.

In a large bowl, beat egg whites with an electric mixer until soft peaks form. Add sugar substitute and remaining 1/2 teaspoon coconut extract. Continue beating until stiff peaks form. Spread meringue mixture evenly over filling mixture, being sure to seal to edges of pie crust. Evenly sprinkle coconut over top.

Bake for 12-15 minutes or until meringue starts to turn golden brown. Allow pie to cool.

Lime Raspberry Cream Pie

Shortbread pie crust

1 package (4 serving) sugar-free instant vanilla pudding mix

1 package (4 serving) sugar-free lime gelatin

2/3 cup nonfat dry milk powder

1-1/3 cups water

1 cup fat free whipped topping

1-1/2 cups fresh red raspberries

Lime slices for garnish, optional

In a bowl, combine pudding mix, gelatin, and milk powder. Add water. Mix well. Blend in 1/4 cup whipped topping. Reserve 8 raspberries. Fold remaining raspberries into pudding mixture. Spread mixture into pie crust. Refrigerate for 10 minutes.

Spread remaining 3/4 cup whipped topping over set filling. Garnish top with reserved raspberries and lime slices. Refrigerate for at least 1 hour.

Key Lime Pie

1 cup graham cracker crumbs

3 tablespoons melted margarine

1 teaspoon sugar-free sweetener

1 envelope (1/4 ounce) unflavored gelatin

1-3/4 cups skim milk, divided

1 package (8-ounces) reduced-fat cream cheese, softened

1/3-1/2 cup fresh lime juice

3-1/2 teaspoons sugar free sweetener

Lime slices, raspberries and fresh mint sprigs, for garnish, optional

Combine graham cracker crumbs, margarine and 1 teaspoon sweetener in bottom of 7-inch springform pan. Pat evenly on bottom and 1/2 inch up side of pan. (If in a hurry, a 9-inch prepared reduced fat graham cracker crust can be used.)

Sprinkle gelatin over 1/2 cup milk in small saucepan. Let stand 2-3 minutes. Cook over low heat, stirring constantly, until gelatin is dissolved. Beat cream cheese in small bowl until fluffy. Beat in remaining 1-1/4 cups milk and gelatin mixture. Mix in lime juice and 3-1/2 teaspoons sweetener. Refrigerate pie until set, about 2 hours.

Garnish with lime slices, raspberries and mint, if desired.

Farmhouse Lemon Meringue Pie

9-inch baked reduced-fat pie
crust

4 large eggs, at room
temperature

3 tablespoons lemon juice

2 tablespoons reduced-fat
margarine

2 teaspoons lemon peel

3 drops yellow food coloring
(optional)

1 cup cold water

2/3 cup sugar, divided

1/4 cup cornstarch

1/8 teaspoon salt

1/4 teaspoon vanilla

Separate eggs and discard two of the egg yolks; set aside. Mix lemon juice, margarine, lemon peel and food coloring in small bowl; set aside.

Combine water, all but 2 tablespoons sugar, cornstarch and salt in medium saucepan and whisk until smooth. Heat over medium-high heat, whisking constantly, until mix begins to boil. Reduce heat to medium. Continue boiling for 1 minute, stirring constantly. Remove from heat.

Stir 1/4 cup boiling sugar mixture into egg yolks; whisk constantly until completely blended. Slowly whisk egg yolk mixture back into boiling sugar mixture. Cook over medium heat for 3 minutes, whisking constantly. Remove from heat and stir in reserved lemon juice mixture until well blended. Pour into baked pie crust.

Beat egg whites in large bowl with electric mixer at high speed until soft peaks form. Gradually beat in remaining 2 tablespoons sugar and vanilla. Beat until stiff peaks form. Spread meringue over pie filling, making sure it completely covers filling and touches edge of pie crust.

Bake for 15 minutes at 425 degrees. Remove from oven and cool completely on wire rack. Cover with plastic wrap and refrigerate for 8 hours or overnight until setting is firm and pie is thoroughly chilled.

Heavenly Lemon Pie

1 (6-ounce) shortbread pie crust

1 package (8-ounces) fat free cream cheese

1/2 cup low fat whipped topping

1 teaspoon lemon juice

Sugar substitute to equal 2 tablespoons sugar

1 package (4 serving) sugar-free instant vanilla pudding mix

1 package (4 serving) sugar-free lemon gelatin

2/3 cup nonfat dry milk powder

1 cup (8-ounces) crushed pineapple, undrained

3/4 cup Diet clear soda

1 teaspoon coconut extract

2 tablespoons (1/2-ounce) chopped pecans

2 tablespoons flaked coconut

In a bowl, stir cream cheese until soft. Stir in 1/4 cup topping, lemon juice, and sugar substitute. Spread mix into pie crust. In a large bowl, combine pudding mix, gelatin and milk powder. Add undrained pineapple and soft drink. Mix well using a wire whisk.

Blend in remaining 1/4 cup whipped topping and coconut extract. Spread mixture evenly over cream cheese mixture. Sprinkle pecans and coconut over top. Refrigerate for at least 1 hour.

Black Bottom Lemon Cream Pie

1 (6-ounce) shortbread pie crust

1 package (4 serving) sugar-free instant chocolate pudding mix

1-1/3 cup nonfat dry milk powder

2-1/4 cups water

1 package (4 serving) sugar-free instant vanilla pudding mix

1 package (4 serving) sugar-free lemon gelatin

1/2 cup fat free whipped topping

1 tablespoon (1/4-ounce) miniature chocolate chips

(Continued on next page.)

(Black Bottom Lemon Cream Pie - *continued*)

In a bowl, combine chocolate pudding mix, 2/3 cup milk powder, and 1 cup water. Mix well using a wire whisk. Spread mix into pie crust.

In large bowl, combine vanilla pudding mix, gelatin, remaining 2/3 cup milk powder, and remaining 1-1/4 cups water. Mix well. Blend in fat free whipped topping.

Spread mix evenly over chocolate layer. Evenly sprinkle chocolate chips over the top. Refrigerate for at least 1 hour.

Mandarin Orange Pie

1 (6-ounce) graham cracker pie crust

2 packages (4 serving) sugar-free instant vanilla pudding mix

1 package (4 serving) sugar-free orange gelatin

1-1/3 cups nonfat dry milk powder

2-1/3 cups water

1 cup (11-ounces) mandarin oranges, rinsed and drained

1 teaspoon coconut extract

1/2 cup fat free whipped topping

1/4 cup flaked coconut

In a bowl, combine 1 package pudding mix, gelatin, 2/3 cup milk powder, and 1-1/3 cups water. Mix well using a wire whisk. Add oranges. Mix gently to combine. Spread mix into pie crust; refrigerate while preparing topping.

In another medium bowl, combine remaining package dry pudding mix, remaining 2/3 cup milk powder, and remaining 1 cup water. Mix well using a wire whisk. Blend in coconut extract, fat free whipped topping and 2 tablespoons coconut. Spread mix evenly over orange filling. Evenly sprinkle remaining 2 tablespoons coconut over top. Refrigerate for at least 1 hour.

Rum Raisin Cream Pie

1 package (4 serving) sugar-free instant vanilla pudding mix

2/3 cup nonfat dry milk

1-1/2 cups water

1 teaspoon rum extract

1 cup lite whipped topping

1 cup raisins

Graham cracker pie crust

Combine dry pudding mix, milk powder, and water. Mix well. Blend in rum extract and 1/4 cup whipped topping. Add raisins. Mix well to combine. Spread pudding mix into pie crust.

Refrigerate for at least 2 hours. To serve, top each piece with 1 tablespoon whipped topping.

Hawaiian Crumb Pie

1 (6-ounce) chocolate pie crust

1 package (4 serving) sugar-free chocolate cook and serve pudding mix

2/3 cup nonfat dry milk powder

1 cup (8 ounces) crushed pineapple, undrained

1 cup water

1 teaspoon coconut extract

1 cup (1 medium) diced banana

6 (2-1/2 inch) chocolate graham cracker squares made into fine crumbs

2 tablespoons flaked coconut

2 tablespoons (1/2 ounce) chopped pecans

Preheat oven to 375 degrees. In saucepan, combine pudding mix, milk powder, undrained pineapple and water. Cook over medium heat until mix thickens and starts to boil, stirring often. Remove from heat. Stir in coconut extract and banana. Place saucepan on a wire rack and let set for 5 minutes. Spread pudding mixture into piecrust.

In a small bowl, combine graham cracker crumbs, coconut and pecans. Evenly sprinkle crumb mixture over top.

Bake for 10-12 minutes. Place pie plate on a wire rack and allow to cool completely.

Pina Colada Pie

1 (6-ounce) shortbread pie crust

2 cups (2 medium) diced bananas, mixed with lemon juice to prevent browning

1 package (4 serving) sugar-free instant vanilla pudding mix

2/3 cup nonfat dry milk powder

1 cup (8-ounces) crushed pineapple, packed in fruit juice, drained, and 1/4 cup liquid reserved

3/4 cup water

1 teaspoon rum extract

1-1/2 teaspoons coconut extract

1 cup fat free whipped topping

2 tablespoons flaked coconut

Layer bananas in bottom of pie crust. In bowl, combine pudding mix and milk powder. Add reserved pineapple liquid and water. Mix well using a wire whisk. Blend in pineapple, rum extract, 1 teaspoon coconut extract, and 1/4 cup whipped topping. Spread mix evenly over bananas.

Refrigerate for 15 minutes. In a small bowl, combine remaining whipped topping and remaining 1/2 teaspoon coconut extract. Spread mix evenly over set filling. Evenly sprinkle coconut over top. Refrigerate for at least 1 hour.

Almond Raisin Pie

Shortbread pie crust

8 maraschino cherries, divided

1 package (4 serving) sugar-free instant vanilla pudding mix

1/3 cup nonfat dry milk powder

3/4 cup water

3/4 cup fat-free plain yogurt

3/4 cup fat free whipped topping

1 teaspoon brandy extract

1 cup raisins

1/4 cup chopped almonds

Chop 4 maraschino cherries. Set aside. In a large bowl, combine pudding mix, milk powder, water and yogurt. Mix well. Blend in whipped topping and brandy extract. Fold in raisins, almonds, and chopped maraschino cherries. Spread mix evenly into pie crust. Cut remaining 4 maraschino cherries in half and garnish top of pie with them. Refrigerate for at least 1 hour.

Low Cal Banana Split Cream Pie

1 (6-ounce) graham cracker pie crust

1 cup (1 medium) diced banana

2 cups sliced fresh strawberries

1 package (4 serving) sugar-free vanilla cook-and-serve pudding mix

1 package (4 serving) sugar-free strawberry gelatin

2 cups diet clear soda or water

1 package (4 serving) sugar-free instant banana cream pudding mix

2/3 cup nonfat dry milk powder

1 cup (8-ounces) crushed pineapple, undrained

1/2 cup fat free whipped topping

2 tablespoons (1/2-ounce) chopped pecans

Layer banana and strawberries in bottom of crust. In saucepan, combine pudding mix, gelatin, and 1-1/2 cups soda or water. Cook over medium heat until mix thickens and starts to boil, stirring constantly. Spoon hot mix evenly over fruit. Refrigerate for 1 hour or until set.

Combine pudding mix, milk powder, undrained pineapple, and remaining 1/2 cup soda. Mix well. Blend in whipped topping. Spread pudding mix evenly over set filling. Sprinkle pecans evenly over top. Refrigerate for at least 30 minutes.

Sugarless Cheese Cake

Low-fat graham cracker crust
Filling:
2 packages (8-ounces each) cream cheese, softened

3 large eggs, room temperature, separated

1/2 cup honey

1 teaspoon vanilla or almond extract

Topping:
1 pint sour cream, low calorie

1/8 cup honey

1 teaspoon vanilla or almond extract

(Continued on next page.)

Mix egg yolks, cream cheese, honey and vanilla until creamy and smooth. Whip egg whites until stiff, fold lightly into cheese mixture; do not blend. Pour into chilled crust. Bake at 350 degrees for about 40 minutes or until pie does not shake in center. It will be browned on top. Remove and cool for 10 minutes and add topping.

Bake at 400 degrees for 3-5 minutes. Remove and cool. Chill about 8 hours before serving. Serve with fresh fruit.

Low Fat Fake Pecan Pie

Crust:
2 large flour tortillas
Butter flavored nonstick cooking spray
1/2 teaspoon butter flavor sprinkles

Filling:
3/4 cup reduced fat egg product

1/2 cup light corn syrup
1 cup brown sugar
1 teaspoon flour
1 tablespoon butter flavor sprinkles
1 teaspoon vanilla extract
1/3 cup Grape Nuts cereal

For crust, place 1 tortilla in 9-inch pie plate and spray with nonstick cooking spray. Spray tortilla and sprinkle with butter flavor sprinkles. Repeat with second tortilla. Using another 9-inch pie plate, spray outside bottom and place on top of tortillas. This helps press and form pie "crust". Bake with pie plate on top at 350 degrees for 7 minutes. Cool slightly while preparing filling.

In a large bowl, combine all ingredients except cereal and mix with electric mixer. Pour into partially baked crust. Sprinkle cereal over top of filling and bake at 350 degrees for 35 minutes. Do not over cook as it may spill over. Do not worry about how it puffs up while baking. It will go back down as soon as it cools.

Carrot Ice Cream Pie

Graham cracker crust
1/3 cup lemonade concentrate
2-1/4 cups chopped carrots

1/4 cup sugar
1 quart vanilla ice cream, softened

Place lemonade concentrate, carrots and sugar in a food processor or blender; cover and process until carrots are finely chopped and mixture is blended. Transfer to a bowl; stir in ice cream until well blended. Pour into crust.

Cover and freeze for 8 hours or overnight. Remove from the freezer 15-20 minutes before serving.

Honey-Oatmeal Pie

9-inch unbaked pastry shell
2 eggs
1-1/4 cups quick-cooking oats
3/4 cup honey
1/2 cup unsalted sunflower seed kernels
1/2 cup raisins
1/2 cup packed light brown sugar

1/2 cup sweetened shredded coconut
1/2 cup melted butter or margarine
1/4 cup chopped dried apricots
1 teaspoon cinnamon

Heat oven to 350 degrees. Line 9-inch pie plate with pastry; flute edge. Combine remaining ingredients in bowl; mix well. Spoon into pastry. Bake for 40 to 45 minutes or until set. Cool on wire rack for 1 hour.

Homemade Sweet Potato Pie

9-inch unbaked pastry shell

1-1/4 cups firmly packed brown sugar

4 medium (1-1/2 cups) sweet potatoes, cooked, skins removed, mashed*

3/4 teaspoon cinnamon

1/2 teaspoon salt

1/2 teaspoon ground ginger

1/4 teaspoon ground cloves

1/4 teaspoon ground nutmeg

1 cup evaporated milk

3 eggs

Sweetened whipped cream, optional

Heat oven to 350 degrees. In large mixer bowl, combine all filling ingredients except evaporated milk, eggs and whipped cream. Beat at medium speed, scraping bowl often, until well mixed (1 to 2 minutes). Reduce speed to low; add milk and eggs. Beat until well mixed (1 to 2 minutes).

Pour filling into pie shell. Bake for 45 to 55 minutes or until knife inserted in center comes out clean. Cool completely.

Garnish with whipped cream, if desired. Store in refrigerator.

 * Substitute 1-1/2 cups canned mashed sweet potatoes

Sweet Potato Pie Supreme

10-inch unbaked pastry shell

4 eggs

1-1/2 cups mashed cooked sweet potatoes

1/3 cup sugar

2 tablespoons honey

2/3 cup milk

1/2 cup crushed black walnuts

1/2 cup orange juice

Salt to taste

1 teaspoon vanilla

1 tablespoon grated orange rind

1/2 teaspoon nutmeg

1 cup whipping cream, whipped

Combine first three ingredients and beat until smooth. Add honey and milk; mix well. Add walnuts, orange juice, salt and vanilla; mix well. Spoon into pie shell. Bake for 10 minutes in a 450 degree oven. Reduce oven temperature to 300-350 degrees. Bake for an additional 30 minutes or longer or until set. Cool to room temperature. Sprinkle with orange rind and nutmeg. Serve with whipped cream.

Sweet Potato Chocolate Pie

10-inch deep dish unbaked
pastry shell
Filling:
2-3/4 pounds sweet potatoes
1-1/4 cups sugar
1/3 cup light brown sugar
1/4 teaspoon cinnamon
1/8 teaspoon freshly grated
nutmeg
1/8 teaspoon salt

5 large eggs
2-ounces semisweet chocolate
at room temperature, cut into
1-inch-long match sticks or
grated
Whipped Cream:
1 cup cold heavy cream
1 tablespoon sugar
1 tablespoon bourbon
1/2 teaspoon cinnamon

Filling: Preheat the oven to 350 degrees. Bake the sweet potatoes on a baking sheet for about 1 hour or until soft when pierced. Let cool; remove skins and puree the potatoes in a food processor.

In a medium bowl, combine sugars, spices and salt. In a large bowl, lightly whisk eggs. Whisk in 3 cups of the pureed sweet potatoes (reserve any extra for another use). Whisk in the sugar mixture. Spoon half of the sweet potato custard into the pie shell and sprinkle half of the chocolate on top. Cover with the remaining sweet potato custard and distribute the remaining chocolate decoratively on top.

Bake the pie in the center of the oven for about one hour or until the custard is almost set in the middle. Turn off the oven but leave the pie inside until cool.

In a chilled bowl, combine the cream with the sugar, bourbon and cinnamon. Beat until stiff. Serve pie at room temperature and pass the whipped cream separately.

Kahlua-Cappuccino Pie

9-inch chocolate cookie or
graham cracker pie shell

2 cups vanilla ice cream,
softened

1 teaspoon instant coffee
granules

2 tablespoons coffee liqueur

2 cups chocolate-almond fudge
ice cream, softened

1 tablespoon coffee liqueur

1 cup whipping cream

1 tablespoon coffee liqueur

1/4 cup toasted sliced
almonds, optional

Freeze pie shell until firm. Combine vanilla ice cream with
mixture of instant coffee granules and 2 tablespoons liqueur in
bowl; mix well. Spoon into pie shell. Freeze until firm. Combine
chocolate-almond fudge ice cream with 1 tablespoon liqueur in
bowl; mix well. Spread over frozen layer. Freeze until firm. Whip
cream with 1 tablespoon liqueur in mixing bowl. Spread over
pie. Freeze until firm. Top with sliced almonds.

Eggnog Pie

9-inch baked pastry shell

1 tablespoon unflavored
gelatin

1/4 cup cold water

1/3 cup sugar

2 tablespoons cornstarch

1/4 teaspoon salt

2 cups eggnog

1 teaspoon vanilla

1 teaspoon rum extract

1 cup whipping cream,
whipped

In a small bowl, sprinkle gelatin over water; let stand 1 minute.
In a saucepan, combine sugar, cornstarch and salt. Stir in
eggnog until smooth. Bring to a boil; cook and stir for 2 minutes
or until thickened. Stir in gelatin until dissolved. Remove from
the heat; cool to room temperature. Stir in extracts; fold in
whipped cream. Pour into pastry shell. Refrigerate until firm.

Creamy Watermelon Pie

9-inch graham cracker crust

1 can (14-ounces) sweetened condensed milk

1/4 cup lime juice

1-2/3 cups cubed seeded watermelon

1-2/3 cups whipped topping

Watermelon balls and fresh mint, optional

In a bowl, combine milk and lime juice. Fold in whipped topping and cubed watermelon. Pour into crust. Refrigerate for at least 2 hours before slicing. Garnish with watermelon balls and mint if desired. Yield: 6-8 servings

Homemade Eggnog Pie

9-inch baked pastry shell

1-1/8 teaspoons unflavored gelatin

1/4 cup cold water

3/4 cup sugar

2 tablespoons cornstarch

2/3 cup milk

3 egg yolks, lightly beaten

1 teaspoon vanilla extract

1-1/2 cup whipping cream, whipped

1/8 teaspoon ground nutmeg

In a small bowl, soften gelatin in cold water; set aside. In a saucepan, combine sugar and cornstarch. Gradually stir in milk until smooth. Bring to a boil; cook and stir for 2 minutes or until thickened. Remove from heat. Stir a small amount of hot mixture into egg yolks. Return all to the pan; bring to a gentle boil, stirring constantly.

Remove from the heat; stir in gelatin and vanilla. Cool to room temperature, stirring occasionally. Fold in whipped cream. Pour into pie shell. Sprinkle with nutmeg. Refrigerate until set, about 2 hours.

Transparent Pie

9-inch baked pastry shell

1 egg

2 egg yolks

1 cup sugar

1 teaspoon flour

1/3 cup butter

3/4 cup cream

1 teaspoon vanilla

(Continued on next page)

Beat egg and egg yolks well and gradually add sugar and flour, beating after each addition. Add butter and cream. Add vanilla. Pour into unbaked crust and bake at 425 degrees for 10-15 minutes. Reduce heat to 350 degrees and bake until filling sets.

Mock Apple Pie

Pastry for double-crust pie
18 saltine crackers, halved
1-1/2 cups sugar
1-1/4 cups water
3 tablespoons lemon juice

1 teaspoon cream of tartar
1/2 to 1 teaspoon ground cinnamon
1/2 to 1 teaspoon ground nutmeg

Place bottom pastry in a 9-inch pie plate. Layer crackers in shell; set aside.

In a small saucepan, combine remaining ingredients; bring to a boil. Carefully pour over crackers (filling will be very thin). Cool for 10 minutes.

Cut lattice strips from remaining pastry; place over filling. Seal and flute edges. Bake at 400 degrees for 25-30 minutes or until golden brown.

Green Tomato Pie

Pastry for double crust pie
1-1/4 cups sugar
7 tablespoons flour
1 teaspoon ground cinnamon
3 cups thinly sliced green tomatoes about 4 to 5 medium)

Pinch of salt
1 tablespoon cider vinegar
1 tablespoon butter or margarine

In a bowl, combine sugar, flour, cinnamon and salt. Add tomatoes and vinegar; toss to mix. Line a pie plate with bottom crust. Add filling, then dot with butter. Top with a lattice crust. Bake at 350 degrees for 60 minutes or until tomatoes are tender.

Shamrock Chiffon Pie

10-inch graham cracker pie crust

2 envelopes unflavored gelatin

1 can (9-ounce) crushed pineapple, undrained

1/3 cup water

3 eggs, separated

1/2 cup sugar

1/4 teaspoon salt

2 tablespoon lemon juice

1 cup heavy whipping cream

1/2 cup chopped maraschino green cherries

2 tablespoons creme de menthe

Soften gelatin in 1/2 cup cold water. Combine pineapple, 1/3 cup water, egg yolks, sugar, salt and lemon juice. Cook over low heat, stirring constantly, until thickened. Add gelatin and stir until dissolved. Cool until mixture begins to thicken.

Beat egg whites until stiff, but not dry. Fold egg whites, whipped cream, chopped cherries and creme de menthe into gelatin mixture.

Pile lightly into crust and chill until ready to serve. Garnish with shamrocks of green cherries.

Caramel Meringue Pie

9-inch baked pastry shell

2 cups sugar, divided

1/3 cup all-purpose flour

Pinch of salt

2 cups milk

5 egg yolks, lightly beaten

2 tablespoons butter or margarine

1 teaspoon vanilla extract

Meringue:

4-6 egg whites

1/2 to 3/4 teaspoon cream of tartar

1/2 cup sugar

1/2 teaspoon vanilla extract

Whisk together 1 cup sugar, flour, salt, milk, and egg yolks in a heavy saucepan. Cook over medium heat, whisking constantly until mix is hot.

(Continued on next page.)

Sprinkle remaining 1 cup sugar in a heavy skillet and cook over medium heat, stirring constantly until sugar melts and turns light golden. Gradually add to hot custard mixture, stirring constantly. Cook, stirring constantly until mixture thickens and comes to a boil. Stir in butter and vanilla. Spoon into pastry shell.

For meringue, beat egg whites and cream of tartar at high speed with an electric mixer just until foamy. Add sugar, 1 tablespoon at a time, beating until stiff peaks form and sugar dissolves (2-4 minutes). Add vanilla, beating well. Spread meringue over hot filling, sealing to edge of pastry.

Bake at 325 degrees for 25-28 minutes.

Pie au Pineapple Brule

9-inch unbaked pastry shell
4 eggs
1/2 cup sugar
1/4 teaspoon salt
1/4 teaspoon nutmeg
1 teaspoon vanilla
2 cups light cream
1/2 cup syrup, drained from pineapple

Topping:
1/2 cup flaked coconut
3 tablespoons brown sugar
1 tablespoon melted butter
5 pineapple slices

Beat eggs slightly and beat in sugar, salt, nutmeg and vanilla. add cream and pineapple syrup. Pour mixture into pastry shell. Bake on lower shelf in 425 degree oven until filling is barely set in center, about 30 minutes.

Remove pie from oven and let stand 5-10 minutes. For topping, combine coconut, brown sugar and butter. Arrange drained pineapple slices on top of pie and sprinkle with topping. Cover edge of crust with foil to prevent excessive browning.

Place pie under broiler for 1-2 minutes or until topping is bubbly. Cool

Oatmeal Pie

9-inch unbaked pastry shell
2 large eggs, slightly beaten
2/3 cup sugar
3/4 cup dark syrup
1/2 cup margarine, melted

1 teaspoon vanilla
2 tablespoons flour
3/4 cup quick-cooking oats
1/2 cup flaked coconut

Combine all ingredients and pour into crust. Bake in moderate 350 degree oven for 30-40 minutes.

Vinegar Pie

9-inch baked pastry shell
3 egg yolks (save whites for meringue)
1 cup sugar
4 tablespoons flour

1/2 cup vinegar
2 cups boiling water
1 teaspoon lemon flavoring or juice
Recipe of meringue

Mix egg yolks, sugar, flour with just enough cold water to mix. Add vinegar and boiling water. Cook over medium heat until thick. Add lemon flavoring or juice. Pour into baked pie shell and top with meringue Bake at 375 degrees for 10-15 minutes or until golden.

Seafoam Pie

9-inch baked pastry shell
1 cup brown sugar
2 heaping tablespoons flour
2 eggs, separated (save whites for meringue)

2 cups milk
1 teaspoon vanilla
Pinch of salt
2 tablespoons butter or margarine

Cook 3/4 cup brown sugar, flour, egg yolks, milk, vanilla and salt in top of double boiler until thick, stirring constantly. Add butter and set aside to cool. Pour into pie shell. Cover with meringue made of stiffly beaten egg whites to which remaining brown sugar has been added.

Bake in 325 degree oven 15 minutes or until meringue is lightly browned.

Custard Blender Pie

2 cups milk
1 cup sugar
1/2 cup baking mix
1/4 cup margarine or butter

1 teaspoon vanilla
4 eggs
1 cup coconut
Nutmeg

Combine milk, sugar, baking mix, margarine, vanilla and eggs in a blender jar. Blend well. Pour into a well-greased 9-inch pie pan. Sprinkle coconut and nutmeg on top. Bake at 350 degrees for 45 minutes

Fresh Peach-Almond Upside-Down Pie

Pastry for 9-inch double crust pie
2 tablespoons soft butter
2/3 cup toasted sliced almonds or pecans
Brown sugar

3/4 cup white sugar
5 cups sliced fresh peaches
2 tablespoons tapioca
1/2 teaspoons nutmeg
1/4 teaspoons cinnamon

Line 9-inch pie pan with 12-inch square of foil. Let excess foil overhand edge. Spread with butter. Press nuts and 1/3 cup brown sugar into butter. Fit bottom crust into pie pan over nuts and brown sugar.

Mix remaining ingredients with 1/4 cup brown sugar. Pour into pastry shell. Cover with top crust. Seal, flute and prick with fork. Brush lightly with milk.

Bake at 450 degrees for 10 minutes. Lower heat to 375 degrees and bake 35-50 minutes more. Cool thoroughly. Turn upside down on serving plate and remove foil.

Peppermint-Fudge Pie

24 Oreo cookies, finely
crushed

1/4 cup margarine, melted

4 cups miniature
marshmallows

1/2 cup milk

1 cup cream, whipped

1/2 cup crushed peppermint
candy

Mix the crushed cookies and the margarine together and press
into 9-inch pie plate. Save 1/2 cup crushed crumbs for a border
on top of the pie. Melt 3 cups of marshmallows in milk in a
double boiler. Stir until smooth. Chill until slightly thickened.
Mix well. Fold in cream, remaining marshmallows and crushed
candy. Pour into crust. Border with reserved crumbs and chill
until served.

Ritz Pie

3 egg whites

1/4 teaspoon cream of tartar

1 teaspoon vanilla

22 Ritz crackers, crushed
medium fine

1 cup sugar

1 cup chopped pecans

1 package whipped topping

Grated German sweet
chocolate

Beat egg whites with cream of tartar until frothy, add vanilla
and beat stiff. Add sugar gradually, beat very stiff. Lightly fold
in cracker crumbs and pecans. Pour into heavily greased and
floured 9-inch pie pan and bake at 300 degrees for 30 minutes.
Chill. Cover with whipped topping and grate chocolate over the
top. Chill 2 hours before serving. Keep refrigerated.

Creativity Pie

Pastry for 9-inch double crust
pie

1-1/2 cup sugar

2 cups water

2 teaspoons cream of tartar

24 Ritz crackers

1 teaspoon lemon juice

1/4 teaspoon lemon rind

Cinnamon

Butter

Cook sugar, water and cream of tartar for 2 minutes and add
Ritz crackers. Cook for 2 minutes longer without stirring. Cool.
Add lemon juice and rind. Pour into an unbaked shell and
sprinkle with cinnamon and dot with butter. Place top crust on
filling. Bake 30 minutes at 425 degrees.

Paradise Pie

3 egg whites
1 cup sugar
1 teaspoon vanilla
20 soda crackers
1 cup pecans or walnuts,
chopped

1 cup whipping cream
1 small can crushed pineapple,
drained
1/2 cup coconut

Beat egg whites, add sugar, slowly add vanilla. Stir in crushed crackers and add nuts. Pour in greased pie pan. Bake 20 minutes at 325 degrees. Cool 1 hour. Mix whipping cream, pineapple, coconut and spread on top of cooled pie. Chill or freeze until firm.

Golden Squash Pie

Two 9-inch unbaked pastry
shells
4 eggs
4 cups butternut squash,
cooked and mashed
1/4 cup butter or margarine,
melted
1 cup buttermilk

2 teaspoons vanilla extract
2 cups sugar
2 tablespoons flour
1 teaspoon salt
1/2 teaspoon baking soda
Nutmeg, optional

Combine squash, buttermilk, eggs, butter and vanilla. Combine the dry ingredients; add to squash mixture and mix until smooth.

Pour into pastry shells. Cover edges with pie shield and bake in a 350 degree oven for 35 minutes. Remove shield and bake 25 minutes longer or until a knife inserted in the middle comes out clean. Cool on a wire rack.

Sprinkle with nutmeg if desired. Store in refrigerator.

This recipe makes 2 pies. For one pie, cut recipe in half.

Amber Pie

9-inch unbaked pastry shell
2 eggs
1 teaspoon cloves
1 teaspoon cinnamon
1/2 cup sugar

3/4 cup buttermilk
1/2 cup chopped raisins
1 tablespoon flour
1 tablespoon butter

Beat eggs. Combine spices and sugar. Add to eggs. Blend in buttermilk and raisins mixed with flour.

Pour into crust and dot with butter. Bake at 425 degrees for 10 minutes then at 325 degrees for 25 minutes more.

Sour Cream Pie

9-inch unbaked pastry shell
2 eggs
1 tablespoon cornstarch
1/2 cup milk
1 cup sour cream

1 cup raisins
1/8 teaspoon salt
1 teaspoon cinnamon
1/4 teaspoon cloves
1 cup brown sugar

Blend eggs and cornstarch. Add milk, slowly stirring until smooth. Add all other ingredients and mix well. Pour into crust. Bake at 425 degrees for 10-12 minutes, then at 325 degrees for 20 minutes or until a knife inserted in filling comes out clean.

Sawdust Pie

9-inch unbaked pastry shell
7 egg whites, unbeaten
1-1/2 cups granulated sugar
1-1/2 cups graham cracker crumbs

1-1/2 cups pecans
1-1/2 cups coconut
Sliced bananas
Whipping cream

Mix egg whites, sugar, graham cracker crumbs, pecans, and coconut together and stir. Pour into crust. Bake at 325 degrees until glossy and set, about 25-30 minutes. Do not over bake. Serve warm with sliced bananas and whipped cream.

Maple-Butternut Squash Pie

Crust:

1 cup flour

1/4 cup walnuts, finely chopped (about 1-ounce)

1/4 teaspoon salt

1/3 cup chilled solid vegetable shortening

5-6 tablespoons ice water

Filling:

2 (11-ounce each) packages frozen butternut squash, thawed

1 cup evaporated milk

1/2 cup granulated sugar

1/2 cup pure maple syrup

1/2 teaspoon ground cinnamon

1/2 teaspoon ground ginger

1/4 teaspoon ground cloves

3 large eggs

Glaze and Garnish:

1 egg white, slightly beaten

Whole walnuts

Whipped cream

Preheat oven to 400 degrees. In medium bowl, mix flour, nuts and salt. Using a pastry cutter or two knives, cut shortening into flour mixture until coarse crumbs form. Add water, 1 tablespoon at a time, tossing with a fork until a soft dough forms. shape dough into a disk; wrap in plastic wrap and chill for 1 hour.

Roll dough to fit into a 9-inch pie plate.

To prepare filling, beat squash, evaporated milk, sugar, maple syrup and spices at medium speed until smooth. Beat in eggs, 1 at a time, beating well after each addition.

Pour filling into prepared crust. Bake until filling is set, 55-60 minutes. Cool on wire rack. Garnish each slice with a whole walnut and a dollop of whipped cream.

For a decorative touch, cut maple leaves out of extra dough from crust. Arrange leaves on top of filling before baking and brush with egg white.

Gooseberry Meringue Pie

9-inch baked pastry shell
2 cups canned, fresh or frozen
gooseberries
2 tablespoons water
1-1/2 cups sugar, divided

3 tablespoons cornstarch
1 cup milk
2 eggs, separated

In a covered saucepan over medium heat, cook gooseberries and water for 3 to 4 minutes or until tender. Stir in 3/4 cup sugar; set aside.

In another saucepan, combine 1/2 cup sugar and cornstarch. Gradually add milk until smooth; bring to a boil. cook and stir over medium-high heat until thickened. Reduce heat and cook and stir 2 minutes longer. Remove from heat.

In a bowl, beat egg yolks. Gradually whisk a small amount of hot filling into yolks; return all to pan. Bring to a gentle boil; cook and stir for 2 minutes. Remove from the heat; stir in gooseberry mixture. Pour into pastry shell.

In a small mixing bowl, beat egg whites until soft peaks form. Gradually add remaining sugar, beating on high until stiff peaks form. Spread evenly over hot filling, sealing meringue to crust. Bake at 350 degrees for 10-15 minutes or until golden. Refrigerate leftovers.

Buttermilk Pie

9-inch unbaked pastry shell
3 eggs
3/4 cup sugar
1 cup buttermilk

1 teaspoon cornmeal
1 teaspoon vanilla
1 teaspoon nutmeg

Beat eggs, sugar and buttermilk. Add remaining ingredients. Mix well and pour into pie crust. Bake at 350 degrees for 30 minutes.

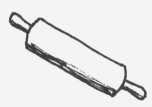

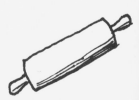

Roast Beef Quiche
A great dish for that leftover roast beef!

9-inch unbaked pastry shell

1-3/4 cups roast beef, cooked and finely chopped

1/4 cup green onion, chopped

1/2 cup green pepper, chopped

1 tablespoon flour

4 eggs

1/2 cup evaporated milk

1 tablespoon steak sauce

1/8 teaspoon dill weed

1/8 teaspoon dried basil

1/8 teaspoon dried oregano

8-ounces cheddar cheese (2 cups)

Salt and pepper to taste

Line an unpricked pastry shell with a double thickness of heavy duty foil. Bake for 5 minutes in a 450 degree oven. Remove foil and bake an additional 5 minutes. Reduce heat to 375 degrees.

Sprinkle beef and onions into the crust. In a bowl, beat flour and eggs until smooth. Add seasonings, milk and steak sauce. Mix until smooth. Stir in cheese and green pepper. Pour into crust and bake for 25 minutes or until center is set. Let stand for about 10 minutes before cutting.

Roast Beef Turnovers

Pastry for double crust pie

2 cups cooked roast beef, cubed in 1/4-inch pieces

1-1/2 cups cooked potatoes, cubes

1 cup beef gravy

1/2 cup cooked carrots, diced

1 tablespoon chopped fresh parsley

1/2 cup cooked onion, diced

1/4 teaspoon dried thyme

1/2 teaspoon salt

1/8 teaspoon pepper

Half and Half cream

Combine first nine ingredients; set aside. Roll out one-fourth of the pastry into an 8-inch circle. Mound 1 cup filling on half of the circle. Moisten edges with water; fold dough over and press edges with fork to seal. Place on an ungreased baking sheet. Repeat with remaining pastry and filling. Cut slits in top of each; brush with cream. Bake at 450 degrees for 20-25 minutes or until golden brown.

Mini Ground Round Quiches

1/4 pound ground round
1/8 teaspoon pepper
1/4 teaspoon garlic powder
1 cup biscuit mix
1/4 cup cornmeal
1/4 cup cold butter or margarine
2-3 tablespoons boiling water
1 egg

1/2 cup Half and Half cream
1 tablespoon green onion, diced
1 tablespoons sweet red pepper, diced
1/4 teaspoon salt
1/8 teaspoon cayenne pepper
1/2 cup cheddar cheese, finely shredded

Cook beef, pepper and garlic powder until meat is no longer pink over medium heat in a saucepan; drain then set aside.

In a bowl, combine biscuit mix and cornmeal. Cut in butter. Add enough water to form a soft dough. Press onto the bottom and up the sides of greased miniature muffin tins.

Place teaspoonfuls of beef mixture into each shell. Next combine the egg, cream, onion, red pepper, salt and cayenne. Pour over beef mixture. Sprinkle each quiche with cheese and bake in a 375 degree oven for 20 minutes or until a knife inserted near the center comes out clean.

Easy Beef Pot Pie

Pastry for single crust pie
1 (10-3/4 ounce) can golden mushroom soup, undiluted
1 (8-ounce) container light sour cream
1-1/2 teaspoons dried thyme
1/2 teaspoon pepper
1 pound lean ground beef

1 (14-1/2 ounce) can sliced carrots, drained
1 (14-1/2 ounce) can whole new potatoes, drained and sliced
1 (4-ounce) can mushroom stems and pieces, drained
1 (12-ounce) can asparagus spears, drained

(Continued on next page.)

Combine first four ingredients. Brown ground beef in a large skillet stirring until it crumbles. Drain well. Add soup mixture, carrots, potatoes, and mushrooms.

Spoon half the mixture into a lightly greased 2-quart baking dish. Arrange half the asparagus on top. Repeat layers.

Place pastry over casserole; fold edges under and crimp pressing crust to edges of baking dish. Cut a 1/2-inch hole in center to allow steam to escape.

Bake at 450 degrees for 15 minutes then reduce heat to 375 and bake 10 minutes or until crust is golden brown and pie is thoroughly heated, shielding with aluminum foil to prevent excessive browning if necessary.

Meat Shell Potato Pie

1 pound ground round

1 (10-3/4 ounce) can condensed cream of mushroom soup, undiluted, divided

1/4 cup onion, chopped

1 egg

1/4 cup dry bread crumbs

2 tablespoons fresh parsley, chopped

1/4 teaspoon salt

Dash of pepper

2 cups mashed potatoes

4 bacon strips, cooked and crumbled

1/2 cup shredded cheddar cheese

Combine beef, 1/2 cup soup, onion, egg, bread crumbs, parsley, salt and pepper in bowl. Mix well. Press onto the bottom and up the sides of a 9-inch pie plate. Bake at 350 degrees for 25 minutes. Drain.

Combine potatoes and remaining soup in a bowl. Mix until fluffy. Spread over meat crust. Sprinkle with bacon and cheese. Bake for 15 minutes. Let stand for several minutes before cutting into wedges to serve.

Spicy Bean and Beef Pie

Pastry for double crust 10-inch pie

1 pound ground beef

2 garlic cloves; minced

1 (11-1/2 ounce) can condensed bean with bacon soup, undiluted

1 (16-ounce) jar thick and chunky picante sauce, divided

1/4 cup cornstarch

1 tablespoon fresh parsley, chopped

1 teaspoon paprika

1 teaspoon salt

1/4 teaspoon pepper

1 (16-ounce) can kidney beans, rinsed and drained

1 (15-ounce) can black beans, rinsed and drained

3/4 cup sliced green onions, divided

8-ounces cheddar cheese, shredded and divided

8-ounces sour cream

1 (2-1/4 ounces) can black olives, sliced and drained

Cook beef and garlic together in skillet until beef is browned; drain. Combine soup, 1 cup picante, cornstarch, parsley, paprika, salt and pepper in a bowl and mix well. Fold in beans, 1/2 cup onions, 1-1/4 cups cheese, and beef and garlic mixture.

Line pie plate with bottom crust. Fill with bean mixture. Top with remaining crust and seal and flute edges. Cut slits in top.

Bake for 30 to 35 minutes in a 425 degree oven or until lightly browned. Let stand for 5 minutes before cutting. Serve with sour cream, olives and remaining cheese, onions and picante sauce.

Topsy Turvy Meat Pie

1 pound ground beef

1/2 cup celery, chopped

1/2 cup onion, chopped

1/4 cup green pepper, chopped

1 (10-3/4 ounce) can condensed tomato soup, undiluted

1 teaspoon prepared mustard

1-1/2 cup biscuit mix

1/3 cup water

3 slices process American cheese, halved diagonally

Green pepper rings, optional

(Continued on next page.)

(Topsy Turvy Meat Pie - *continued*)

Cook beef, celery, onion and green pepper over medium heat in skillet until meat is no longer pink and veggies are tender; drain. Stir in soup and mustard. Mix well. Transfer to a greased 9-inch pie plate.

In bowl, combine the biscuit mix and water until a soft dough forms. Roll into a 9-inch circle. Place over meat mixture. Bake at 425 degrees for 20 minutes or until golden brown. Cool 5 minutes. Run a knife around edge to loosen biscuit. Invert onto a serving platter. Arrange cheese slices in a pinwheel pattern on top. Garnish with green pepper rings if desired.

Meat Pie

2 cups flour
1 teaspoon salt
2/3 cup plus 2 tablespoons shortening
1 beaten egg
2-3 tablespoons cold water or milk
__Filling:__
1-1/2 pounds ground round

1 medium onion, chopped
1 garlic clove, minced
1/4 cup water
1 teaspoon salt
1/2 teaspoon rubbed sage
1/2 teaspoon dried thyme
1/4 teaspoon pepper
1/8 teaspoon ground cloves

Combine flour and salt in bowl. Cut in shortening until mixture looks like coarse crumbs. Add egg and water or milk; mix with fork until dough forms a ball. Divide dough in half; refrigerate.

In a frying pan over medium heat, cook beef, onion and garlic until meat is no longer pink; drain. Stir in remaining ingredients; heat thoroughly.

Roll out one portion of dough. Line a 9-inch pie plate with bottom crust. Spoon filling into crust. Roll out remaining crust to fit top of pie. Place over filling; seal and flute edges. Brush crust with milk and cut slits in top to vent.

Bake at 375 degrees for 30-35 minutes or until golden brown. Cover edges with pie shield to prevent over browning. Let stand for 15 minutes before cutting.

"Mon Ami" Meat Pie

This recipe makes two pies. If you need just one pie, cut recipe in half!

Pastry for two double-crust 9-inch pies

1 pound ground beef

3/4 ground pork

3/4 cup onion, chopped

2 celery ribs, chopped

2 garlic cloves, minced

6 cups hot mashed potatoes (do not add milk or butter, just mash the potatoes)

1/4 cup chicken broth

1/2 teaspoon thyme

1/4 teaspoon marjoram

1/2 teaspoon rosemary, crushed

1/2 teaspoon sage

Salt and pepper to taste

Milk, optional

Cook beef, pork, onion, celery and garlic over medium heat in a large skillet until meat is no longer pink and veggies are tender. Drain. Remove from heat and stir in potatoes, broth and seasonings.

Line two 9-inch pie plates with pastry. Divide meat mixture between the two crusts. Top each with remaining pastry. Trim, seal and flute the edges. Cut slits in top and brush with milk if desired. Bake at 375 degrees for 30-35 minutes or until golden brown.

Tamale Pie

1 pound ground beef

1 cup yellow corn meal

2 cups milk

2 eggs, beaten

1 (1.48 ounce) package Spices & Seasonings for Chili

2 teaspoons seasoned salt

1 (17-ounce can) whole kernel corn, drained

1 (14-1/4 ounce) can whole tomatoes, cut up

1 (2-1/4-ounce) can sliced ripe olives, drained

4-ounces cheddar cheese, shredded

In medium frying pan, cook beef until browned and crumbly; drain.

(Continued on next page.)

(**Tamale Pie** - *continued*)

In 2-1/2 quart casserole, combine corn meal, milk and eggs. Mix well. Add beef and remaining ingredients except cheese; mix well. Bake uncovered in 350 degree oven 1 hour and 15 minutes. Add cheese and continue baking until cheese melts. Let stand 10 minutes before serving.

Guadalupe Chili Pie

<u>Crust:</u>
2-1/4 cups biscuit mix
1/2 cup cold water
<u>Filling:</u>
1 pound ground round
8-ounces sour cream
1 cup cheddar cheese, shredded (4-ounces)

2/3 cup mayonnaise or salad dressing
2 tablespoons onion, chopped
2 medium tomatoes, thinly sliced
3/4 cup green pepper, chopped
Paprika

Preheat oven to 375 degrees. Grease a 13x9x2-inch baking pan; set aside.

<u>Crust:</u> In a medium bowl, stir biscuit mix and water together until moistened and soft dough is formed. Press mixture into the bottom and 1/2 inch up the sides of the pan. Bake approximately 12 minutes or until lightly browned.

In a large frying pan, cook ground round until brown; drain fat and set aside.

In another medium bowl, combine sour cream, shredded cheese, mayonnaise and onion together. Mix well; set aside.

Sprinkle cooked ground round on top of crust. Layer tomatoes over beef then sprinkle with green pepper. Spread sour cream mixture over layers. Sprinkle with paprika. Bake about 30 minutes more or until bubbly around the edges.

For a reduced-fat pie, prepare as directed except use light dairy sour cream, light mayonnaise and reduced-fat cheddar cheese.

Meat and Tater' Pie

Crust:
2 tablespoons shortening

1-1/2 cups biscuit/baking mix

3 to 4 tablespoons cold water

Filling:
1-1/2 pounds ground round

1 medium onion, chopped

1 can (10-3/4 ounces) condensed cream of mushroom soup, undiluted

1/2 teaspoon salt

1/2 teaspoon dried rosemary, crushed

1/2 teaspoon dried thyme

1 can (15-ounces) sliced carrots, drained

1 can (8-ounces) mushroom stems and pieces, drained

2 cups hot mashed potatoes (prepared with milk and butter)

1/2 cup sour cream

1/2 cup shredded cheddar cheese

Cut shortening into biscuit mix in a bowl until mixture resembles coarse crumbs. Add water, 1 tablespoon at a time, tossing lightly with a fork until dough forms a ball.

On a lightly floured surface, roll out pastry to fit a 9-inch pie plate. Line ungreased pie plate with pastry; trim and flute edges. Set aside.

In a skillet, cook beef and onion over medium heat until meat is no longer pink; drain. Stir in soup and seasonings; bring to a boil. Reduce heat and simmer, uncovered, for 5 minutes. Pour into pie shell. Top with carrots and mushrooms. Combine potatoes and sour cream; spread over pie. Bake, uncovered, at 425 degrees for 15 minutes. Reduce heat to 350 degrees and bake an additional 15 minutes or until golden brown. Sprinkle with cheese; let stand 5-10 minutes.

Taco Chili Pie - makes two pies

1 pound ground beef

2 cups sliced fresh mushrooms

1 cup chopped onion

4 cups torn fresh spinach

1 can (16 ounces) kidney beans, rinsed and drained

1 can (15 ounces) pinto beans, rinsed and drained

1 can (15 ounces) tomato sauce

1 can (14-1/2 ounces) stewed tomatoes, undrained

2 tablespoons taco seasoning

1 tablespoon sugar

1 tablespoon molasses

Crust:

4-1/2 cups all-purpose flour

4 teaspoons sugar

2 teaspoons salt

2 cups cold butter or margarine

12 to 14 tablespoons cold water

Preheat oven to 400 degrees. In a skillet, cook beef, mushrooms and onion over medium heat until meat is browned; drain. Stir in the next eight ingredients. Bring to a boil. Reduce heat; simmer, uncovered, for 20-30 minutes.

Meanwhile, combine the flour, sugar and salt in a bowl. Cut in butter until crumbly. Gradually add water, tossing with a fork until dough forms a ball. Divide dough into fourths; flatten each portion into a circle. Cover with plastic wrap. Refrigerate for at least 30 minutes.

Line two 9-inch pie plates with crust. Divide beef mixture in half between crusts. Roll out remaining pastry to fit tops of pies; place over filling. Trim, seal and flute edges. Cut slits on tops of crusts.

Bake for 20 minutes. Reduce heat to 375 degrees and bake 30-35 minutes longer or until crust is golden brown. Let stand for 10-15 minutes before cutting.

Beef Stew Pie

Pastry for 9-inch single-crust pie

6 tablespoons flour, divided

1-1/2 teaspoons salt

1/2 teaspoon pepper

1 pound boneless beef round steak, cut into 1-inch pieces

2 tablespoons vegetable oil

1/2 cup chopped onion

2 garlic cloves, minced

2-1/4 cups water, divided

1 tablespoon tomato paste

1/2 teaspoon Italian seasoning

1/2 teaspoon dried basil

1 bay leaf

2 cups cubed cooked potatoes

1-1/2 cups sliced cooked carrots

2 tablespoons minced fresh parsley

Preheat oven to 425 degrees. In a large resealable plastic bag, combine 3 tablespoons of the flour with salt and pepper. Add beef to bag in batches, shaking each time to coat. In a large skillet, saute beef in vegetable oil until browned. Add onion and garlic; cook and stir until onion is tender. Add 1/4 cup water, stirring to scrape browned bits.

Combine 1-1/2 cups water, tomato paste, Italian seasoning and basil; stir into skillet ingredients. Add bay leaf. Bring to a boil. Reduce heat; cover and simmer for 1-1/4 to 1-1/2 hours or until meat is tender.

Combine the remaining flour and water until smooth; gradually stir into skillet ingredients. Bring to a boil; cook and stir for 2 minutes or until thickened and bubbly. Discard bay leaf. Stir in vegetables and parsley. Transfer into a greased 2-quart baking dish.

On a floured surface, roll out crust to fit dish. Place crust over filling; flute edges if desired. Cut slits in top. Bake for 25-30 minutes or until golden brown. Let stand for 10 minutes.

Beef-Stuffed Sopaipillas

Crust:
2 cups flour
1 teaspoon salt
1 teaspoon baking powder
1/2 cup water
1/4 cup evaporated milk
1-1/2 teaspoons vegetable oil,
additional oil needed for frying

Filling:
1 pound ground beef
3/4 cup chopped onion

1/2 teaspoon salt
1/2 teaspoon garlic powder
1/4 teaspoon pepper

Sauce:
1 can (10-3/4 ounces)
condensed cream of chicken
soup, undiluted
1/2 cup chicken broth
1 can (4 ounces) chopped
green chilies
1/2 teaspoon onion powder
2 cups shredded cheddar
cheese

In a bowl, combine the flour, salt and baking powder. Stir in water, milk and oil with a fork until a ball forms. On a lightly floured surface, knead dough gently for 2-3 minutes. Cover and let stand for 15 minutes. Divide into four portions; roll each into a 6-1/2 inch circle.

In an electric skillet or deep-fat fryer, heat oil to 375 degrees. Fry circles, one at a time, for 2-3 minutes on each side or until golden brown. Drain on paper towels.

In a skillet, cook beef and onion until meat is browned; drain. Stir in salt, garlic powder and pepper. For sauce, combine soup, broth, chilies and onion powder in a saucepan; cook for 10 minutes or until heated throughout. Cut a slit on one side of each sopaipilla and fill with 1/2 cup of meat mixture. Top with cheese. Serve with sauce.

Spinach-Beef Spaghetti Pie

6-ounces uncooked angel hair pasta

2 eggs, lightly beaten

1/2 cup Parmesan cheese, grated

1 pound ground beef

1/2 cup chopped onion

1/4 cup chopped green pepper

1 jar (14-ounces) meatless spaghetti sauce

1 teaspoon Creole seasoning

3/4 teaspoon garlic powder

1/2 teaspoon dried basil

1/2 teaspoon dried oregano

1 package (8-ounces) cream cheese, softened

1 package (10-ounces) frozen chopped spinach, thawed and squeezed dry

1/2 cup shredded mozzarella cheese

Cook pasta according to package directions; drain. Add eggs and Parmesan cheese to pasta. Press onto the bottom and up the sides of a greased 9-inch deep-dish pie plate. Bake at 350 degrees for 10 minutes.

Meanwhile, in a skillet, cook the beef, onion and green pepper over medium heat until meat is browned; drain. Stir in spaghetti sauce, Creole seasoning, garlic powder, basil, and oregano. Bring to a boil. Reduce heat to simmer, keep covered for 10 minutes.

Roll out cream cheese into a 7-inch circle between two pieces of waxed paper. Place inside the crust. Top with spinach and meat sauce. Sprinkle with mozzarella cheese.

Bake at 350 degrees for 20-30 minutes or until set.

Cheesy Veal Pie

1/2 cup flour

1 pound veal or boneless skinless chicken breasts, cubed

1/4 cup butter or margarine

1 can (14-1/2 ounces) diced tomatoes, undrained

1 can (8-ounces) tomato sauce

1/4 cup chopped onion

1 teaspoon dried basil

1/2 teaspoon garlic salt

1/2 teaspoon dried oregano

1/8 teaspoon pepper

3 tablespoons grated parmesan cheese

Herb-Cheese Crust:

1-1/2 cups all-purpose flour

1/4 cup grated Parmesan cheese

1 teaspoon garlic salt

1 teaspoon dried oregano

1/2 cup cold butter or margarine

4 to 6 tablespoons cold water

1/2 cup shredded cheddar cheese

Preheat oven to 400 degrees. Place flour in a large resealable plastic bag; add meat in batches and shake to coat. In a skillet, cook meat in butter until no longer pink. Add tomatoes, tomato sauce, onion, basil, garlic salt, oregano, and pepper. Bring to a boil. Reduce heat; cover and simmer for 30 minutes or until meat is tender. Stir in parmesan cheese.

In a bowl, combine the first four crust ingredients until mixed. Cut in butter until crumbly. Gradually add water, tossing with a fork until dough forms a ball. Divide dough in half. Roll out one portion to fit 9-inch pie plate and place in plate. Flute edges. Add filling and top with cheddar cheese.

Roll out remaining pastry to 1/8-inch thickness. With a 2-inch biscuit cutter, cut out circles and place over cheese, overlapping slightly. Bake for 35-40 minutes or until golden brown.

Asparagus Ham Quiche

2 packages (10-ounces each) frozen cut asparagus, thawed

1 pound fully cooked ham, chopped

8-ounces shredded Swiss cheese

1/2 cup chopped onion

6 eggs

2 cups milk

1-1/2 cups biscuit mix

2 tablespoons dried vegetable flakes

1/4 teaspoon pepper

In two greased 9-inch pie plates, layer asparagus, ham, cheese and onion in that order.

In a bowl, beat eggs. Add remaining ingredients and mix well. Divide in half and pour over asparagus mixture in each pie plate.

Bake at 375 degrees for about 30 minutes. Check by inserting a knife near the center of the dish . . if it comes out clean it is done.

Breakfast Quiche

9-inch unbaked pastry shell

12 strips bacon, cooked and crumbled

1/2 cup sharp cheddar cheese, shredded

1/2 cup Pepper Jack or Monterey Jack cheese, shredded

1/3 cup onion, finely diced

4 eggs

2 cups whipping cream

1/4 teaspoon sugar

3/4 teaspoon salt

1/8 teaspoon cayenne pepper

Line unpricked pastry shell with double thickness of heavy duty foil. Bake for 5 minutes in a 450 degree oven. Remove foil and bake an additional 5 minutes. Remove from oven and cool. Reduce heat to 425 degrees.

Sprinkle bacon, cheeses and onion over the crust. In a bowl, beat eggs, cream, salt, sugar and cayenne. Pour mixture into crust. Bake 15 minutes at 425 degrees then reduce heat to 300 degrees and continue to bake 30 minutes longer or until a knife inserted near middle comes out clean.

Sausage Pie

1 (16-ounce) package hot roll mix

1 pound bulk sweet or hot Italian sausage

4 cups sliced fresh mushrooms

1 cup chopped onion

1 cup chopped red sweet pepper

2 cloves garlic, minced

1 (8-ounce) can pizza sauce

2 cups smoked mozzarella or provolone cheese, shredded

1 egg

1 tablespoon water

Prepare hot roll mix according to package directions through the kneading step. Cover; let dough rest 5 to 10 minutes.

Preheat oven to 350 degrees. In a large frying pan cook sausage over medium heat until meat is brown. Drain off fat, reserving 1 tablespoon fat in skillet. Add mushrooms, onion, red pepper and garlic. Cook over medium heat until vegetables are tender. Drain off any liquid. Stir in pizza sauce.

In a small bowl beat egg and water together. Set aside. Grease bottom and sides of a 9-inch springform pan. Roll three-fourths of the dough into a 15-inch circle. Fit into the bottom and press up the sides of the springform pan. Sprinkle bottom of dough with 1/2 cup of the cheese. Spoon meat mixture over cheese. Sprinkle remaining cheese over meat. Press lightly into meat filling.

Roll remaining dough into a 9-inch circle and place on top of meat-cheese mixture. Fold bottom dough over top dough and pinch to seal. Brush top of pie with egg-water mixture; allow to dry 5 minutes. Score top of pie in a diamond pattern but do not cut all the way through the dough.

Bake 45-50 minutes or until golden brown. Cool in pan on a wire rack for about 20 minutes then cut into wedges and serve.

Swiss Asparagus Quiche

9-inch unbaked pastry shell
1 pound fresh asparagus, trimmed
4-ounces Swiss cheese, shredded
10 strips bacon, diced
1/2 cup onion, chopped

1 tablespoon flour
1/4 teaspoon salt
1/8 teaspoon pepper
3 eggs
1/2 cup half and half cream

Fry bacon over medium heat until crisp. Remove to paper towels; drain. reserve 1 tablespoon bacon grease and sauté onion until browned; drain.

Cut eight asparagus spears into 4-inch long spears for garnish. cut in remaining spears into 1-inch pieces. Cook all the asparagus in a small amount of boiling water until crisp tender. Drain.

Toss bacon, onion, asparagus pieces, cheese, flour, salt and pepper in a bowl. Pour into pastry shell. In another bowl, beat eggs and cream. Pour over bacon mixture. Top with long asparagus spears and bake at 400 degrees for 30-35 minutes or until a knife inserted near the center comes out clean and crust is golden brown. Allow to stand 10 minutes before cutting.

Corn Tortilla Quiche

3/4 pound pork sausage
5 (6-inch) tortillas
4-ounces Monterey Jack cheese, shredded
4-ounces cheddar cheese
6 eggs, beaten
1/4 cup canned green chilies, diced

1/2 cup whipping cream
1/2 cup small-curd cottage cheese
1/2 teaspoon chili powder
1/4 cup minced fresh cilantro or parsley

(Continued on next page.)

(Corn Tortilla Quiche - continued)

In frying pan, cook sausage until it is no longer pink. Drain well. Place four tortillas in a greased 9-inch pie plate, overlapping and extending 1/2-inch beyond rim. Place remaining tortilla in the middle. Layer with sausage, cheeses and chilies.

Combine eggs, cream, cottage cheese and chili powder. Slowly pour over chilies. Bake in a 350 degree oven for 45 minutes or until the center is set and puffed. Sprinkle with cilantro or parsley.

Mama's Pork Turnovers

6 cups flour

1-1/2 teaspoons salt

1 cup shortening

2 teaspoons sugar

1 cup cold butter or margarine

12-18 tablespoons cold water

Filling:

1/2 cup onion, chopped

2 cups potatoes, cooked and cubed

2 pounds ground pork

3 tablespoons butter or margarine

2 cups tart apples, peeled and diced

3 tablespoons flour

1 tablespoon brown sugar

1 teaspoon pepper

1-1/2 teaspoons rubbed sage

1/2 teaspoon salt

2 egg yolks

2 tablespoons water

Combine flour, sugar and salt in bowl; cut in the shortening and butter until crumbly. Add 1 tablespoon water at a time tossing lightly with a fork until dough forms a ball. Cover and chill for at least 1 hour.

In a Dutch oven, brown pork until no longer pink over medium heat. Add butter and onion; sauté until onion is tender. Add apples, potatoes, flour, sage, brown sugar, salt and pepper. Cook and stir for 2 minutes longer. Cool.

Meanwhile, on a heavily floured surface, roll pastry to 1/8-inch thickness. Cut into 3-1/2 inch circles. Place between 1 to 2 tablespoons of the filling on each circle. Moisten edges with water and fold dough in half. Seal edges with fingers or a fork. Place on ungreased baking sheets. Beat egg yolks and water; brush over turnovers. Bake at 375 degrees for 20-25 minutes or until golden brown.

Deep Dish Ham Pie

Pastry for single crust 9-inch pie
1/4 cup butter or margarine
1/2 teaspoon salt
1/4 cup flour
1/4 teaspoon ground mustard
1/8 teaspoon pepper

1 cup milk
1 teaspoon dried minced onion
2-1/2 cup fully cooked ham, cubed
1 cup frozen peas, thawed
2 hard-boiled eggs, chopped

Melt butter in saucepan; stir in flour, salt, mustard and pepper until smooth. Gradually add milk and onion. Bring to a boil. Cook and stir for 2 minutes or until thickened. Add peas, ham and eggs. Pour into an ungreased deep dish plate and cover with single crust. Flute edges and cut slits in top. Bake at 425 degrees for 25 minutes or until crust is golden brown and filling is bubbly.

Pork Potato Pie
Leftover pork roast works great in the recipe!

2-1/2 cups cubed cooked pork
2 pounds potatoes, peeled and cubed
4 tablespoons butter or margarine, divided
1/3 cup whipping cream
3/4 teaspoon salt
1/8 teaspoon pepper
1 medium onion, chopped

1 garlic clove, minced
1/4 cup flour
1 can (14-1/2 ounces) beef broth
1 tablespoon Dijon mustard
1 teaspoon dried thyme
4 tablespoons minced fresh parsley, divided

Put potatoes in saucepan and cover with water; bring to boil. cover and cook for 20-25 minutes or until tender. Drain well. Mash potatoes with cream, 2 tablespoons butter, salt and pepper. Spread 1-1/2 cups of mashed potatoes into a greased shallow 1-1/2 quart baking dish.

(Continued on next page.)

(Pork Potato Pie - continued.)

In a skillet, sauté onion and garlic in remaining butter until tender. Stir in flour until blended. Gradually add broth, mustard, thyme and 2 tablespoons parsley. Bring to a boil and cook and stir for 2 minutes or until thickened.

Add pork; stir and heat through. Pour over potato crust. Pipe or spoon remaining mashed potatoes over top. Bake uncovered at 375 degrees for 35 to 40 minutes or until the potatoes are lightly browned. Sprinkle with remaining parsley.

Bacon-Tomato Pie

<u>Crust:</u>
1-1/4 cups flour
1/2 teaspoon salt
1/2 teaspoon dried basil
2 teaspoons baking powder
1/2 cup shortening
1/2 cup sour cream
<u>Filling:</u>
4-ounces cheddar cheese, shredded

3/4 cup mayonnaise
1 (4-1/2 ounce) can mushroom pieces and stems, drained
8 bacon strips, cooked and crumbled
1 tablespoon onion, diced
1 tablespoon green pepper, diced
3 medium tomatoes, peeled and sliced

Combine flour, salt, basil and baking powder in bowl. Cut in shortening until crumbly. Stir in sour cream; cover and refrigerate for 30 minutes. Press dough into a 9-inch pie plate. (This dough can also be rolled.) Flute edges if desired. Bake for 10 minutes in a 375 degree oven. Cool completely.

In medium bowl, combine cheese, mayonnaise, mushrooms, bacon pieces, green pepper and onion. Layer half of the tomatoes in the cooled crust. Top with half of the cheese mixture. Repeat layers. Bake at 350 degrees for 30 to 35 minutes or until golden brown. Be sure to refrigerate leftovers.

Mona's Shepherd's Bean Pie

1-1/4 pounds each of fresh green beans and fresh wax beans, cut into 2-inch pieces

1/2 small onion, diced

3 medium carrots, cut into 2-inch julienne strips

1 teaspoon butter or margarine

1 (10-3/4 ounce) can condensed cream of chicken soup, undiluted

1/2 cup whipping cream

1/2 cup chicken broth

3-1/4 teaspoons dill weed, divided

6-ounces fully cooked ham, cubed

1-1/2 cups (6-ounces) Swiss cheese, shredded and divided

1/4 cup slivered almonds

7 cups hot mashed potatoes (prepared with milk and butter)

Place beans and carrots in a saucepan; cover with water and bring to a boil. Cook, uncovered, for about 10 minutes or until crisp tender. Drain and set aside.

In a small skillet, sauté onion in butter until tender, about 3 minutes.

In a large bowl, combine soup, cream, broth and 3 teaspoons of dill. Whisk until well blended. Add the beans, carrots and onion. Gently stir to coat. Transfer to a greased shallow 3-quart baking dish. Top with ham and 1 cup cheese and almonds. Spread mashed potatoes over the top.

Cover and bake for 30 minutes in a 350 degree oven. Uncover; sprinkle remaining cheese and dill on top. Bake 5-10 minutes longer or until heated through and the cheese is melted.

Down on the Farm Pork and Apple Pie

1 pound bacon, sliced and cut into 2-inch pieces
3 medium onions, chopped
3 pounds boneless pork, cubed
Vegetable oil
3 tart apples, peeled and chopped
1 teaspoon rubbed sage
1/2 teaspoon ground nutmeg
1 teaspoon salt
1/4 teaspoon pepper
1 cup apple cider
1/2 cup water
4 medium potatoes, peeled and cubed
1/2 cup milk
5 tablespoons butter or margarine, divided
Additional salt and pepper
Snipped fresh parsley, optional

In an ovenproof 12-inch skillet, cook bacon until crisp. Remove with a slotted spoon to paper towels to drain. Sauté onions in bacon grease until tender; remove with slotted spoon and set aside.

Dredge pork lightly with flour. Brown in drippings, adding more oil if needed. Remove from the heat and drain.

To pork, add bacon, onions, apples, sage, nutmeg, salt and pepper. Stir in cider and water. Cover and bake at 325 degrees for 2 hours or until pork is tender.

In a saucepan, cook potatoes in boiling water until tender. Drain and mash with milk and 3 tablespoons butter. Add salt and pepper to taste. Remove skillet from the oven and spread potatoes over pork mixture. Melt remaining butter; brush over potatoes.

Broil about 6 inches from the heat for 5 minutes or until topping is browned. Sprinkle with parsley if desired.

Farmer's Market Sausage Pie

Pastry for double crust pie

4 Italian sausage links, casings removed, halved and cut into 1/2-inch pieces

1 medium tomato, cut into chunks

1 small yellow tomato, cut into chunks

1 cup thinly sliced zucchini

1 cup thinly sliced yellow summer squash

1/2 cup julienned sweet red pepper

1/2 cup julienned green pepper

1 tablespoon Italian salad dressing

1/2 teaspoon garlic powder

1/4-1/2 teaspoon crushed fennel seed

1 cup (4-ounces) shredded cheddar cheese

1 cup (4-ounces) shredded mozzarella cheese

Preheat oven to 375 degrees. In a large skillet, cook sausage over medium heat until browned; drain. Add tomatoes, squash, peppers, salad dressing mix, garlic powder, fennel seed. Cook and stir for 10 minutes; drain. Cool for 10 minutes.

Line a 9-inch pie plate with bottom pastry and trim even with the edge. Fill with the sausage mixture. Sprinkle with cheeses. Roll out remaining pastry to fit top of pie and place over filling. Trim, seal and flute edges. Cut slits in top of pastry to vent. Bake for 35 to 40 minutes or until filling is bubbly and crust is golden brown. Let stand 10 minutes before cutting and serving.

Spinach and Sausage Turnovers

1 pound bulk pork sausage

1/2 cup onion, chopped

1 (10-ounce) package frozen chopped spinach, thawed and squeezed dry

1-1/2 cups sharp cheddar cheese, shredded

2 teaspoons prepared mustard

1 teaspoon dried marjoram

Salt and pepper to taste

1 loaf (16-ounces) frozen bread dough, thawed

1 egg white, beaten

Cook sausage and onion over medium beat in a frying pan until meat is no longer pink. Drain well. Stir in spinach, cheese, mustard, marjoram, salt and pepper. Cook and stir until cheese is melted. Remove from heat and cool slightly.

(Continued on next page.)

362

Divide dough into eight portions. Roll each portion into a 6-inch circle. Spoon about 1/2 cup meat mixture on half of each circle. Brush edges with egg white; fold dough over filling and press edges with a fork to seal. Place on greased baking sheets; cover and let rise in a warm place about 20 minutes.

Brush tops with egg white; cut slits in the top of each. Bake at 350 degrees for 20 minutes or until golden brown.

Spiced Pork Potpie

1-1/2 pounds cubed pork shoulder roast

1/2 cup butter or margarine, divided

2 cups apple cider or juice

1 cup water

1 cup chopped peeled tart apple

1/2 cup dried cranberries

1/2 cup dried pitted prunes, chopped

2 teaspoons ground cinnamon

1-1/2 teaspoons ground ginger

2 whole cloves

6 tablespoons flour

1 (15-ounce) can sweet potatoes, drained and cubed

Crust:

1 cup flour

1-1/2 teaspoons baking powder

1/2 teaspoon salt

3/4 cup milk

1/2 cup butter or margarine, melted

Preheat oven to 400 degrees. In a Dutch oven, cook pork in 2 tablespoons butter until browned. Add cider and water; bring to a boil. Reduce heat to simmer for 10 minutes. Stir in the fruit and seasonings; simmer 10 minutes longer.

Melt remaining butter and stir in flour until smooth. Slowly add to meat mixture. Bring to a boil; cook for 1-2 minutes or until thickened. Discard cloves. Stir in sweet potatoes. Pour into a greased 3-quart baking dish.

For crust, combine the flour, baking powder and salt in a bowl. Combine the milk and butter; stir into dry ingredients until smooth. Spread over filling. Bake for 28-32 minutes or until crust is browned.

Herbed Pork Pie

Pastry for double crust pie
1-1/2 pounds ground pork
1 cup celery, chopped
1 medium onion, diced
1 clove garlic, minced
2 medium potatoes, peeled and shredded
1-1/2 cups water
1 teaspoon salt
1/4 teaspoon ground cinnamon

1 tablespoon fresh sage, minced or 1 teaspoon rubbed sage
1/4 teaspoon dried savory
1/4 teaspoon ground allspice
1 bay leaf
1 tablespoon flour
2 tablespoons cold water

<u>Glaze:</u>
1 egg, lightly beaten
1 teaspoon water

Line a 9-inch pie plate with bottom pastry. Trim edge even. Set aside.

In a large frying pan, cook pork, onion, celery and garlic until meat is no longer pink and vegetables are tender; drain. Add potatoes, water and seasonings. Bring to a boil. Reduce heat; cover and simmer for 15 minutes.

Combine flour and cold water until smooth; stir into pork mixture. Bring to a boil. Reduce heat; cover and simmer for 5 minutes or until slightly thickened. Discard bay leaf. Beat egg and water; brush over bottom pastry.

Bake at 400 degrees for 5 minutes. Increase heat to 450 degrees. Pour pork mixture into crust. Roll out remaining pastry to fit top of pie. Place over filling; cut slits in top. Trim, seal and flute edges.

Bake for 10 minutes. Reduce heat to 350 degrees; bake 10 to 15 minutes longer or until golden brown.

Special Chicken Potpie

3 to 3-1/2 pound broiler/fryer chicken, quartered
4 cups water
4 teaspoons chicken bouillon granules
4 carrots, halved crosswise
3 medium onions
1 bay leaf
1/2 pound fresh mushrooms, quartered
2 celery ribs, halved crosswise
3 tablespoons butter or margarine
5 tablespoons flour

1 teaspoon poultry seasoning
1 teaspoon salt
1/4 teaspoon pepper
1 cup frozen peas
1/2 cup whipping cream
Biscuits:
1-1/2 cups flour
2 teaspoons baking powder
1/4 teaspoon salt
1-1/4 teaspoons sugar
4 tablespoons shortening
1/2 cup milk

In a Dutch oven, combine chicken, water, bouillon, carrots, onions and bay leaf. Bring to a boil. Reduce heat and cover and simmer for 1-1/4 hours.

Add mushrooms and celery; cover and simmer for 15 minutes or until chicken and vegetables are tender. Remove chicken and vegetables. Debone chicken and dice meat. Set aside. Strain broth; set aside. Slice vegetables and set aside.

Melt butter in a saucepan; stir in flour until smooth. Cook and stir over medium heat until slightly thickened and bubbly. Gradually stir in cream and reserved broth; bring to a boil. Cook and stir for 2 minutes. Add poultry seasoning, salt, pepper, peas, chicken and vegetables. Pour into a 2-quart round baking dish. Set aside and keep warm.

Biscuits: Combine flour, sugar, salt and baking powder. Cut in shortening until mixture resembles coarse crumbs. Stir in milk just until mixed. Roll to 1/2-inch thickness. Cut with a 2-inch biscuit cutter. Place biscuits on top of chicken mixture and bake for 20 minutes in a 400 degrees oven or until biscuits are golden brown.

Turkey Pot Pie

1 (10-3/4 ounce) can
condensed cream of mushroom
soup, undiluted

1 (5-ounce) can evaporated
milk

1/4 cup minced fresh parsley
or 1 tablespoon dried parsley
flakes

1/2 teaspoon dried thyme

3 cups cooked turkey, cubed

1 (10-ounce) package frozen
mixed vegetables, thawed

1/4 teaspoon salt

1/4 teaspoon pepper

Crust:

3/4 cup instant mashed
potato flakes

3/4 cup flour

1/4 cup grated parmesan
cheese

1/3 cup cold butter or
margarine

1/4 cup ice water

Half-and-Half cream

Combine soup, evaporated milk, parsley and thyme together. Stir in turkey, vegetables, salt and pepper. Spoon into a greased 11x7x2-inch baking dish.

Crust: Combine potato flakes, flour and parmesan in a bowl. cut in butter until crumbly. Add water, 1 tablespoon at time, tossing lightly with a fork until dough forms a ball.

Roll the dough to fit the baking dish. Cut vents in crust. Place over filling; flute edges. Brush pastry with cream and bake in a 400 degree oven for 25-30 minutes or until golden brown. (If necessary, cover edges of crust with foil to prevent over browning.)

Homestyle Chicken Pot Pie

Pastry for single crust pie

2 tablespoons margarine or butter, divided in half

1 pound boneless skinless chicken breasts, cut into 1-inch pieces

1/2 teaspoon salt

1/2 teaspoon dried thyme leaves

1/4 teaspoon black pepper

1 package (16-ounces) frozen mixed vegetables, such as potatoes, peas and carrots, thawed and drained

1 can (10-3/4 ounces) condensed cream of chicken or mushroom soup, undiluted

1/3 cup dry white wine or milk

Preheat oven to 425 degrees. Melt 1 tablespoon margarine in medium broiler proof skillet over medium-high heat. Add chicken; sprinkle with salt, thyme and pepper. Cook 1 minute, stirring frequently.

Reduce heat to medium-low. Stir in vegetables, soup and wine; simmer 5 minutes.

While soup mixture is simmering, prepare pie crust. Using small cookie cutter, make 4 decorative cut-outs from pastry to allow steam to escape.

Remove chicken mixture from heat; top with pie crust. Melt remaining tablespoon margarine. Brush pie crust with 2 teaspoons melted margarine. Arrange cut-outs attractively over crust, if desired. Brush cut-outs with remaining 1 teaspoon melted margarine.

Bake 12 minutes. Turn oven to broil; broil 4 to 5 inches from heat source 2 minutes or until crust is golden brown and chicken mixture is bubbly.

Turkey & Stuffing Pie

1 egg, beaten
1 cup chicken broth
1/3 cup butter or margarine, melted
5 cups herb-seasoned stuffing
Filling:
4-ounces mushroom stems and pieces, drained
1/2 cup onion, diced
1 tablespoon butter or margarine

1 tablespoon flour
3 cups turkey, cubed and cooked
1 cup frozen peas
1 tablespoon minced fresh parsley
1 teaspoon Worcestershire
1/2 teaspoon thyme
1 (12-ounce) jar turkey gravy
5 slices process American cheese, cut into strips

Combine egg, broth and melted butter in large bowl. Add stuffing and mix well. Pat onto the bottom and up the sides of a greased 9-inch pie plate. Set aside.

In a skillet, sauté mushrooms and onion in butter until tender. Sprinkle with flour, add peas, parsley, turkey, worcestershire and thyme; mix well. Stir in gravy then bring to a boil. Boil and stir for 2 minutes. Spoon into the crust.

Bake for 20 minutes in a 375 degree oven. Arrange cheese strips in a lattice pattern over filling. Bake 5-10 minutes longer or until the cheese melts.

Delicious Turkey Pot Pie

1/2 cup Miracle Whip salad dressing
2 tablespoons flour
1 teaspoon instant chicken bouillon
1/8 teaspoon pepper
3/4 cup milk

1-1/2 cups turkey or chicken, cooked and chopped
1 (10-ounce) package frozen mixed vegetables
1 (4-ounce) can refrigerated crescent rolls

(Continued on next page.)

(Delicious Turkey Pot Pie - continued.)

Combine salad dressing, flour, bouillon and pepper in medium saucepan. Gradually add milk.

Cook, stirring constantly, over low heat until thickened. Add turkey and vegetables; heat thoroughly, stirring occasionally.

Spoon into 8-inch square baking dish. Unroll dough into two rectangles. Press perforations together to seal. Place rectangles side-by-side to form square. Press edges together to form seam. Cover turkey mixture with dough.

Bake for 15 to 20 minutes in a 375 degree oven.

Potato Baskets with Chicken

Baskets:

4-1/2 cups frozen shredded hash brown potatoes, thawed

6 tablespoons butter or margarine, melted

1-1/2 teaspoons salt

1/4 teaspoon pepper

Filling:

1/2 cup onion, chopped

1/4 cup butter or margarine

1/4 cup flour

2 teaspoons chicken bouillon granules

1 teaspoon Worcestershire

1/2 teaspoon dried basil

2 cups milk

3 cups cubed cooked chicken

1 cup frozen peas, thawed

In a bowl, combine potatoes, butter, salt and pepper. Press into six greased 10-ounce custard cups; set aside.

In a saucepan, sauté onion in butter. Add flour, bouillon, Worcestershire and basil. Stir in milk. Bring to a boil; cook and stir for 2 minutes or until thickened. Add chicken and peas. Spoon into prepared crusts.

Bake uncovered at 375 degrees for 30-35 minutes or until crusts are golden brown.

Chicken Potpies

1 recipe Pastry for Double-Crust Pie or Pastry for Single-Crust Pie

1 package (10 ounces) frozen mixed vegetables

1/2 cup chopped onion

1/2 cup chopped fresh mushrooms

1/4 cup margarine or butter

1/3 cup all-purpose flour

3/4 teaspoon crushed, dried sage, marjoram, or thyme

1/2 teaspoon salt

1/3 to 1/4 teaspoon pepper

2 cups chicken broth

3/4 cup milk

3 cups (1 pound) cubed cooked chicken or turkey

1/4 cup snipped parsley

1/4 cup chopped pimento

Milk

Sesame seed, optional

For filling, cook vegetables according to package directions; drain. In a medium saucepan cook onion and mushrooms in butter until tender. Stir in flour; sage, marjoram or thyme; salt; and pepper. Add broth and 3/4 cup milk all at once. Cook and stir until thickened and bubbly. Stir in vegetables, poultry, parsley, and pimiento; cook and stir until bubbly. Pour chicken mixture into six (10-ounce) casseroles or 2-quart round casserole.

To make six individual casseroles, roll double-crust pastry to a 15x10-inch rectangle; cut into six 5-inch circles. To make the 2-quart casserole, roll a single-crust pastry into a 10-inch circle.

Cut out shapes or cut slits in center of pastry. Place crusts on top of casserole. Flute edges. Brush with milk; top with cutouts, if desired. Sprinkle with sesame seeds. Bake at 450 degrees until pastry is golden brown: 12-15 minutes for individual casseroles or 15-20 minutes for 2 quart casserole.

Biscuit-Topped Potpies:

Prepare as above, except omit pastry. Cut dough rounds from one package of six refrigerated biscuits into quarters; arrange on top of chicken mixture in casserole. Bake in a 400 degree oven for about 15 minutes or until biscuits are golden brown.

Greek Shepherd's Pie

4 large potatoes, peeled and cubed

1/2 cup sour cream

1/4 cup butter or margarine

5-1/2 cups eggplant, cubed

2 teaspoons salt

2 tablespoon flour

1/4 cup vegetable oil

1 pound ground lamb

1/2 pound ground turkey

1 teaspoon garlic powder

1 (26-ounce) jar meatless spaghetti sauce

2 tablespoons dried minced onion

2 tablespoons minced fresh parsley

1/2 teaspoon dried rosemary, crushed

1/2 teaspoon dried basil

1/2 teaspoon pepper

1 cup (4-ounces) crumbled feta cheese

In a large saucepan, cook potatoes in boiling water until tender then drain. Mash potatoes with sour cream and butter. Set aside.

In a mixing bowl, combine eggplant and salt. Let stand for 10 minutes then drain. Add flour and toss to coat.

In a frying pan, cook eggplant in oil over medium heat until browned and oil is absorbed. Transfer to a greased 3-quart baking dish.

In the same pan, cook lamb and turkey over medium heat until no longer pink; drain. Stir in spaghetti sauce, onion, parsley and seasonings. Cook until heated through . . . about 5 minutes.

Pour over eggplant; sprinkle with feta cheese. Spread mashed potatoes over the top and bake, uncovered in a 350 degree oven for 35-45 minutes or until top begins to brown. Let stand for 15 minutes before serving.

Chicken Cordon Bleu Calzones

Puff pastry recipe or 1
package (17-1/4 ounces)
frozen puff pastry, thawed4
boneless skinless chicken
breasts (1 pound)

1 cup sliced fresh mushrooms

1/2 medium onion, chopped

2 tablespoons butter or
margarine

3 tablespoons cornstarch

1-1/4 cups milk

1 tablespoon minced fresh
basil or 1 teaspoon dried basil

1 teaspoon salt

1/4 teaspoon pepper

8 thin slices of deli ham

4 slices provolone cheese

Additional milk, optional

Preheat oven to 350 degrees. Place chicken in a greased 2-quart baking dish; cover with water. Cover and bake for 30 minutes or until juices run clear.

Meanwhile, sauté mushrooms and onion in butter in a skillet until tender. Combine cornstarch and milk until smooth; stir into skillet mixture. Add seasonings. Bring to a boil; cook and stir for 2 minutes or until thickened.

Drain chicken. Cut pastry sheets in half widthwise. On one side of each half, place a chicken breast, 1/4 cup mushroom mixture, two ham slices and one cheese slice. Fold pastry over filling and seal edges.

Place on a greased baking sheet. Brush tops of pastry with milk, if desired. Bake at 400 degrees for 15-20 minutes or until puffed and golden.

Chili Shrimp Quiche

Pastry:
1 cup flour
1/8 teaspoon salt
2 tablespoons butter or margarine
2 tablespoons shortening
2-4 teaspoons water
Filling:
4 eggs
1/2 cup milk

1/2 cup light cream
1/2 clove garlic, crushed
1 cup cheddar cheese, grated
3 green onions, chopped
2 green chilies, seeded and chopped
8-ounces cooked and peeled shrimp
salt (to taste)

Crust: Sift flour and salt; cut in shortening and butter until the mixture resembles corn meal. Gradually mix in the liquid adding enough to bring the pastry together. Wrap the pastry and chill for 20-30 minutes. Roll out pastry on well floured board. Place pastry into 10-inch flan dish, taking care not to stretch it. Remove excess pastry with rolling pin or knife; flute as desired.

Filling: Mix eggs, milk, cream and garlic together. Sprinkle with cheese, onion, chilies and shrimp. Pour into pastry lined pan. Bake at 400 degrees for 30-40 minutes until firm and golden brown.

Potato Broccoli Cheddar Cheese Pie

9-inch unbaked pastry shell
3-ounces cheddar cheese
1 medium potato, boiled without skin
1 (10-ounce) package frozen broccoli, chopped and thawed

1/2 cup skim milk
2 large eggs
2 tablespoons flour
3/4 teaspoon salt
1/8 teaspoon pepper
1/8 teaspoon nutmeg

Preheat oven to 350 degrees. Shred cheese and sprinkle 1-ounce into unbaked pie shell. Bake for 5 minutes. Remove from oven. Shred potato; mix in broccoli and combine with remaining ingredients. Stir to combine and pour into pie shell. Place on baking sheet. Bake at 350 degrees for 1 hour or until done.

Salmon Asparagus Delight

1 pound asparagus

1/4 cup finely chopped onion

1/4 cup chopped sweet red or yellow pepper

2 tablespoons butter or margarine

4 ounces cream cheese, softened

1/2 cup mayonnaise

2 tablespoons flour

2 eggs, lightly beaten

1/2 cup half-and-half cream

1 teaspoon dill weed

1/2 teaspoon dried basil

1/4 teaspoon pepper

1 (15-ounce) can salmon, drained, bones and skin removed

2 tablespoons grated parmesan cheese

1/2 cup Swiss cheese

Trim asparagus and cut into 2-inch pieces. In a saucepan, bring 1-inch of water to a boil. Add asparagus in a steamer basket over water; cover and stem for 4-5 minutes or until crisp-tender. Drain; set aside.

In a frying pan, sauté onion and red pepper in butter until tender; set aside. Combine cream cheese, mayonnaise, flour, eggs, cream, dill, basil and pepper in mixing bowl. Fold in salmon, asparagus, onion mixture and Swiss cheese.

Transfer to a greased 9-inch pie plate. Sprinkle with parmesan cheese and bake at 350 degrees for 35 minutes or until a knife inserted near middle comes out clean.

Salmon-Mango Pockets

1 pound fresh or frozen
skinless salmon fillets

1/2 cup chopped onion

1 tablespoon olive oil

1/2 cup finely chopped mango

1/2 cup walnuts, finely
chopped

12 sheets frozen phyllo dough,
thawed (18x4-inch
rectangles)

1/2 cup butter, melted

Mango-Curry Mayonnaise

1/2 cup mayonnaise

1/2 teaspoon curry powder

1 cup coarsely chopped mango

Heat oven to 375 degrees. Thaw salmon, if frozen. Rinse salmon and pat dry. Cut into four pieces. Sprinkle light with salt and pepper; set aside.

In a large skillet, sauté onion in hot oil over medium-high heat about 3 minutes. Stir in walnuts, mango, 1 teaspoon salt and 1/2 teaspoon pepper. Set aside.

Unfold phyllo; cover with plastic wrap, then a dampened towel. Lay 1 sheet of phyllo flat on a work surface. With short side facing you, brush with some melted butter. Add 2 more sheets, brushing each with butter. Spoon 1/4 cup of the mango mixture in middle of dough about 4-inches from bottom edge. Place a salmon piece on top of mango mixture so that a long side of salmon is parallel to bottom edge. Fold bottom edge of phyllo over salmon. Fold long side in. Roll up from bottom.

Place seam side down in a greased 15x10x1-inch baking pan. Bake for 25-30 minutes or until phyllo is golden and fish flakes easily when tested with a fork.

Serve with Mango-Curry Mayonnaise. Prepare mango-curry mayonnaise by combining mayonnaise with curry powder then gently folding in 1 cup chopped mango. Mix until mango is coated.

Colonial Game Pie

This is for meat lovers only!

Puff pastry recipe or one
package (17-1/4 ounces)
frozen puff pastry thawed

1/2 pound sliced bacon, diced

1-1/2 pounds beef stew meat,
cubed

2 cans beef broth (14-1/2
ounces each)

1/2 cup red currant jelly

2 dressed rabbits (about 3
pounds each), cut up

1 can chicken broth (14-1/2
ounces)

1/4 cup Worcestershire sauce

1 bay leaf

1/4 teaspoon pepper

1 teaspoon salt

1/4 teaspoon cayenne pepper

1/4 pound pearl onions

2 medium potatoes, diced

2 medium carrots, diced

1/2 cup sliced fresh
mushrooms

1 dressed duck (4-1/2
pounds), cut up

6 tablespoons flour

3/4 cup cold water

In heavy kettle, cook diced bacon until crisp. Drain, reserving
1/4 cup drippings in pan. Set bacon aside.

Brown stew meat in bacon grease. Add beef broth and jelly;
cover and simmer for 45 minutes.

Cover rabbits with water in a pot; simmer for 1 hour or until
meat falls from bones. Remove meat and set aside. Discard
bones.

To beef mixture, add chicken broth, Worcestershire, bay leaf,
salt, pepper and cayenne; simmer for 20 minutes. Add onions,
carrots, potatoes and mushrooms; simmer another 20 minutes
or until tender. Remove bay leaf.

In another pot, cover duck with water. Simmer until meat nearly
falls from the bones. Remove meat and set aside. Mix flour and
water; stir into beef mixture. Cook until thickened. Add rabbit
and duck meat.

Cut puff pastry into 3-inch squares and place on a greased
baking sheet. Bake at 400 degrees for 10-12 minutes; place on
individual servings of meat mixture.

Pheasant Potpie

Pastry for single crust pie
2 pheasants about 2-1/2 pounds each
1 medium onion, quartered
1 rib celery, quartered
4 cups water
1 garlic clove, mined
2 tablespoons lemon juice
1-1/4 teaspoons salt
1/2 teaspoon pepper

1/4 teaspoon Worcestershire
1/8 teaspoon ground nutmeg
3/4 cup flour
1 (16-ounce) jar whole onions, drained
1 (10-ounce) package frozen peas
1-1/2 cups sliced carrots
1 (2-ounce) jar sliced pimientos, drained
1/4 cup minced fresh parsley

Place pheasants, water, onion, celery and garlic in large saucepan or Dutch oven. Bring to a boil then reduce heat; cover and simmer for 1 hour or until tender. Remove pheasants; cool.

Remove meat from bones and set aside. Strain the broth and discard vegetables. Measure 3-1/2 cups of the broth and pour into a saucepan. Add lemon juice, Worcestershire, salt, pepper and nutmeg. Remove 1/2 cup of liquid and stir in flour; set aside

Bring broth in saucepan to a boil; add flour mixture and boil 1 minute until thick and bubbly. Add onions, carrots, peas, pimientos, parsley and pheasant. Mix well.

Spoon into a 2-1/2 quart baking dish. Roll pastry out to fit dish; place over meat mixture and seal edges to dish. Cut steam vents in crust. Bake for 35-40 minutes in a 425 degree oven or until bubbly and golden.

Chicken or turkey can be substituted for pheasant.

Mushroom Quiche

9-inch unbaked pastry shell

4 cups fresh mushrooms, sliced

1 tablespoon butter or margarine

1 cup Swiss cheese, shredded

2 tablespoons flour

3 eggs, lightly beaten

1-1/4 cups milk

1 tablespoon minced fresh savory or 1 teaspoon dried savory

1/2 teaspoon salt

1/4 teaspoon pepper

Line unpricked pastry shell with a double thickness of heavy-duty foil. Bake at 425 degrees for 10 minutes or until edges begin to brown. Remove foil; set crust aside.

Sauté mushrooms in butter. Remove with a slotted spoon; set aside. Toss cheese with flour in a bowl; add eggs, milk, savory, salt and pepper. Stir in mushrooms. Pour into crust.

Bake at 350 degrees for 60 minutes or until knife inserted near middle comes out clean. Let stand 10 minutes before cutting.

Vidalia Tomato Pie

9-inch deep dish pastry shell

6 medium tomatoes, peeled, seeded and coarsely chopped

1 medium Vidalia onion, finely chopped (1/2 cup)

1 teaspoon dried basil, crushed

1/4 teaspoon salt

1/4 teaspoon pepper

1 cup shredded Monterey Jack cheese (4-ounces)

1 cup light mayonnaise dressing or salad dressing

1/2 teaspoon garlic powder

Place tomatoes in a colander and let stand for 30 minutes.

Sprinkle half of the onion into the pastry shell. Top with half of the tomatoes. Sprinkle with basil, salt and pepper. top with remaining onion and remaining tomatoes. In a small bowl, stir together cheese, mayonnaise dressing, and garlic powder. Spread over tomato layer to cover.

Bake, uncovered, in a 400 degree oven for 30-35 minutes or until golden brown. Cool slightly before serving. Makes 8 to 10 side-dish servings.

Asparagus Quiche

9-inch unbaked pastry shell

1 pound fresh asparagus, trimmed

3 tablespoons butter or margarine

3 tablespoons flour

1/2 teaspoon salt

1-1/2 cups milk

4 eggs, beaten

1/2 cup Swiss cheese, shredded

1/4 cup bread crumbs

Cut eight asparagus spears into 4-inch pieces. Cut remaining asparagus into 1/2-inch pieces. Cook all the asparagus in a small amount of water until tender. Drain and set aside.

Line the unpricked pastry shell with a double thickness of heavy duty foil. Bake at 450 degrees for 5 minutes. Remove foil and bake an additional 5 minutes. Remove from oven and set aside.

Melt butter in a saucepan over medium heat. Stir in flour and salt. Gradually add milk. Cook and stir until thickened. Stir a small amount of hot mixture into eggs. Pour egg mixture into thickened sauce. Stir in cheese and the 1/2-inch asparagus pieces. Pour into crust; sprinkle with bread crumbs.

Bake at 400 degrees for 35 minutes or until a knife inserted in the middle comes out clean. Arrange the 4-inch asparagus pieces in a spoke pattern on top.

Tomato Quiche

Crust:
3/4 cup flour
1/2 cup cornmeal
4-5 tablespoons cold water
1/2 teaspoon salt
1/3 cup shortening
1/8 teaspoon pepper

Filling:
2 cups plum tomatoes, chopped
1/2 cup green onions, chopped
1/2 cup cheddar cheese, shredded
1/2 cup Swiss cheese, shredded
1 teaspoon salt
1/2 teaspoon dried basil
1/8 teaspoon pepper
2 tablespoons flour
1 cup evaporated milk
2 eggs

Combine the flour, cornmeal, salt and pepper in a bowl. Add shortening and cut into dry ingredients until crumbly. Add water, tossing with a fork until dough will form a ball. Place in refrigerator for 30 minutes.

Roll out dough to fit a 9-inch pie plate. Transfer to plate and trim to 1/2 inch beyond edge of plate. Flute edges then bake in a 375 degree oven for 10 minutes. Cool completely.

Arrange tomatoes in the crust; sprinkle with salt, basil, pepper, onions and cheeses. In a bowl, combine milk, flour and eggs. Whisk until smooth then pour over filling. Bake at 375 degrees 40-45 minutes or until a knife inserted near middle comes out clean. Let stand 10 minutes before cutting.

Spring Vegetable Quiche

9-inch unbaked pastry shell
2 cups whole milk
1 box spring vegetable soup ,
dip and recipe mix

4 large eggs
4-ounces Swiss cheese,
shredded (1 cup)

Preheat oven to 350 degrees. Pour milk into a 4-cup measure; add soup mix and let soak for at least 10 minutes.

Beat eggs in a medium bowl with a fork until blended. Sir in milk mixture.

Sprinkle 3/4 cup cheese over crust. Add egg mixture: sprinkle remaining cheese on top.

Bake 45 minutes or until tip of a knife inserted in center comes out clean. Let stand 10 minutes before cutting into wedges.

Winter Squash Quiche

2 tablespoons onion, diced
2 teaspoons vegetable oil
8-ounces shredded Swiss cheese
1 cup mashed cooked winter squash

3 eggs
1/4 teaspoon salt
1/8 teaspoon pepper
1/8 teaspoon ground nutmeg
1-1/2 cups milk

Sauté onion in oil until tender. Transfer to a greased 9-inch pie plate. Sprinkle with cheese.

In a bowl, whisk milk, squash, eggs, salt, pepper and nutmeg until smooth; pour over cheese. Bake for 50-60 minutes in a 325 degree oven, until knife inserted near middle comes out clean.

Quick Italian Spinach Pie

2 cups cottage cheese

1 (10-ounce) package frozen chopped spinach, thawed and drained

1 cup low-moisture part skim mozzarella cheese

4 eggs, beaten

1 (7-ounce) jar roasted red peppers, well drained, chopped

1/3 cup grated parmesan cheese

1 teaspoon dried oregano leaves

Combine all the ingredients and pour into a buttered 9-inch pie plate.

Bake at 350 degrees for 40 minutes or until center is set. Garnish with red pepper slivers.

Variation: Substitute 1/2 cup chopped red pepper for roasted red pepper.

Special Onion-Tomato Phyllo Pizza

5 tablespoons butter or margarine, melted

7 sheets phyllo dough (18"x14")

7 tablespoons Parmesan cheese, grated and divided

1 cup mozzarella cheese, shredded

1 cup thinly sliced onion

7 to 9 plum tomatoes, sliced

1-1/2 teaspoons minced fresh oregano or 1/2 teaspoon dried oregano

1 teaspoon minced fresh thyme or 1/4 teaspoon dried thyme

Salt and pepper to taste

Brush a 15x10x1-inch baking pan with some of the melted butter. Lay a sheet of phyllo in pan, folding edges in to fit. Keep remaining dough covered with waxed paper to avoid drying out. Brush dough with butter and sprinkle with 1 tablespoon Parmesan. Repeat layers five times, folding edges for each layer.

Top with remaining dough, folding edges to fit pan; brush with remaining butter. Sprinkle with mozzarella. Arrange onions and tomatoes over the cheese. Sprinkle with oregano, thyme, salt, pepper and remaining Parmesan.

Bake at 375 for 20-25 minutes or until edges are golden brown.

Mexican Pizzas

4 fat-free flour tortillas (12-inches)

16-ounces fat-free refried beans

2 medium plum tomatoes, diced

1 (4-ounce) can green chilies, drained

1 cup salsa

1/2 cup green pepper chopped

1/4 cup onion, chopped

1 (2-1/4 ounce) can ripe olives, sliced and drained

1 cup reduced-fat cheddar cheese, shredded

Place tortillas on two ungreased baking sheets; spread with beans. Layer with salsa, tomatoes, chilies, green pepper, onion, olives and cheese.

Bake at 350 degrees for 10 minutes or until cheese is melted.

Borekas...Israeli Spinach Turnovers

17-1/4 ounce package frozen puff pastry (2 sheets)

1 (10-ounce) package frozen chopped spinach

1 cup fat-free ricotta cheese

8-ounces feta cheese, crumbled

Milk

Thaw puff pastry according to directions. Cook spinach following directions; drain well. In medium bowl, combine spinach, ricotta and feta. Line baking sheets with foil. Grease foil. Set aside.

Preheat oven to 375 degrees. Unfold thawed puff pastry. Cut each sheet into 16 squares. Place 1 generous tablespoon of the spinach mixture just off center on each pastry square. For each pastry square, brush one pastry point with milk. Bring the point brushed with milk over the filling to the opposite point. Press to seal. Brush with milk.

Place on prepared baking sheets. Bake for 15 to 20 minutes or until golden brown. Serve warm.

Green Bean Quiche

1 (10-ounce) package frozen cut green beans
1/2 cup water
1/2 cup onion, chopped
2 tablespoons butter or margarine
1/4 cup green pepper, diced
1/2 cup fresh mushrooms, sliced
1/2 cup mayonnaise
1/4 cup sour cream
1/4 teaspoon salt
1/4 cup saltines, crushed (about 8 crackers)
6 eggs, beaten
1 medium tomato, chopped and seeded
3/4 cup shredded sharp cheddar cheese

Put water and beans in a saucepan; bring to boil. Reduce heat and cover then simmer for 6-8 minutes or until crisp-tender. Drain and set aside.

In a small frying pan, sauté onion in butter until tender. Add mushrooms and green pepper; sauté until tender.

In a large bowl, combine mayonnaise, sour cream and salt. Stir in beans, mushroom mixture and cracker crumbs. Gradually stir in beaten eggs. Pour into a greased deep-dish 9-inch pie plate. Sprinkle with tomato and cheese.

Bake at 350 degrees for 25-30 minutes or until a knife inserted near the middle comes out clean.

Ham and Mushroom Breakfast Pizza

Pizza Crust:
1 cup warm water
1 package yeast
2 tablespoons oil
2-1/2 cup flour
1 teaspoon salt
1 teaspoon sugar
1/2 teaspoon poppy seed

Topping:
1 (4-ounce) package sliced cooked ham
1 (6-ounce) package sliced Swiss cheese
1/4 pound mushrooms sliced
3 green onions, chopped
2 tablespoons butter or margarine
3 eggs
3/4 cups milk

(continued on next page)

Combine water, yeast, and oil together. Set aside. Mix flour, salt, sugar and poppy seeds with yeast mixture. Beat for 20 strokes and let stand for 5 minutes. Roll out on board and transfer to pizza pan.

Bake pastry crust 5 minutes on lowest rack of preheated 425 degree oven. Gently press down bubbles. Top with ham and cheese. Sauté mushrooms and onions in butter until tender. Spread over ham and cheese. Beat eggs and milk; pour over pizza. Return to oven and bake 18 to 20 minutes longer.

Mini Broccoli Quiches

Pastry for double crust pie

Half of a 10-ounce package frozen chopped broccoli, thawed and drained

3/4 cup finely shredded Swiss cheese

1 cup half-and-half or light cream

2 eggs

1/2 teaspoon salt

Preheat oven to 400 degrees. Grease and lightly flour thirty-six 1-3/4 inch muffin cups. Set aside.

On a lightly floured surface, roll pastry to slightly less than 1/8-inch thickness. Using a fluted round 2-1/2-inch biscuit or cookie cutter, cut the dough into circles. Reroll scraps, cutting additional circles. Gently line each muffin cup with a pastry circle, patting to fit.

Pat broccoli dry with paper towels. Divide broccoli and cheese evenly among muffin cups. Combine half-and-half, eggs, and salt; spoon about 2 teaspoons mixture into each muffin cup.

Bake for about 25 minutes or until puffed and set. Cool in pans or wire racks for 5 minutes. Loosen and remove from pans. Serve warm. Makes 36 little quiches.

This can also be made ahead and frozen until needed. To reheat, place frozen quiches on baking sheet and bake uncovered in a 400 degree oven for about 10-12 minutes or until heated through.

Mushroom and Green Bean Pie

Crust:
2-1/2 cups flour
2 teaspoons baking powder
1 teaspoon dill weed
1/4 teaspoon salt
1 cup cold butter or margarine
8-ounces sour cream
1 egg
1 tablespoon whipping cream

Filling:
3 cups fresh mushrooms, sliced
4 tablespoon butter or margarine, divided
2-1/2 cups onions, chopped
6 cups fresh green beans, cut into 1-inch pieces
2 teaspoons minced fresh thyme or 3/4 teaspoon dried thyme
1/2 teaspoon salt
1/4 teaspoon pepper
8-ounces cream cheese, cubed
1/2 cup milk

In a large frying pan, sauté mushrooms in 1 tablespoon butter until tender. Drain and set aside. In the same frying pan, sauté onions and beans in remaining butter for 18-20 minutes or until beans are crisp-tender. Add thyme, salt, pepper, cream cheese, milk and mushrooms. Cook and stir until the cheese is melted. Remove from the heat and set aside.

In a bowl, combine flour, baking powder, dill and salt. Cut in butter until mixture resembles coarse crumbs. Stir in sour cream to form a soft dough. Divide dough in half. On a well-floured surface, roll out one portion to fit a deep-dish 9-inch pie plate. Trim pastry even with edge.

Pour green bean mixture in the crust. Roll out remaining pastry and make a lattice crust. Trim, seal and flute edge.

In a small bowl, beat the egg and cream; brush over lattice top. Bake for 25-35 minutes or until golden brown in a 400 degree oven.

Eggplant Pot Pie

1/4 cup olive oil

1 medium eggplant, peeled and cut into 1/2-inch pieces (Eggplant should be about 1 pound)

1 green or yellow bell pepper, chopped

1 large onion, chopped

1-1/2 teaspoons bottled minced garlic

1 teaspoon dried basil leaves

2 cups (8-ounces) mozzarella cheese, shredded and divided

1 (14-1/2 ounce) can pasta ready diced tomatoes with garlic and herbs or Italian stewed tomatoes, undrained

1/2 teaspoon red pepper flakes

1/4 teaspoon salt

1 tablespoon balsamic vinegar

1 package (10-ounces) refrigerated pizza dough

Preheat oven to 425 degrees. Heat oil in large skillet over medium heat until hot. Add eggplant, onion, peppers and garlic.

Cook 10 minutes or until eggplant begins to brown; stir occasionally. Stir in tomatoes with juice, basil, pepper flakes and salt. Cook, uncovered, over medium-low heat for 5 minutes.

Remove from heat and stir in vinegar. Let stand 10 minutes; stir in 1 cup cheese. Transfer mixture to an ungreased 11x7-inch casserole dish. Sprinkle with remaining cheese.

Unroll pizza dough and arrange over top of casserole. Make decorative cut-outs using a small cookie cutter, if desired. Spray dough with nonstick cooking spray and bake for 15 minutes or until crust is golden brown and vegetable mixture is bubbly. Let it stand for 5-10 minutes before serving.

Notes: